Financial Crises, 1929 to the Present, Second Edition

To my father, John Hsu.

Financial Crises, 1929 to the Present, Second Edition

Sara Hsu

Assistant Professor of Economics, State University of New York at New Paltz, USA

Cheltenham, UK • Northampton, MA, USA

Published by
Edward Elgar Publishing Limited
The Lypiatts
15 Lansdown Road
Cheltenham
Glos GL50 2JA
UK

Edward Elgar Publishing, Inc.
William Pratt House
9 Dewey Court
Northampton
Massachusetts 01060
USA

A catalogue record for this book
is available from the British Library

Library of Congress Control Number: 2016949988

This book is available electronically in the **Elgar**online
Economics subject collection
DOI 10.4337/9781785365171

ISBN 978 1 78536 516 4 (cased)
ISBN 978 1 78536 517 1 (eBook)

Typeset by Servis Filmsetting Ltd, Stockport, Cheshire
Printed and bound in Great Britain by TJ International Ltd, Padstow

Contents

About the author

Sara Hsu is an Assistant Professor of Economics at the State University of New York at New Paltz. Dr Hsu specializes in Chinese economic development, sustainable development, financial crises, and trade. Prior to working at the State University of New York at New Paltz, Dr Hsu was a Visiting Professor at Trinity University in San Antonio, Texas. She earned her PhD from the University of Utah in 2007 and her BA from Wellesley College in 1997.

Dr Hsu also worked in the dot-com industry in New York in the late 1990s and early 2000s, at which time she became interested in the origins and behavior of financial crises. The Asian financial crisis, Russian financial crisis, Brazilian financial crisis, and Argentine financial crisis unfolded over this period, just as the dot-com industry entered a mini-crisis of its own.

1. The financial system and roots of crisis

Financial crises have occurred for centuries, and after the Great Recession of 2008 which began in the United States (US) and spread globally, both economists and policy makers have realized that economically developed countries are not immune from such phenomena. After the Asian financial crisis that began in 1997, much literature was generated which sought to decrease the volatility of capital flows, but in most studies, these short-term flows were seen as problematic only in combination with underdeveloped financial systems. Yet at this point, we have witnessed the final death knell of the efficient-markets hypothesis (according to reasonable economists) which holds that prices immediately reflect all available information. We have also watched a key economic figurehead, former US Federal Reserve Chairman Alan Greenspan, admit that he was wrong in approaching monetary policy from a free market ideology. Free market ideology, in which markets are viewed as self-correcting and symmetric, remains prevalent in the United States, but cracks in the system can no longer be ignored. As history has shown, rather than reaching equilibrium, markets can descend into stagnation without active policy maneuvers. The correct policies are still subjects of sharp debate.

This book seeks to describe and analyze the events, causes, and outcomes of crises from the Great Depression to the Great Recession, unifying a vast amount of literature on each crisis. We start from a general discussion of the global financial system and the roots of crises, both theoretical and empirical. We then discuss crises between 1929 and 2011. We briefly discuss select events before 1929, but focus on the Great Depression and beyond since these crises were created within or bore the current policies and institutions of our current financial system. Our approach differs from what we consider the two leading texts on financial crises (in terms of comprehensive content coverage and analysis), *Manias, Panics and Crashes* by Kindleberger (1978),[1] and more recently, *This Time is Different*, by Reinhart and Rogoff (2009). While Kindleberger discusses major themes in financial crises from the Dutch Tulip Crisis to the Asian financial crisis, and while Reinhart and Rogoff analyze empirically several centuries of crises, we analyze major crises separately to view them in light

1

of the scholarly consensus on each crisis and of more recent understanding of financial fragility.

FINANCIAL CRISIS, DEFINED

First we must agree on a definition for financial crises. We know that we can clearly define a recession in economic terms. Even though there are alternative definitions outlining the time spans in which a downturn occurs, a recession is considered a decline in gross domestic product (GDP) or GDP growth. Financial crises are bigger, confidence-negating episodes. Liquidity may be lost or frozen, in the case of banking crises, or currency may lose its value, in the case of currency crises. At what point does a recession, a credit crunch, an inflationary or deflationary episode, a payment default, or a change in currency value, become a crisis?

The two classic definitions of financial crises, posed by Hyman Minsky (1977) and Charles Kindleberger (1978), make use of the notion of financial fragility. In both definitions, an excessive boom leads to an inevitable crisis or contraction as part of the natural business cycle and the unstable nature of finance. In Minsky's definition, there is a forced liquidation of assets, a credit crunch, and then a sharp drop in asset prices, leading to a depression. A lack of prudence and undue financial fervor (a "mania" in Kindleberger's terms) bring about a financial crisis.

Minsky, whose work was not popularized in the mainstream media until the Great Recession of 2008, after his death, viewed financial markets as essentially fragile and crisis prone, and described three financial postures that the market can take. The first is hedge financing, in which financial institutions have sufficient cash to cover principal and interest on debts. The second is speculative financing, in which institutions can cover interest but not principal; and the third is Ponzi financing, in which financial institutions cannot cover either principal or interest on debts (Minsky 1991; originally in Minsky 1980).

Within Minsky's framework, procyclical credit expansions, or increases in flows of credit in conjunction with an expansionary period during economic growth, can reverse during contraction and lead to financial fragility. Finance is stable when the market is successfully operated, and unstable when events in an uncertain environment push the market into a precarious position. The increase in the number of financial transactions and the speed at which they have been performed in the past 30 years have demonstrated the fragile nature of finance, as the world economy has of late spent a great deal of time in speculative and Ponzi mode.

In his original work, Kindleberger (1978) first describes the beginning of a crisis as a speculative mania, of which there are two stages. The first stage of a mania is a response to an external shock, such as war; while the second is related to profit seeking. Secondly, credit expansion aggravates the mania, and over time, expectations reverse. Kindleberger dubs the sequence "biological in its regularity." Financial distress may then develop into a crisis, triggered by a *causa proxima*, any event that causes investors to sell. Hence a crash or panic may ensue. Unlucky countries engaged in financial activity with the country in turmoil may experience contagion of the crisis. A wide range of policy responses, from simply doing nothing to enforcing bank holidays, to using a domestic or international lender of last resort, may be and have been used.

However, researchers have also used various quantitative measures to determine crises. Carmen Reinhart and Kenneth Rogoff, American economists who have written extensively on crises and other macroeconomic events, construct a database that extends over a period of eight centuries and provides indicators on the existing financial environment (Reinhart and Rogoff 2009). Reinhart and Rogoff define inflation crises as inflationary episodes of greater than 20 percent per year, currency crises as exchange rate depreciations over 15 percent per year, banking crises as events in which important or besieged (run upon) banks submit to government takeovers, sovereign default as failure to meet a payment on the due date, and domestic debt crises as situations where payments cannot be met or bank deposits are frozen or forced to convert to local currency.

As a result of their analysis, themes emerge from descriptive and econometric analysis. Reinhart and Rogoff find that almost all countries experience serial default during the intermediate stages of economic development, and these occurrences are often accompanied by high inflation, currency crashes, and devaluation. The authors also find that periods of extensive financial opening are often followed by domestic banking crises. Looking at data on crises between 1800 and 2006, Reinhart and Rogoff find that there are five long periods in which countries are in default or financial restructuring. These conclusions are in line with the idea that finance is generally unstable, and that increased instability leads to crisis.

Less comprehensive definitions also exist. Carron and Friedman (1982) define a financial crisis from a microeconomic perspective, in which some borrowers face a risk premium arising from unrelated financial developments, which may induce solvency and liquidity problems. This causes a banking crisis. Bordo and Wheelock (1998) also define a financial crisis as a banking panic. These definitions, however, do not account for currency crises. At the opposite end of the spectrum, Andrade and Teles (2004) define a financial crisis from a macroeconomic perspective, in which there is a shift from a good equilibrium with low country risk to a bad equilibrium with high country risk.

Additional crises have been defined as periods in which there is a general consensus that risk has dramatically increased. For example, although financial fragility in the Southeast Asian countries had increased leading up to the Asian financial crisis, a crisis situation was not recognized until a single event occurred: the devaluation of the Thai baht on July 2, 1997 (a *causa proxima*); the *causa proxima* date of a crisis is a definition that researchers like Johnson and Mitton (2001) have used. In this book, we define crises in terms of the consensus starting dates while also providing more specific economic evidence of financial decline, in an attempt to reconcile the technical with the popular view.

THE CONTEXT OF MODERN CRISES

Major crises have occurred sporadically since the Dutch Tulip Crisis in 1637, but became increasingly global and closer together as the twentieth century approached. Crises moved even closer together at the end of the twentieth century. This is in part due to normal economic expansion and growth, and along with it, rapid changes in production technologies. However, speculative investment sometimes accompanied real expansion, bringing about crises. The major reason for the increase in the occurrence of financial crises at the end of the twentieth century is the immense growth and liberalization of finance, which began with the breakdown of the Bretton Woods system that was constructed in the 1940s, the spread of eurocurrency markets in the 1960s, and the rise of portfolio investment in the 1980s (D'Arista 2002), which are discussed in later chapters.

The US political economy of the 1970s in particular aligned the interests of the banking sector with those of the political arena. This is because the US played a large role in the global economy and led both deregulation and bank standardization. On the one hand, politicians faced the threat of a loss of competition, and on the other, they feared the consequences of a lack of regulation. The relatively recent high-level development of finance has, since then, been a balancing act between the two specters.

The debate over fiscal spending or prudence during crisis, and the beginning of the modern financial architecture, has its roots in the Great Depression. Although banking crises and asset price bubbles were not unique throughout history, the Great Depression was so severe that widely accepted economic policy responses at the time failed to ameliorate the descent into economy-wide failure. New policies, categorized as the "First New Deal," were tried and failed, until at last government intervention in public assistance, labor, and industrial regulation put the economy on the track to recovery (Bordo et al. 1998). The powerful insights of Keynesian theory were also brought to light during the later period of the Great Depression, and underscored an expanded role for government intervention. Keynesian perspectives dominated economic thought for some time thereafter, and even after their demise in the 1970s, they have been revived to a large extent today, due to desperate measures undertaken during the Great Recession of 2008.

Of equal importance, the transition from the gold standard, destroyed once and for all during the Great Depression, to pegged exchange rates under the Bretton Woods System created in 1944, established the US dollar (at first tied to gold, later used alone) as the international reserve currency. World leaders set up an adjustable peg system of currencies fixed to the dollar, which was in turn exchangeable for gold (Bordo and Eichengreen 1993). These new global monetary structural changes ushered in years of relative financial stability. After the ravages of the Great Depression and World War II, global financial security was greatly desired. And global financial security was indeed gained, in a period of relative peace, until the 1960s. The lasting element of the Bretton Woods architecture was, and remains, the centrality of the US dollar.

The Bretton Woods meeting was truly singular in that it represented a major global effort to establish monetary and financial rules, for the sake of both stabilizing the world economy and enhancing trade and financial relations. Due to fixed exchange rate regimes, inflation was maintained in most countries at low levels. International monetary cooperation, in conjunction with existing capital controls, brought about a period of calm in the global economy. Pegging currencies to the dollar secured US global economic hegemony through the present day, and has had a lasting impact on the dynamics of international financial power and the anatomy of financial crises down the line. Financial and ideological power was concentrated in the US, has influenced patterns of global trade and investment, and produced directives to developing countries for proper measures for economic development. The historical Bretton Woods meeting also brought into existence international financial and monitoring institutions, namely the International Monetary Fund (IMF) and the World Bank.[2]

The second half of the Bretton Woods regime, the 1960s, saw the rise of eurocurrencies, which are deposits located in banks outside the home country. The use of eurocurrencies allowed domestic banks to bypass capital controls in international lending. Eurocurrencies also allowed banks to avert domestic reserve requirements, deposit insurance, interest rate ceilings, and quantitative controls on credit growth (D'Arista 2002). Due to an increase in popularity, eurodollars began to affect countries' domestic balance of payments after a period of only a few years, and by the late 1960s the US Federal Reserve began to loosen requirements of domestic lending in order to compete with eurocurrencies, ushering in a period of financial liberalization in the 1970s.

Although Bretton Woods institutions remain in the form of the World Bank and IMF, an important feature of the Bretton Woods exchange system was shattered unilaterally in 1971 by US President Nixon, who ended the dollar's convertibility to gold. Nixon closed the "gold window" due to the United States' perpetual balance-of-payments deficits resulting largely from engagement in the Vietnam War, which had greatly reduced the supply of gold reserves (Bordo 2008). This led to the return of inflation and monetary imbalances and, coupled with capital account liberalization in the early 1970s, signaled the prospective return of financial crises. The dollar became the de facto reserve currency, without a commodity anchor.

A vigorous rise in oil prices in the 1970s caused a global recession, and the recycled petrodollars that had been lent in force to developing nations in Asia, Latin America, and Africa during this period led to a chain of banking and sovereign debt crises years later (Reinhart and Rogoff 2009). Both governments and commercial banks lent exorbitant amounts to developing nations to finance their oil imports, setting the stage for the debt crises of the 1980s. Eurocurrency markets spread through the 1970s, in large part due to petrodollar lending, and came into competition with more restricted commercial bank lending in the 1980s. Financial liberalization continued, particularly with the rapid expansion of portfolio investment in this same period. This greatly increased capital mobility and the quantity of cross-border transactions in bonds and equities (D'Arista 2002).

Due to a global environment of increased financial liberalization, the 1980s saw the emergence of debt default crises in Latin America as banks refused to continue financing developing countries' interest payments. Crises then came closer together, with the European Exchange Rate Mechanism Crisis and Nordic banking crises of the late 1980s and early 1990s. Policy conditions imposed by the IMF on developing and developed countries alike in exchange for emergency loans required financial austerity and later came under sharp criticism. The "Washington Consensus," a set of policies so dubbed in 1989 and pushed forward by the IMF for countries enmeshed in crisis, incorporated two of the policy prescriptions that had so emphatically failed in the immediate aftermath of the Great Depression: fiscal policy discipline and expansion of the tax base. The recommendations also included policies that increased the level of risk and exposure to foreign and domestic shocks, such as privatization and trade liberalization.

The prolonged Japanese real estate bust occurred in 1992, followed on its heels by the Mexican peso crisis. Then, just as the 1990s were roaring in the US, the rest of the world went into crisis, hitting the Southeast Asian tigers, Russia, Brazil, and Argentina. Clearly, something was amiss in the global financial architecture. Even the genius mathematical models constructed for long-term credit management under the supervision of Nobel laureates Myron Scholes and Robert Merton failed to decode the complex movements of international finance.

After the Asian financial crisis of 1997, some economists recognized that the collapse of Bretton Woods had led to global financial and monetary instability. The long series of crises after 1971 that came closer together indicated that there may be something fundamentally volatile about the modern financial architecture. The longed-for era of stability under the Bretton Woods system could not be forgotten, and some called for eliminating what has been dubbed the "dollar standard," in which the dollar gained inherent value with the closing of the gold window, and replacing it with a more globally oriented basis of monetary transactions. Also due to short-term capital reversals that occurred during the Asian crisis, the wave of thinking that led to large-scale capital account liberalizations – that is, the Washington Consensus – has become less prominent, if not outmoded in some circles.

The crisis that began in the US in 2007 and 2008 spread quickly across the globe. Because of the centrality of the US economy in terms of both finance and trade, other economies in Europe, Asia, Latin America, and elsewhere were all affected. Those in many strata of income suffered real losses, as individuals directly involved in finance experienced stock market and asset declines, as currencies were devalued, and as export laborers and migrant workers lost jobs.

Although a second radical global change toward economic stability, another "Bretton Woods," is unlikely to occur in the near future, it has been recognized that, at least, more sophisticated and coordinated monitoring of the world economy must take place. It behooves us to examine in detail the panoply of crises that have occurred since 1929, in order to better understand the economic and financial context in which these crises arose, and how they were affected by policies designed, for better or worse, to cushion their impact. With international cooperation and greater understanding of historical missteps, we hold the optimistic view that solutions toward stability can be formulated and implemented.

GLOBAL FINANCE TODAY

We next look at the global financial architecture as it stands today. Since there are too many details to discuss all aspects of the global financial architecture, we focus on a few features that affect capital flow and regulation and currency volatility. These features include:

Existence of a Global Reserve Currency Hegemony Comprised of Limited Countries or Regions

Currently, the dollar is the most widely used global reserve currency. The willingness of foreign governments to hold dollar-denominated foreign currency securities has allowed the US to operate under prodigious national and trade deficits. Because of this, the US has had de facto unlimited credit to purchase goods and services from abroad. Some scholars and financiers, such as George Soros (see Chinn and Frankel 2008; Conway 2008) predicted that the euro would overtake the dollar as the largest international reserve currency (although this has been a subject of debate due to Europe's deep involvement in the global crisis of 2008), but this may simply shift the balance of financial and purchasing power to another region, and concentrated reserve currency power will continue to exacerbate trade and financial imbalances. A better solution would be what Frankel (2009) promotes as "a multiple international currency system." In this type of system, the dollar would lose its dominance as a global reserve currency and other currencies, such as the euro, yen, and in time, the renminbi, could join the dollar as important stores of international reserves.

An associated problem is the issue of "original sin," in which emerging markets in particular cannot borrow abroad in their own currency. Therefore, when these countries accumulate a net debt, they develop an aggregate currency mismatch on their balance sheets. As Eichengreen et al. (2004) show, "original sin" has important stability and economic implications in terms of both policies and outcomes. Developing country domestic policies cannot be used wholesale to encourage growth within the country; many of the policies must be oriented toward servicing the international debt and maintaining a stable exchange rate. Debt denominated in foreign currency, in emerging markets with pegged exchange rates, requires developing countries to balance foreign currency borrowing with the trade deficit and foreign currency reserves in order to maintain a pegged exchange rate. Foreign exchange reserves are necessary to sell in order to uphold the value of the domestic currency when exports decline or currency demand falls. Balance sheet crises can occur, either from holding debt in short-term foreign currency, or from a currency mismatch in corpo-

Table 1.1   International bonded debt, by country groups and currencies,
*   1991–2001*

	Total debt instruments issued by residents (%)	Total debt instruments issued by residents in own currency (%)	Total debt instruments issued in groups' currency (%)
Major financial centers	45	61	68
Eurozone	33	37	30
Other developed countries	8	2	1
Developing countries	8	0	1
International organizations	7	0	0
ECU	0	0	0

Note: Major financial centers include the US, Japan, the United Kingdom, and Switzerland.

Source: Eichengreen et al. (2004), Bank for International Settlements.

rate balance sheets (Jeanne and Zettelmeyer 2004). The label "original sin" is appropriate since denominating debt in foreign currency can cause many other problems originating from the currency regime.

As a mirror image of the problem, US data from 2001 show that developed countries are more often willing to expose themselves to developing country credit risk rather than developing country currency risk, which may be more financially fragile. Table 1.1 describes total debt issued in countries' own currencies.

As seen in Table 1.1, the major financial centers are able to issue much or most of their debt in their own currencies, while other countries do not share that privilege. If developing countries experience "original sin," developed countries encourage the sinners.

Persistence of Unregulated International Capital Flows

Some international capital flows remain unregulated or less regulated than those under banking supervision. These consist of capital flowing through the carry trade market, in which investors borrow in low-yielding currencies and invest in high-yielding currencies. Although hedge funds must now be registered with the Securities and Exchange Commssion (SEC) in the US and in Europe, these and other actors, counting on interest rate differentials and exchange rate appreciation, have played a large role in procyclical carry trades (D'Arista and Griffith-Jones 2009). Carry trades, during downturns as yields reverse, can create deepening currency mismatches that necessitate international intervention, as in the case of Iceland and Hungary in 2008. Eurocurrency markets, which consist of dollar or other deposits held by banks in foreign countries, were subjected to some regulation after Basel I, but continue to evade regulation, and are the main suppliers of funds for the carry trade (D'Arista 2006). American and European regulation implemented in the wake of the Great Recession has not put specific controls on the eurocurrency market.

These evasive capital flows are dangerous. Trade in goods and trade in capital are not equal (Bhagwati 1998). The argument for free trade does not extend to free capital; restricted capital mobility is not tantamount to protectionism. This is because free capital flows can experience sharp reversals, harming economies in their wake. Because of this, some countries have instituted capital controls to curb this maleffect of international financial flows.

Mix of Capital Control Regimes

Countries' control over capital inflows and outflows vary across the world, from capital openness to tight capital control. Capital controls create stability by preventing the flow of real and financial assets as recorded in the capital account in the balance of payments. Such controls can take the form of taxes, quantity or price controls on capital inflows or outflows, or restrictions on trade in assets abroad. These were first used on a larger scale by the belligerents beginning during World War I, restricting capital outflows, in order to keep capital in the domestic economy for taxation purposes (Neely 1999).

Although throughout the 1990s, financial openness was encouraged, studies have shown that financial openness has mixed effects. After the Asian financial crisis, China was lauded for maintaining capital controls, which helped the country to evade accelerating capital reversals, and capital controls once again were back in vogue. Later research, such as that of Chinn and Ito (2005), finds that financial openness is beneficial only in countries above a particular level of institutional development. Indeed, the Great Recession has shown that capital controls may be applicable to countries with an even higher level of institutional development, since without capital controls, contagion of declining assets can quickly spread to foreign-investing countries.

Edwards (2005) creates an index of capital controls to determine countries' vulnerability to and depth of financial crises, looking at crises that manifest themselves in sudden stops of capital inflows and current account reversals. He finds that openness may worsen a financial crisis once it has begun. Other authors, such as Chang and Velasco (1998) and Williamson and Mahar (1998), find that financial openness may also increase vulnerability to crises.

Implementation of Basel I, Basel II, and (soon) Basel III

Basel I and II set standards for banks around the world. Basel I was created in 1988, Basel II in 2004, in order to improve and coordinate banking supervision, regulation, and capital adequacy requirements across countries (Balin 2008). The accords are not enforced by any supranational body, but are guidelines for best banking practices. The Group of Ten (G-10) comprised the Basel Committee during the first round of Basel guidelines, and Basel I was considered applicable mainly to these developed countries.

Basel I protected against banking risk, and was not drawn up to prevent other sources of systemic risk created by lack of diversification or market risk (Balin 2008). Basel I grouped assets into categories according to credit risk, requiring banks to hold minimum capital levels according to their risk levels (Elizalde 2007). Most Basel Committee members implemented Basel I by 1992.

Banks found loopholes around Basel I, and for this reason, and because of the need to increase coverage of systemic risk and improve applications to developing countries, Basel II was created. Basel II created three pillars to expand on Basel I in order to cover these gaps. These pillars were: Pillar 1, capital requirements; Pillar 2, supervisory review; and Pillar 3, market discipline. The latter two are the newer components, while Pillar 1, which largely comprised Basel I, expanded risk sensitivity. Pillars 2 and 3 are less extensive than Pillar 1 and have been largely left to the discretion of supervision of national officials (Elizalde 2007). Basel III was put forward in June 2011 to improve systemic banking oversight, as well as to improve banks' risk management and transparency (BIS 2011). It is comprised of the same three pillars as in Basel II. Box 1.1 illustrates the Basel III Three-Pillar model.

Due to shortcomings of the previous Basel Models, Basel III was created to set up stronger requirements for banks. These include ensuring better quality and transparency of the capital base, in particular since the crisis revealed the inconsistency of capital definitions across regions and a lack of full disclosure of the capital base (BIS 2010). They also include enhancing risk coverage to raise capital requirements for trading and complex securitizations using a stressed value-at-risk capital requirement, since the Great Recession revealed that exposure to on- and off-balance sheet risk was not captured. Basel III also seeks to supplement the risk-based capital

BOX 1.1   BASEL III THREE-PILLAR MODEL

Pillar I Capital Requirements
Capital:

- Quality and level of capital.
- Greater focus on common equity. The minimum will be raised to 4.5% of risk-weighted assets, after deductions.
- Capital loss absorption at the point of non-viability.
- Contractual terms of capital instruments will include a clause that allows – at the discretion of the relevant authority – write-off or conversion to common shares if the bank is judged to be non-viable. This principle increases the contribution of the private sector to resolving future banking crises and thereby reduces moral hazard.
- Capital conservation buffer.
- Comprising common equity of 2.5% of risk-weighted assets, bringing the total common equity standard to 7%. Constraint on a bank's discretionary distributions will be imposed when banks fall into the buffer range.
- Countercyclical buffer.
- Imposed within a range of 0–2.5% comprising common equity, when authorities judge credit growth is resulting in an unacceptable build-up of systematic risk.

Risk coverage:

- Securitizations.
- Strengthens the capital treatment for certain complex securitisations. Requires banks to conduct more rigorous credit analyses of externally rated securitization exposures.
- Trading book.
- Significantly higher capital for trading and derivatives activities, as well as complex securitizations held in the trading book. Introduction of a stressed value-at-risk framework to help mitigate procyclicality. A capital charge for incremental risk that estimates the default and migration risks of unsecuritized credit products and takes liquidity into account.
- Counterparty credit risk.
- Substantial strengthening of the counterparty credit risk framework. Includes: more stringent requirements for measuring exposure; capital incentives for banks to use central counterparties for derivatives; and higher capital for inter-financial sector exposures.
- Bank exposures to central counterparties (CCPs).
- The Committee has proposed that trade exposures to a qualifying CCP will receive a 2% risk weight and default fund exposures to a qualifying CCP will be capitalized according to a risk-based method that consistently and simply estimates risk arising from such default fund.

Containing leverage:

- Leverage ratio.
- A non-risk-based leverage ratio that includes off-balance sheet exposures will serve as a backstop to the risk-based capital requirement. Also helps contain system-wide build-up of leverage.

Pillar II Risk Management and Supervision

- Supplemental Pillar 2 requirements.
- Address firm-wide governance and risk management; capturing the risk of off-balance sheet exposures and securitization activities; managing risk concentrations; providing incentives for banks to better manage risk and returns over the long term; sound compensation practices; valuation practices; stress testing; accounting standards for financial instruments; corporate governance; and supervisory colleges.

Pillar III Market Discipline

- Revised Pillar 3 disclosures requirements.
- The requirements introduced relate to securitization exposures and sponsor-ship of off-balance sheet vehicles. Enhanced disclosures on the detail of the components of regulatory capital and their reconciliation to the reported accounts will be required, including a comprehensive explanation of how a bank calculates its regulatory capital ratios.

Source: Bank for International Settlements (2012).

requirement with a leverage ratio, which would constrain leverage and reduce the risk created by deleveraging processes. Procyclicality has also been addressed in the hopes of dampening cyclical amplifications of the minimum capital requirement and preventing excess credit growth. Finally, Basel III seeks to address systemic risk by increasing capital requirements for trading activities and inter-financial sector exposures and by using central counterparties for over-the-counter derivatives.

Large, Unwieldy Financial-Banking Institutions

Policies that emerged in the 1980s and 1990s in developed countries allowed commercial banks to merge with investment banks, securities firms, and insurance companies. This resulted in the rise of mammoth financial institutions that lacked transparency and appropriate regulation. This, coupled with large, procyclical bonuses in the banking sector and the lack of a global financial regulator resulted in the Great Recession of 2008.

Simon Johnson (2009b) of Massachusetts Institute of Technology (MIT) and other major economists have dubbed the new financial organizations as "too big to fail." "Too big to fail" creates moral hazard, in which banking managers take excessive risks because they assume the government will bail them out should the risky investments fail. Buiter (2009) notes that although firms can be closely interconnected, it is large firms that threaten the stability of financial systems. These firms can become so large that they no longer exploit economies of scale and scope, but lose control over their own organizational activities and efficiency. Bailouts based on "too big to fail" were eliminated in the US Dodd–Frank Act of 2010 but specific legislation preventing the build-up of large financial institutions was not part of the bill, and was left to the discretion of the Financial Stability Oversight Council.

Procyclical and Short-Term Risk Measurement

The Great Recession of 2008 showed that risk modeling can be so deeply flawed as to allow banking officials to overlook entrenched banking instability. D'Arista and Griffith-Jones (2009) point out that the value-at-risk measurement is procyclical, and additional, non-cyclical measures of risk must be used. The value-at-risk (VaR) measurement provides the probability that an asset or bundle of assets will decline by a particular amount over a given time period. Capital requirements given by VaR are inherently procyclical, since banks experience more losses during recessions than during booms, decreasing the lending capacity of the institution. Dodd–Frank and Basel III mandated changes that require countercyclical capital requirements (Kowalik 2011). The Basel III changes designate a buffer of 0–2.5 percent above the minimum capital requirements, while Dodd–Frank also includes countercyclical capital requirements and requirements that holding companies assist subsidiaries of insured depository institutions.

These are the major aspects of the current global financial architecture. As noted above, many changes within the world economic structure still need to be made, yet regulatory and institutional change has been ongoing. It will become apparent that institutional change in the face of financial instability is the only consistent feature of the global financial architecture.

STRUCTURE OF THE BOOK

Having looked at aspects of the financial architecture and at the general context of modern crises, we are now ready to look at individual crises themselves. In order to do this, we discuss crises by time period. Some time periods are long and are occupied by one large crisis, such as the Great Depression, while other time periods are relatively short and encompass several crises, such as the early 1990s in which several countries experienced economic reversals.

We move through the twentieth and early twenty-first centuries in chronological order. Chapter 2 analyzes the Great Depression and its aftermath, in which many economies struggled to recover. We first touch upon the political economy before 1929, discussing the crisis of 1907 and the destabilizing influence of World War I, then discuss at length the causes and economic debate surrounding the Great Depression. We look at the transmission of the Great Depression through the mechanism of the gold standard, which was once and for all abandoned during this period. Finally, we discuss policies implemented in the US and Europe to overcome the depression, and the impact of World War II on the global economy.

Chapter 3 examines the 1950s through 1970s, under the Bretton Woods system, which experienced a relatively low level of crises with increasing financial instability. We look at the factors that allowed for this relative stability and debate its sustainability. Although the 1950s brought on a period of general financial stability, increasingly, a high level of global coordination was required in the 1960s as imbalances threatened to undermine the system due to increasing pressures on the US balance of payments. The US could not maintain its level of spending while upholding credibility in the dollar–gold standard. Because of the United States' growing current account deficit, the Bretton Woods dollar–gold parity was unsustainable and unilaterally canceled in the 1970s, which brought about great changes in the global financial architecture. The end of Bretton Woods coincided with unrest in the Middle East and a consequential large movement of capital from both oil-rich and developed countries to oil-poor developing nations, which set the stage for increased financial liberalization that allowed such transfers of funds.

The expansion of financial instruments and global economic and political forces gave rise to the 1980s' emerging markets debt default crises when the indebted Latin American countries found themselves unable to repay loans at higher interest rates, the subject of Chapter 4. In this chapter, we examine the processes at work in these crises, both from the prevailing perspective at the time of the crisis, as well as from a historical perspective of sovereign debt crises.

Much to the chagrin of the developed world, crises in advanced countries were not far ahead. The Nordic crises, the Exchange Rate Mechanism crisis, and the Japanese crisis in the early 1990s are examined in Chapter 5. The Nordic crises began at the end of the 1980s and were exacerbated by the European Exchange Rate Mechanism crisis of 1992. The Japanese crisis began with the bursting of the asset bubble at the end of the 1980s, extended through the early 1990s, and culminated in a larger systemic crisis in 1997.

The mid- and late 1990s saw a return to emerging markets crises, with the Mexican peso crisis and the Asian financial crisis, the focus of Chapter 6. The Asian financial crisis was a shock to those who had considered the Southeast Asian tigers to be growth machines, and threatened global contagion. Global contagion indeed arose in Russia and Brazil. Chapter 7 elaborates on the Russian, Brazilian, and Argentine financial crises, all connected to the Asian financial crisis but also to varying degrees products of domestic economic shortcomings.

Chapter 8 covers the Great Recession of the late 2000s. We study the reasons for the initiation and spread of the crisis, as well as outcomes and changes in the global economy. Chapter 9 covers global imbalances and shows how some economists have referenced these imbalances in discussing the reasons for the rise of financial crises.

Finally, as an appeal to concerned individuals, Chapter 10 looks at policy recommendations for preventing future crises. Some of the recommendations resulted from the Asian financial crisis and endured, while others have arisen from the most recent international crisis. We study the viability of these proposals and the implications for the future global financial architecture.[3]

NOTES

1. Most recently published in 2005 with Robert Aliber.
2. At the time, the World Bank was known as the International Bank for Reconstruction and Development.
3. The author would like to thank Jane d'Arista and an anonymous referee for their invaluable comments on the manuscript.

2. 1930s and 1940s: the Great Depression and its aftermath

The Great Depression was an unprecedented event that began in the United States (US) and spread to both developed and developing countries globally. Although serious crises had occurred previously, the Great Depression changed the way in which policy makers around the world responded to a flagging economy and notably ended permanently the gold standard, which had been used in varying capacities for decades. Countercyclical fiscal policy was first used on a grand scale in the US, after insufferable months of cyclical budget tightening in which economic grievances caused great social unrest.

PRE-1929 CRISES AND CONDITIONS

Financial crises prior to the Great Depression occurred consistently around the world throughout the nineteenth century, as well as in the beginning of the twentieth century. Some of these crises were similar in nature to crises that came later (for example, caused by excessive foreign lending, as in 1826). The crisis of 1873 in the US, which lasted more than 20 years, is sometimes seen as even more devastating than the Great Depression of 1929 (Kindleberger 1986). In the nineteenth century, the largest national banks in Europe and Canada led the way out of crises. In the US, bankers coordinated at a regional level to suspend convertibility and establish rules for interbank clearing of transactions over this period (Calomiris and Gorton 1991).

The crises of the twentieth century brought about significant banking regulation at a national level in the US (Calomiris and Gorton 1991). Unlike some European countries, whose central banks provided monetary and financial stability for decades, even centuries,[1] the US lacked a central bank, which had dissolved in 1836. The US crisis of 1907, significantly, gave rise to the Federal Reserve and highlighted the instability of US banks and markets in a crisis compared to the relative stability found elsewhere in the world. During the crisis of 1907, New York banker J.P. Morgan pledged his own funds to assist the financial system (Bruner and Carr 2007). In the aftermath of the crisis, and soon after the death of J.P. Morgan in 1913, legislation was passed to revive a central bank.

When World War I began in 1914, the US was strongly isolationist, but nevertheless the economy was affected by the war. Stock markets the world over declined and the price of gold soared, reflecting a rush of uncertainty in the global economy (Sobel 1968). In time, American securities appeared safer than European securities. Trade for both American and European merchants was at risk as freight ships were attacked on the seas. However, trade continued and increased for US munitions producers, with demand for weapons and other war materials on the rise. Even after the US declaration of war in 1917, on the whole, wealth was lost in Europe and much was transferred to the US.

Europe suffered greatly from World War I as a result of losing many of its youth and experiencing destruction of its lands. The United Kingdom's future had been compromised to guarantee its victory in the war (Sobel 1968). France was deeply scarred. Germany was made to pay reparations to the opposing nations, the Allies, for its instigating role in the Great War. The payments were forced despite the great opposition of John Maynard Keynes, at the time an advisor to the British government (Keynes 1920). Keynes's views in this regard were later upheld.

The Dawes Plan of 1924 was drawn up by Allied nations, and sought to collect German war reparations more effectively, demanding 1 billion Marks in the first year of the plan, rising to 2.5 billion Marks over a period of four years (*Columbia Electronic Encyclopedia* 2001). Within a short period of time, the Dawes Plan was largely recognized as excessively onerous. The Young Plan of 1929 brought together a group of experts in Paris to discuss German reparations, and was negotiated, rather than imposed upon Germany (Bergmann 1930).

Since there was at the time no other commodity or currency that was considered outside money, save for gold, Europe and the US returned to the gold standard in 1925 under the Gold Standard Act of 1925 enacted in Britain. Small countries favored the gold standard for its stabilizing properties, while larger countries wanted stability in exchange rates for foreign trade (Kindleberger 1986). After the Great Depression, the return to the gold standard was for the most part regarded as an error, which we discuss below. France in particular struggled to regain monetary stability, suffering speculative attacks on the franc and large depreciations under political chaos, between 1924 and 1926. The franc was finally stabilized under the strong leadership of Raymond Poincaré (Eichengreen 1992).

CAUSES AND EVENTS OF THE GREAT DEPRESSION

Much of the debate among economists surrounding the Great Depression has to do with the reasons for its propagation and, in accordance, with the policies used to combat the deep trough. There has also been controversy, over the years, about the causes of the Great Depression (Were the fundamental reasons monetary, real, financial, or some combination of these factors?), descriptively, we can at least say that in the short run the "roaring twenties," in which loose credit and expanding industrial production led to stock market gains, gave way to declining industrial production and an increasingly overvalued stock market. While a handful of countries suffered from recession (including the United Kingdom, Italy, and Japan), the boom took place mainly in the United States, Australia, Canada, and France[2] (Romer 2004).

Economic expansion was based on the rise of the automobile and its associated industries, production of electrical appliances, and motion pictures. Eichengreen (2014) paints a colorful picture of the period leading up to the Great Depression, underscoring the fact that good times generated a false sense of security. Faster productivity brought about by the assembly line, used in successful factories such as that owned by Henry Ford, led to higher incomes and had the effect of inflating asset prices. Security brought about by the creation of the Federal Reserve gave rise to the delusion that monetary stability was there to stay.

Although economic growth was based on a moderate increase in production, by the late 1920s, US investors were borrowing large sums to finance stock purchases for speculation. Canadian and most European stock markets turned downward, starting in 1927. As the end of the decade approached, brokers' loan contracts increased interest rates and initial margins, revealing increasing uncertainty in the US (Rappoport and White 1994). John Kenneth Galbraith (1955) eloquently writes on the transformation of the stock market climb into a "speculative orgy" in 1928, which ultimately culminated in September 1929's record high Dow Jones Industrial Average just before the crash in the following month. Paul Krugman (2007) has dubbed this transition from boom to crash a "Wile E. Coyote" moment, referring to a popular television cartoon in which the coyote runs off a cliff, legs spinning in midair, before he looks down and realizes he is about to plunge into the abyss. Galbraith argues that market makers in late 1929 were unaware that they were necessarily pricking the bubble, but were instead reacting to declines in the real economy. In any case, the coyote fell, and far. Brokers' loans dried up as orders to sell stock came rushing in.

The Federal Reserve (Fed) had been unable to deflate the stock bubble and was insufficiently active in its response to the crash. Galbraith and Kindleberger differ in their interpretation of why the Federal Reserve did not deflate the stock market bubble before the crash. Galbraith views the Fed as essentially incompetent, failing to clearly denounce speculation or to implement policies that would accomplish this task. Galbraith notes that the Fed, although limited in its capacity to perform open market operations, could have requested the power to increase margins or issue a strong warning that a bust would ensue. Kindleberger, by contrast, rejects the monetarist and Keynesian explanations of the Great Depression, as well as the assertion that the Fed was incompetent. Kindleberger takes the Minskian view that declines in industrial production and associated prices led to loan defaults and a credit crunch. Although the Fed took an inappropriate stance, this we can see clearly only in hindsight; the going, politically acceptable policy remedy at the time was to execute the policies that were indeed implemented and spectacularly failed.

The stock market boom in the US, combined with the pressure of potential French claims on British gold and the introduction of the Young Plan in 1929 created a climate of uncertainty, which led to an increase in discount rates across Europe and in the US, and a global credit crunch. The stock market then crashed at the end of 1929. As industrial production in the US fell immediately and sharply after the crash, the New York Federal Reserve and European central banks implemented discount rate reductions at the end of 1929 and in the first half of 1930 in order to inject liquidity into the market (Cogley 1999). Open market operations policies, which would have introduced additional liquid funds into the system, were rejected by the main Federal Reserve (Friedman and Schwartz 2008). Declines in the nominal money supply began at the end of 1930 and spread into declines in the real money supply, affecting purchasing power, starting in 1931. During this period, banking panics ensued and bank failures accelerated at the end of 1930.

Deflation spread from the stock market declines to production decreases, and from stock price declines to commodity price declines, then to reduced import prices (Kindleberger 1986). Credit became instantly scarce immediately following the crash. Some international lending revived over 1930 but lagged thereafter. Commodity prices went into a downward spiral as credit dried up, leaving farmers with no choice but to sell off stocks at the cheap market price.

The first banking panic began in December 1930 when the Bank of the United States in New York City went bankrupt (Friedman and Schwartz 1963). The bank was an ordinary commercial bank, but due to its name, many at home and abroad believed it was an official bank, and panicked in response. Clearing house banks did not save the bank and served as a blow

Source: Library of Congress. No known copyright restrictions.

Figure 2.1   Migrant mother, Dorothea Lange, United States, 1936

to the reputation of the Federal Reserve Bank of New York. Additional banking crises followed.

This initiated a tragic period in which unemployment and poverty increased (Figure 2.1), families broke up due to the external stresses, and homeless settlements were built all over the US and dubbed "Hoovervilles." These shanty towns, comprised mainly of cardboard dwellings, were immortalized in John Steinbeck's *Grapes of Wrath* (1939), in which the Joad family settles into a Hooverville in California.

However, despite the slide for many into the abyss of poverty, the correct policy prescription was unknown at the time. As Edwin Gay wrote in 1932: "the deep depression cripples every economic process and discourages

even the most sanguine business leaders. There are many confusing prescriptions offered from all sides. But no one, however skilled, really knows
the character of or the specific cure for what some practitioners diagnose
as a wasting disease."

In retrospect, and from a distance, Friedman and Schwartz (1963) view
American monetary policy as singularly responsible for the crisis, while
at the other extreme Temin (1976) considers the causes of the crisis to be
"real," with the money supply declining in step. Friedman and Schwartz
argue that a credit crunch, led by panic after the failure of a New York
bank, was transformed into the Great Depression through the Fed's use of
contractionary monetary policy and deficiency in addressing banking liquidity shortages. Additional liquidity, they argue, would have eased the credit
crunch, saved banks, and reversed deflation and economic contraction.[3]

Temin (1976) notes that proactive fiscal and monetary policy could have
tempered the depression, but that income and production dropped after
1929 for reasons that were not monetary. Temin found that the monetary
contraction was caused by a passive response of money to sharp declines
in output, particularly in industrial production; his causality the reverse
of Friedman and Schwartz. Falling production resulted in the failure of
businesses and mounting pressures on banks, which lost profitability and
began to fail. Temin finds that deflationary pressure was also transmitted
by international financial collapse.

The Friedman and Schwartz proposition has been disproved both
through academic empirical analysis, and through the events of history.
Calomiris and Mason (2003) show that contractionary monetary policy
alone during the early stages of the crisis itself cannot explain the
descent into the depression. Building on prior research disaggregating
data on banking fundamentals by region (Wicker 1980, 1996), Calomiris
and Mason use three regression models to test the Friedman–Schwartz
hypothesis, which states generally that monetary policy could have prevented the Great Depression. The authors reject the notion that the Great
Depression was created by banking panics that could have been resolved
through monetary policy, and find, rather, that degeneration of banking
fundamentals in 1930 and 1931 were responsible for the deep economic
decline, although they note that after 1932, other factors were also at play.

Despite the type of analysis performed by Calomiris and Mason and due
in part to the writings of Friedman and Schwartz, for quite some time in
recent decades, many policy makers believed that monetary policy could
stabilize the economy and prevent another Great Depression. Later, Fed
Chairman Ben Bernanke's promise to prevent another Great Depression
through proactive monetary policy[4] was checked by the severity of the US
crisis. Notwithstanding the efforts of Bernanke to stabilize the economy,

monetary policy lost its ability to bring the economy out of deep recession. The Great Recession of 2008 revealed that the Federal Reserve's monetary policy alone could not prevent economic disaster.

Ben Bernanke, regarded as one of the leading scholars on the Great Depression, finds that monetary shocks, although not the only source of the initial decline, played a large role in the economic descent by spreading into the real sector. Monetary shocks were effective in wreaking havoc on the economy due to the creation of a deflationary spiral, in which deflation induced increasingly higher demands on debtors, cutting off real economic opportunities to this strata of the economy and creating banking distress (Bernanke 1995). Deflation took place in both the agricultural and industrial sectors, which were experiencing distress around the world. Nominal wage rigidity, through non-indexed debt contracts and slow adjustment of nominal wages, led to increasing real wages as the value of the dollar was worth more domestically (Bernanke and Carey 1996; Bordo et al. 2000). This explains the sharp increase in unemployment.

Importantly, Bernanke (1983) rejects the Kindlebergian theory that industrial declines led to debt defaults and a liquidity shortage. Financial problems led output declines rather than the other way around. What is more, financial shocks unassociated with output declines were also prevalent. Banking constraints, and in some cases failures, led to a decline in output. Countries that experienced banking crises suffered worst during the depression. Operationalizing this, Bernanke (1983) posited that an increase in the costs of financial intermediation led to a severe credit crunch, which affected aggregate demand and in turn reduced output.

Given insights from the Great Recession of 2008 and from history beyond the Great Depression, we find Bernanke's work to be the most insightful with regard to the Great Depression, for the following reasons:

1. We have experienced variable types of monetary policy that have not led to severe recessions; that is, monetary tightening has not caused a depression per se.
2. We know that financial shocks in and of themselves can trigger real declines in output. It is not necessary for real declines in output to be triggered by real economic shocks.
3. We have witnessed a sudden credit crunch due to increases in costs of financial intermediation caused by uncertainty, even in the presence of sufficient liquidity.

These observations strengthen the credibility of Bernanke's work. Whereas before the Great Recession, disproving Friedman and Schwartz or Temin took some doing, today the idea that serious economic trouble can be caused by financial shocks upon the real sector has a very current resonance. And, in light of the fact that we can disprove the causality of the Great Depression as stemming mainly from real or monetary sources (although these factors were endogenous to the process), Bernanke's modeling of the Great Depression emerges as a clear winner.

In addition, Eichengreen (1992) discusses the fact that, on the gold standard, central banks lost the ability to act as the lender of last resort, exacerbating the position of banks. A combination of monetary shocks, rigid nominal wages, and banking constraints offer some explanation for economic collapse.

President Hoover blamed the Great Depression on financial shocks from Europe, but the severity of the contraction convinced voters otherwise. In November 1932, Franklin Delano Roosevelt (FDR) won the presidency in a landslide and in 1933 began a series of policies under the heading of the "New Deal." Hoover continues to be denigrated today for his ineffectiveness in response to the descent into economic depression and, despite FDR's controversial policies, his four-time re-election speaks to his enormous popularity in those hard times.

DISTRESS ABROAD

The crisis spread abroad but was also exacerbated by pre-existing conditions in Europe. In 1930, Germany encountered extremely large unemployment numbers, and unemployment insurance was funded by a government deficit (Rothermund 1996). Political reorganization under an increasingly nationalistic policy led to foreign withdrawal of funds the same year. Banks went into distress as deposits declined, and economic strain mounted.

The return of Italian banks in 1926 to the *quota novanta* led to a sharp appreciation of the lira and stressed the banking system (Rothermund 1996). Government intervention took place through the Bank of Italy. France faced bank failures as commodity and security prices fell, leading to non-performing loans.

Austria's economic troubles after World War I faced no abatement. Austria's largest bank, the Creditanstalt, was forced to declare bankruptcy in 1931. It took almost two years to settle accounts with foreign creditors of the bank and begin financial reconstruction. The failure of Creditanstalt led to panic that flowed over Austria's borders into neighboring nations and abroad (Schubert 1991).

Monetary currents grew stronger in the lead-up to the Great Depression. Both the United States and the United Kingdom wished to restore the gold standard. The Federal Reserve Governor Benjamin Strong lowered interest rates starting in 1924 to help Britain gain necessary reserves for its return to gold (Eichengreen 2014). The interest rate differential between the US and Britain channeled funds to London.

However, after the Great Depression unraveled, claims upon Britain's pound sterling mounted in 1931 as European economic pressures climbed (Eichengreen et al. 1996). Withdrawals of gold thereby increased and became intolerable. Britain was forced to abandon the gold standard at year end and the pound devalued subsequently. Twenty-five countries followed Britain off gold, and it was only a matter of time before countries still on the gold standard began to place gold withdrawal requests on the US. Monetary authorities increased the discount rate, but devaluation in countries off gold further pushed the downward spiral of prices.

The financial crisis spread through declines in the value of securities, contractions in spending and trade, and monetary shocks that broadcast deflation (Kindleberger 1986). Panic was also a factor. The gold standard and war reparations played the largest incipient role in the transmission of financial shocks from the US to Europe. Developing countries were hardest hit through slowdowns in their exports to developed countries. In Table 2.1, Triantis (1967) shows the percentage decline in exports at the beginning of the crisis within 49 exporting countries.

The gold standard was revived after World War I under different

Table 2.1   *49 primary-exporting countries classified by percentage of decline in exports, 1928–29 to 1932–33*

Percentage decline in exports	Country
>80	Chile
75–80	China
70–75	Bolivia, Cuba, Malaya, Peru, Salvador
65–70	Argentina, Canada, Ceylon, Netherlands Indies, Estonia, Guatemala, India, Irish Free State, Latvia, Mexico, Siam, Spain
60–65	Brazil, Dominican Republic, Egypt, Greece, Haiti, Hungary, Netherlands, Nicaragua, Nigeria, Poland, Yugoslavia
55–60	Denmark, Ecuador, Honduras, New Zealand
50–55	Australia, Bulgaria, Colombia, Costa Rica, Finland, Panama, Paraguay
45–50	Norway, Persia, Portugal, Romania
30–45	Lithuania, Philippines, Turkey, Venezuela

Source: Triantis (1967).

circumstances. Claims upon gold against foreign currencies posed a danger, particularly to the British, but also to the French, who held both spot and forward contracts against the British pound sterling (Kindleberger 1986). The gold standard was increasingly a point of contention.

Bernanke (1995) elaborates on the mechanism by which the contraction was channeled abroad through the widely continued use of the gold standard. The tendency to transmit financial contagion through a common monetary standard had earlier been shown in Fisher (1934), and was echoed in later work by Temin (1989) and Eichengreen and Sachs (1985). The gold standard fixed a unit of national currency to a given weight of gold. The ratio of national currency to gold was contracted by the Fed to reign in the mounting stock market speculation beginning in 1928, and monetary contraction spread to the rest of the world beginning in 1931.

The mechanism by which the gold standard created deflation is spelled out in Bernanke (1995). A country's domestic money supply was comprised of a multiple of the money supply to monetary base ratio, the monetary base to international reserve ratio, the international reserves to gold reserve ratio, the price of gold, and the quantity of gold. This is illustrated in the following equation:

$$M1 = (M1/BASE) \times (BASE/RES) \times (RES/GOLD) \times PGOLD \times QGOLD$$

The first variable, the money supply to monetary base ratio, is the money multiplier, which fell as lending transactions declined. Flight away from foreign exchange reserves to gold produced a decline in the international reserve to gold ratio. In many countries, the flight to gold also produced declines in the monetary base to international reserve ratio. Therefore, the money supply within countries on the gold standard dropped, producing deflation.

Deflation had real effects, operating through several channels, including the Fisherian debt–deflation spiral, in which debt contracts become harder to service, leading to a "fire sale" of assets and further price declines. Countries that abandoned the gold standard were able to reflate their economies and begin real economic recovery. The United Kingdom (UK), upon abandoning the gold standard, was able to recover its terms of trade and living standards (Eichengreen 1992). Sweden, which left the gold standard with the UK, was equally successful in recovering stable prices, incomes, and employment. As prices rose more quickly than nominal wages in countries leaving gold, real wages fell, allowing employment to sharply increase (Bernanke 1995).

In addition, post-World War I reparations were repaid by Germany at the expense of its own economic growth and stability. The reparations repayment schedule was interrupted by the Great Depression, since foreign loans from New York that financed reparations repayment were withdrawn, and this led to near financial collapse in Germany (Eichengreen 1992). New York loans to Europe had already declined at the height of the boom as investors redirected their funds into the stock market (Kindleberger 1986). As contagion spread, Austria experienced capital flight[5] from German investors and a loss of reserves, and Hungary also saw short-term capital flow reversals. Importantly, US President Hoover put forth a one-year moratorium on German reparations in 1931 as Germany faced increasing financial difficulties.

Transmission of the contraction was exacerbated by worldwide overproduction in agriculture, which led to steeply declining farm prices. Although in developed countries the business cycle was separated from agricultural harvests beginning in the middle of the nineteenth century, the interaction between agricultural price declines, a sharp reduction in foreign loans, and tariffs exacerbated farm debt and the living circumstances of farmers around the world (Temin 1976). Countries that were still largely agricultural, however, faced hardship in advance of the rest of the world. Global leadership was not strong enough to raise agricultural prices while enforcing the prosecution of violators.

Tariffs were implemented globally after the US passed the Smoot–Hawley Tariff Act in 1930, which placed tariffs on a range of goods in response to growing excess capacity in US factories (Beaudreau 2005). The Smoot–Hawley Tariff attempted to encourage consumption of American-made goods, mainly agricultural products. Although foreign trade was a small part of the American economy constituting only 4.2 percent of gross domestic product (GDP), the agriculture sector was greatly affected by imports. Farming income declined even after enacting the tariffs because the overall economy was worsening and consumers were unable to purchase products across all sectors despite the tariffs. Exports declined as other countries retaliated in response to the Smoot–Hawley Tariff. The tariffs were seen as an effective tax on goods and intensified worldwide deflation.

In time, the pound sterling began to rapidly depreciate and in 1931, Britain moved off the gold standard (Kindleberger 1986). Twenty-five countries then went off gold, including the US somewhat belatedly, in 1933. The cancellation of reparations in 1932 and shift away from the gold standard over the same period put Europe on the road to recovery, even as the shocks of the depression were still spreading to export-oriented developing countries through declining international demand.

DEPRESSION POLICIES

Just as there has been great debate regarding the causes and propagation of the Great Depression, there has been much controversy over the success of America's New Deal policies. It is almost a given, within the literature, that US President Hoover's policies were insufficient to curb the painful effects of the downturn. New Deal policies did not always achieve their lofty goals but were well intentioned and certainly more productive, as a whole, than Hoover's meager endeavors. First, we review President Hoover's policies, then turn to the diverse policies of his successor, Franklin Delano Roosevelt (FDR).

Monetary policy in immediate response to the contraction has been discussed above. Monetary policy under Hoover was minimal and mainly ineffective. Hoover's initial response to the crisis was to revert to traditional policies of balancing the budget, which pushed the economy into further decline. Especially detrimental was the Smoot–Hawley Tariff, mentioned above, instituted in 1930. The tariff provoked international retaliation, and global tariffs on US exported goods effectively made most traded goods more expensive for both consumers and producers. In addition, Hoover attempted to raise tax rates on corporations, trade, and income on Americans, enacting the Revenue Act of 1932, one of the greatest tax increases in American history.

Hoover also requested that employers not lower wages. This move was heavily criticized by mainstream economists, since it meant that the labor market may be prevented from clearing. Hoover then strove to contain deflation through the passage of the first Glass–Steagall Act of 1932, which allowed government securities along with eligible paper to be used as collateral against borrowing from Federal Reserve banks, which temporarily eased the credit crunch.

Construction of the Hoover Dam began in 1931 and was a symbol of hope to unemployed workers, who flooded into Boulder City, Nevada seeking employment. Though only some were employed, under grinding conditions, the public works project was an asset to the economy in this period. In addition, during President Hoover's term in office, the Reconstruction Finance Corporation, created in 1932 to lend to indebted institutions, was considered a boon to spending until 1935 (Sprinkel 1952). These relatively small-scale policy actions helped, but were of limited consequence in the face of high unemployment, which peaked in 1933.

Economic theory did not promote government intervention until Keynes's publication of the *General Theory of Employment, Interest, and Money* (*General Theory*) in 1936. Before that time, neoclassical economics dominated. Marginalists such as William Stanley Jevons, Carl

Menger, and Léon Walras believed that the economy could be described in a mathematical and objective manner in a world with rational agents. This type of model could not account for the Great Depression. What is more, Alfred Marshall, considered by some to be the father of neoclassical economics which incorporated marginal theory, believed that the government stood in the way of markets. Therefore, President Hoover's inaction cannot be criticized based on the economic theory in vogue at the time. Still, his insufficient intervention had disastrous consequences for the flailing American economy.

The political fight between President Hoover and candidate Roosevelt was ugly and polarized. Roosevelt accused Hoover of being entirely responsible for the depression. Although Hoover's policies were lukewarm, we know now that Hoover's inaction was not completely at fault for the unfolding events of this period. Hoover, on the other hand, blamed the Great Depression on Europe and the legacy of World War I.

That being said, more vigorous action was taken after FDR was inaugurated. Roosevelt opposed coordinated international action, such as that proposed at the World Economic Conference in 1933, but his commitment to reviving the US economy was paramount. One of Roosevelt's first actions in office, in March 1933, was to move away from the gold standard, thereby reflating the economy (Eichengreen and Temin 1997). Roosevelt favored ending the US dollar parity to the gold standard rather than maintaining fabricated foreign exchange stability at the expense of domestic growth. This provided the US with substantially greater control over monetary policy.

Also in 1933, Roosevelt passed the Agricultural Adjustment Act to restrict output in order to raise prices, passed the National Industrial Recovery Act to protect labor, created the Tennessee Valley Authority to instill government authority over dam construction, set up the Federal Deposit Insurance Corporation, and signed the Emergency Relief Act with the Civil Works Agency to provide jobs (Schlesinger 2003). The Home Owners Refinancing Act, which set up the Home Owners' Loan Corporation (HOLC), refinanced homes to prevent foreclosures and reduce insolvency among mortgage-holding banks, which was very successful (Davidson 2009).

In 1934, the Securities and Exchange Commission was established to guard against fraudulent stock market practices, and the Federal Communications Commission was created to regulate interstate communications (Schlesinger 2003). In addition, the Reciprocal Trade Agreement Act allowed for a reduction of tariff duties.

FDR's policies could be supported by Keynesian theory of government spending, which arose in 1936 with the penning of the *General Theory.*

Keynes believed that the government could provide much-needed demand where private sector demand fell off due to recession. Keynes stated:

> Whilst, therefore, the enlargement of the functions of government, involved in the task of adjusting to one another the propensity to consume and the inducement to invest, would seem to a nineteenth-century publicist or to a contemporary American financier to be a terrific encroachment on individualism, I defend it, on the contrary, both as the only practicable means of avoiding the destruction of existing economic forms in their entirety and as the condition of the successful functioning of individual initiative.

Essentially, this is what FDR put into practice even before Keynes's theory was formalized.

From the trough of the depression in 1933, the economy began to turn upward, but gradually (Figure 2.2). Figure 2.3 shows the US unemployment rate over this period. As the US and Canada experienced

Source: Photo from the Franklin D. Roosevelt Presidential Library and Museum. Photo in public domain.

Figure 2.2   Unemployed shown at Volunteers of America soup kitchen in Washington, DC, 1936

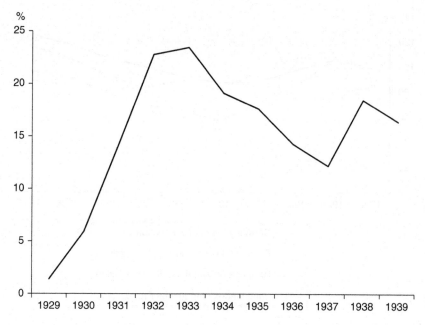

Source: NBER Macrohistory Database (2010).

Figure 2.3 *US unemployment rate, seasonally adjusted yearly average*

recovery, many developing countries entered debt default. But it seemed that the worst, within North America at least, was over.

In 1935, the New Deal changed direction somewhat to assist urban groups; 1935 saw the establishment of the Wagner Act, to strengthen organizing power of labor unions, mortgage refinancing programs, and social security, designed to enhance the welfare of individuals and their dependents (Schlesinger 2003). The Revenue Acts of 1935, 1936, and 1937 moved toward democratizing the tax structure, while the Fair Labor Standards Act of 1938 established a minimum wage.

After 1935, the United Kingdom recovered most swiftly in production, GDP and employment, followed by the US and Japan. Germany, under Hitler, also recovered, but under different circumstances: preparation for war. Those who remained in the gold bloc were the last to emerge from the depression, including France, the Netherlands, Switzerland, and Belgium (Eichengreen 1992). The improved production over time can be viewed in Figure 2.4. The gold bloc faced a tremendously difficult task in defending its trade balance and gold reserves. France, the Netherlands, Switzerland, and Belgium experienced economic recovery after leaving the gold bloc.

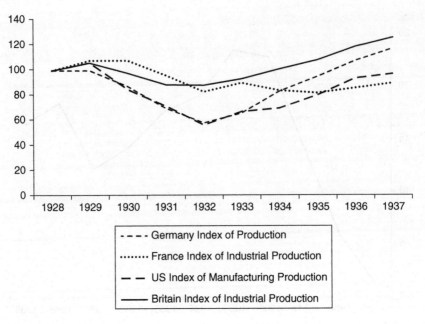

Note: 1928 = 100.

Source: NBER Macrohistory Database.

Figure 2.4   Production indices in the US, UK, Germany, and France, 1928–37

In addition, the US, UK, and France entered the Tripartite Monetary Agreement in 1936 to guard against competitive devaluation and stabilize their currencies. This prompted the dishoarding of gold as confidence in the major currencies increased (Kindleberger 1986).

After a short period of recovery, recession returned in 1937. Davidson (2009) attributes the return of recession to the fiscal austerity FDR was forced to implement to satisfy elements of Congress just before his re-election in 1936. In the US, speculation in commodities was on the rise. European gold was invested in the US, and, due to excessive inflows, was sterilized in December 1936 (Kindleberger 1986). But investors feared the price of gold would in turn fall. Uneasy markets through 1937 led to falling stock prices, and the Fed injected liquidity into the system. In response to the recession, a large fiscal stimulus package was introduced in order to increase funds to public works and the US Housing Authority.

WAR STIMULUS

Fiscal stimulus as well as the return of war signaled the beginning of economic recovery. As Europe and Japan rearmed in the late 1930s, war production was increased to fill government demand. Hitler's rise in Germany began in 1933, and transformed Weimar Germany into the Third Reich. The UK and France led the war against Hitler's Germany beginning in September 1939, and the US joined in 1942 (Robinson 2009). GDP clearly increased between 1938 and 1945 in Allied countries and increased until 1941 in Axis countries (Table 2.2).

As can be seen from Table 2.2, defense spending ratcheted up GDP in militarily successful countries, and war destruction brought about declines in GDP in militarily unsuccessful countries. The end of war left the Axis countries in economic shreds, and the global economy, after the ravages of war and depression, was in need of strict reordering. The appropriate arena for restructuring took place at the 1944 Allied meeting at Bretton Woods, which set up a system of global economic coordination that took effect in 1945, at the end of World War II.

The Great Depression shifted into World War II, both of which revealed the need for a new financial architecture. We skip the economic details of World War II, which are numerous and widely documented, and look at its aftermath. The new global system was put forth in 1944 at Bretton

Table 2.2   Allied versus Axis GDP during World War II

	1938	1939	1940	1941	1942	1943	1944	1945
Allied powers								
USA	800	869	943	1094	1235	1399	1499	1474
UK	284	287	316	344	353	361	346	331
France	186	199	82	–	–	–	–	101
Italy	–	–	–	–	–	–	117	92
USSR	359	366	417	359	318	464	495	396
Allied total	1629	1721	1757	1798	1906	2223	2458	2394
Axis powers								
Germany	351	384	387	412	417	426	437	310
France	–	–	82	130	116	110	93	–
Austria	24	27	27	29	27	28	29	12
Italy	141	151	147	144	145	137	–	–
Japan	169	184	192	196	197	194	189	144
Axis total	686	747	835	911	903	895	748	466
Allies/Axis	2.4	2.3	2.1	2.0	2.1	2.5	3.3	5.1

Source: Harrison (1998).

Woods, in which representatives from 44 countries gathered to coordinate economic policies. As described in Chapter 1, Bretton Woods was put into effect at the end of the war and created a system of exchange rates pegged, within a band, to the dollar, which was exchangeable at $35 per ounce of gold. International institutions, the International Monetary Fund (IMF), and the International Bank of Reconstruction and Development (IBRD), now the World Bank, were also created to help maintain global financial stability. The task of the IMF was to assist in exchange rate coordination, while the task of the IBRD was to finance war reconstruction.[6] The General Agreement on Tariffs and Trade (GATT; now the World Trade Organization, WTO) was to provide stability on tariffs and exchange rates to ease global trade (Galbraith 2008).

The uniting concept behind Bretton Woods was that the global economy required governmental intervention, through collaboration rather than competition. General operating principles took time to establish. Kindleberger's (1951) article on the Bretton Woods institutions discusses the ineffectiveness of the IMF relative to the IBRD, mainly due to differences of opinion in exchange rate policy, and due to the undirected use of IMF funds not for liquidity shortages but for European economic recovery. However, despite initial criticism, ultimately Bretton Woods institutions and policies heralded a two-decade-long period of global financial stability. In the aftermath of the Great Depression and World War II, these circumstances were greatly welcome.

POLITICAL ECONOMY OF THE CRISIS IN THE US

The Great Depression introduced a great shock to a relatively young economy lacking in expertise in reviving credit, production, and consumption. While crises had occurred in the past, extensive government intervention to stimulate the macroeconomy was not de rigueur in the US.

Furthermore, the Federal Reserve was relatively new and inexperienced. The decision to raise interest rates in 1928, 1929, and 1931 negatively impacted the rest of the world through the gold standard and choked off economic growth. Although Eugene Meyer, Governor of the Federal Reserve Board in 1930–1933, advocated for intervention, the Fed failed to act as a lender of last resort during banking panics that lasted from 1930 through 1933 due to differences of opinion.

Wall Street men and working people alike attributed the prosperity of the 1920s to President Calvin Coolidge, viewed as a man of strong character who promoted a small government. Coolidge stated, "I want the people of America to be able to work less for the government and more for themselves. I want them to have the rewards of their own industry. This is the chief meaning of freedom" (Coolidge 1924). Few scholars have attributed the Great Depression to Coolidge's pro-business policies in tenure.

President Herbert Hoover, who took office in March 1929, has by contrast received much of the blame for insufficient government action during the Great Depression, despite maintaining a political economic ideology similar to that of Coolidge. Since times were wretched during the presidency of Herbert Hoover, the American populace viewed him as a weak, incompetent leader. President Hoover did not diverge from received wisdom in his understanding of recessions as a normal part of economic business cycles, nor in his view of a balanced budget as a fiscal responsibility. Hoover thought that the recession would die away in time, particularly if consumers and producers maintained confidence in economic growth.

Hoover was in favor of starting limited public works to improve national infrastructure and of building up agricultural co-operatives to decrease excessive competition among farmers (Hoover 1952). He initiated prison, law enforcement, and child welfare reforms, among many others. He was therefore in favor of government action on several important fronts. However, President Hoover did not believe in government bailouts to ailing sectors, and was steadfast about ensuring a healthy budget that was balanced through the least increase in taxes. Hoover eventually bailed out banks and railroads – firms that were deemed too big to fail – while refusing to bail out farmers in order to preserve the forces of community self-help.

Hoover's efforts to ease the pain of the Great Depression remained insufficient. In defense of his actions, Hoover stated in his memoirs:

> Whatever our apprehensions may have been, it can be said at once that neither the American people nor the Congress would have approved such unprecedented measures before these ill winds began to strike our shores. It is not given to mortals clearly to foresee the violence or the emergence of hidden forces of destruction. (Hoover 1952)

Hoover remained unpopular, making way for Democratic candidate Franklin Delano Roosevelt to win the 1932 election. Roosevelt drew a negative picture of Hoover in his election campaign and, in an ironic twist of fate, accused him of overspending and running up the government debt. Roosevelt won by a landslide. Although the nation was at a historic low point, Roosevelt's Inaugural Address was greeted with hearty approval, and Roosevelt embarked on improving economic conditions mere hours after his inauguration.

In President Roosevelt's first 100 days, 15 major bills were passed through Congress (Cohen 2009). Banks were closed to prevent further bank failures, and were to be reopened once healthy under the Emergency Banking Act. Farmers were given relief in the form of payment not to plant their crops, as crop prices were extremely low. A large-scale social welfare program was enacted to provide a safety net for families falling into dire poverty, indicated by homelessness and starvation. The first 100 days of Roosevelt's presidency changed the role of the government in America.

President Roosevelt created an atmosphere of infectious optimism, which helped turn around the desperation of the Great Depression. The worst of the Depression was over due to strong leadership under Roosevelt and a surge in demand stemming from the government.

ECONOMIC THEORIES OF THE DAY

Neoclassical economic theory, the economic theory that grew out of classical economics in the 1870s and predominated until the late 1930s, viewed individuals as rational actors in a world where equilibrium is a plausible and natural outcome. The economy was viewed as moving toward equilibrium, such that policy implications held that the government should allow free markets to flourish, and should not intervene.

Léon Walras was one of the founders of general equilibrium theory. He laid the mathematical foundation for the theory, setting the number of equations equal to the number of unknowns, and speculated that the way in which society may reach general equilibrium is through a process called *tatonnement*, in which by trial and error, supply is set equal to demand. Walras himself recognized that general equilibrium was not necessarily reached in reality. Vilfredo Pareto later adapted the theory of general equilibrium in a centralized economy with general utility functions (Davar 2015). The economics profession embraced the tenets of general equilibrium, and it became widely believed that economies tend toward this state, despite the hesitation expressed by Walras.

Alfred Marshall had a profound influence on the field of economics, seeking to illustrate economic growth through partial equilibrium analysis. Marshallian economics was developed by 1875, and published in 1890 in his book, *Principles of Economics*. He developed the theory of utility in order to restrict demand functions and strived to consider the representative firm and the real costs of production. Marshall implemented mathematics and diagrams into his study of economics, giving the field a more scientific appearance. As Keynes (1924) later states:

> Marshall's mathematical and diagrammatic exercises in Economic Theory were of such a character in their grasp, comprehensiveness and scientific accuracy and went so far beyond the "bright ideas" of his predecessors, that we may justly claim him as the founder of modern diagrammatic economics – that elegant apparatus which generally exercises a powerful attraction on clever beginners, which all of us use as an inspirer of, and a check on, our intuitions and as a shorthand record of our results, but which generally falls into the background as we penetrate further into the recesses of the subject.

Irving Fisher was an early pioneer of neoclassical economics and laid the foundation for monetary economics, particularly through his work defining and calculating index numbers. Fisher believed that the monetary authority was responsible for price level stability. Like Marshall, Fisher used mathematics in his study of economics. Fisher, however, had little knowledge of financial crises and lost a large amount of money in the stock market crash. One day before the stock market decline, he even commented on October 24, 1929, that if "it is true that 15 billion in stock quotation losses have been suffered in the present break I have no hesitation in saying values are too low" (Fisher 1929 [1931]). Fisher later labelled this a "New Era," as most explanations for the crisis were lacking (Thornton 2008).

LOOKING BACK

It seems apparent that Hoover's relative inaction and budget tightening policies prevented recovery from the Great Depression, but there has been much debate over FDR's actions under the New Deal. Hannsgen and Papadimitriou (2009) argue that when FDR took office, the economy was in great distress, and therefore restoring economic health took several long years. It was not, as some have argued, that New Deal policies were ineffective.

The main criticisms of the New Deal have been directed at policies regarding cartelization and unionization.[7] Hannsgen and Papadimitriou state that those who criticized the 1933 National Industrial Recovery Act (NIRA) and the 1935 National Labor Relations Act (NLRA) for preventing clearing in the labor market and perfect competition by promoting the minimum wage and cartelization had unrealistic views of the economy's ability to return to competitive equilibrium. Galbraith (1994) elaborates on this view: firms cut prices due to declines in demand; price reductions

brought about wage reductions and unemployment. The NIRA was
designed to stop this process by maintaining employment and therefore
demand.

However, whether or not these policies worked, Dobbin (1993) points
out that governments, including those of the US, France, and Britain,
reversed traditional industrial policies to escape the downturn. To some
degree, these policies were experimental. For a short time, and a short time
only, the US rejected antitrust policies and attempted cartelization under
the 1933 NIRA, France rejected statism and attempted liberalism, and
Britain rejected pro-small firm policies and attempted monopoly building.
In the US, cartelization was abandoned in 1935 while labor protection
remained.

Although there has been some criticism of New Deal policies on
grounds other than cartelization and establishment of the minimum
wage, as in Powell (2003),[8] prominent economists such as Paul Krugman,
Christina Romer, and James Galbraith have generally supported FDR's
fiscal spending programs, which prove successful when tested empirically.

Importantly from a scholarship perspective, the Great Depression
refuted Say's Law. Income from production of supply was hoarded and
credit was not extended; supply was unable to create its own demand
(Galbraith 1994). And to this end, Keynes prevailed. John Maynard
Keynes, in fact, wrote his most important work, *The General Theory
of Employment, Interest and Money* (1936), at the tail end of the Great
Depression. His work, although theoretical, justified government economic intervention. After the Great Depression, government spending
became a feature of macroeconomic policy in response to economic downturns. This new mentality of domestic and international policy coordination lasted until the 1970s and provided vital financial security.

NOTES

1. As in the UK, France, Italy, and so on.
2. Britain, Italy, and Japan were in recession in the 1920s.
3. In the context of a credit crunch accompanied by deflation, borrowers face a debt–deflation cycle as elaborated by Fisher (1933). In this situation, real debt increases as deflation
   increases the value of the currency.
4. See Bernanke (2002).
5. "Hot money" earned its name during the Great Depression, describing invisible capital
   flows from Europe to the United States, and was discussed in the work of Robert Warren
   (1937) and Charles Kindleberger (1937).
6. The purpose and mandates of these institutions are described in detail in Pehle (1946).
7. As in Cole and Ohanian (2000) and Taylor (2002).
8. Powell criticizes almost every New Deal policy for various reasons.

3. 1950s through 1970s: the inter-crisis period

The 1950s through 1970s inter-crisis period was the exception rather than the rule, for preventing crisis took a great deal of global coordination and effort that could not be maintained in the face of countries' individual pursuit of sovereign policies. We first look at the Bretton Woods regime that existed during the 1950s and 1960s, then turn to the post-Bretton Woods oil shocks that caused an economic recession in the 1970s.

BRETTON WOODS: THE 1950S AND 1960S

With the introduction of the Bretton Woods regime, the 1950s and 1960s were a period of relative stability, although one that was difficult to maintain. The Bretton Woods period was in fact the most stable period in terms of most real and nominal macro variables, more so than the gold standard regime, the interwar period, or the floating exchange rate system (Bordo 1992). It can be viewed as an important intermediary step between the gold standard and floating exchange rates, but also a period that required a commitment from the center country, the United States (US), that increasingly came into conflict with domestic economic goals.

Importantly, the US emerged as the world's largest economic and political superpower after World War II, and the dollar emerged as the dominant currency. The rest of Europe was in a shambles due to the destruction experienced during the war. At the Bretton Woods meeting in 1944, the US and the United Kingdom (UK) laid out the details of the proposed Bretton Woods system before meeting with the other 40 countries (Eichengreen and Kenen 1994). The question to address was how to stabilize the global financial system and rebuild Europe.

One of the main objectives in seeking to stabilize global finance was to fix exchange rates to the dollar, and the dollar to gold, but also to allow countries to pursue policies that promoted full employment. Yet the fixed exchange rate paradoxically ruled out discretionary monetary policy, since in maintaining a fixed exchange rate, countries would have to give up some control over monetary policy to the extent that complete sterilization of foreign exchange inflows could not be managed, and rely more on fiscal policy. This was not understood at the time, and the goals set at Bretton Woods were not easily attained. There was a commitment to pursue trade and current account liberalization, and to assist countries in the maintenance of a stable balance of payments. While free capital movement was at this time discouraged, 15 years later it was promoted and amplified the difficulties associated with maintaining financial stability.

Within the framework of Bretton Woods, the dollar was exchangeable at $35 per ounce of gold, while other currencies were fixed but adjustable within 1 percent of their dollar parities. While this was desirable for some countries, which had experienced great instability during the Great Depression and World War II, many foreign central banks felt uncomfortable holding large dollar stocks, since this was dependent on the US maintaining the value of the dollar (Eichengreen 2007). But this discomfort belied a lack of confidence in the core currency of the Bretton Woods system, which was the dollar and not gold. Countries were nervous about moving from a peg to gold directly to an indirect peg through a fiat currency, since the dollar held no intrinsic value.

During the Bretton Woods negotiations, both British and American architects of the plan (Keynes and White; Figure 3.1) recommended that the agreement include a requirement of capital controls, while New York bankers strongly objected to this type of control. Capital controls would assist nations in their main focus of maintaining a domestic economic policy of full employment rather than an international economic policy of currency parity (Cesarano 2006). Capital controls in Western European nations were accepted, while they were not implemented in the US.[1]

The end of World War II showed a large increase in per capita income for the United States over European countries, with the US holding a per capita gross domestic product (GDP) 1.7 times that of Western Europe in 1950, and four times that of Southern Europe. It took years for Western Europe to catch up in per capita income to the US, while Southern and Eastern European countries continued to lag behind (Figure 3.2). It is plain to see that at the beginning of the Bretton Woods period, the US had a clear economic hegemony, and its power would have to be tempered with a sense of responsibility in upholding the system.[2]

The US was a clear "winner," and this was reinforced by the currency regime that put the dollar at the center of the world economy. New "rules" of the global order established at Bretton Woods were effected in order to maintain the system.

McKinnon (1993) spells out the rules of the game that came into force for the 1950s and 1960s, as follows. Industrial countries other than the United States should:

Source: IMF, public domain photo.

Figure 3.1   Harry Dexter White and John Maynard Keynes (post-Bretton Woods, in 1946)

1. fix a par value for the national currency with the US dollar as the numeraire, and keep exchange rate within one percent of this par value indefinitely;
2. use free currency convertibility for current-account payments;
3. use capital controls to insulate domestic financial markets, but begin liberalization;
4. use the dollar as the intervention currency, and keep active official exchange reserves in US Treasury Bonds;
5. subordinate long-run growth in the domestic money supply to the fixed exchange rate and to the prevailing rate of price inflation (in tradable goods) in the United States;
6. offset substantial short-run losses in exchange reserves by having the central bank purchase domestic assets to partially restore the liquidity of domestic banks and the money supply (Bagehot's Rule);
7. and limit current account imbalances by adjusting national fiscal policy (government net saving) to offset any divergences between private savings and investment.

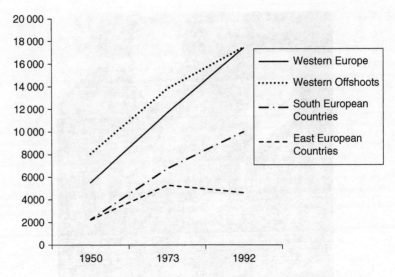

Note: Western Europe includes Austria, Belgium, Denmark, Finland, France, Germany, Italy, the Netherlands, Norway, Sweden, Switzerland, and the UK. Western Offshoots include Australia, Canada, New Zealand, and the US. Southern European Countries include Greece, Ireland, Portugal, Spain, and Turkey. East European Countries include Bulgaria, Czechoslovakia, Hungary, Poland, Romania, the USSR, and Yugoslavia.

Source: Maddison (1995).

Figure 3.2   Per capita income in selected regions, 1950, 1973, and 1992

The United States should:

1. remain passive in the foreign exchanges;
2. practice free trade with neither a balance-of-payments nor an exchange-rate target[;]
3. ... not hold significant official reserves of foreign exchange;
4. keep US capital markets open to foreign governments and private markets as borrowers or depositors;
5. maintain position as a net international creditor (in dollar-denominated assets) and limit fiscal deficits;
6. and anchor the dollar (world) price level for tradable goods by an independently chosen American monetary policy.

The Bretton Woods system was not something that simply functioned once the "rules of the game" were established; it had to be maintained. The Marshall Plan attempted to support the focus of Bretton Woods. Under the Marshall Plan (1948–52), Western European countries were encouraged by the US to export to the US and restrict imports in order to build up dollar reserves (Meltzer 1991). A portion of the dollar reserves was converted to gold. Thereafter, the US maintained a large current account surplus and invested abroad, which upheld confidence in the US economy (Eichengreen 2007). The Marshall Plan also underscored US hegemony, since the US was able to bypass Bretton Woods institutions in lending aid to European nations, and in doing so, was able to require borrower nations to commit to balance their budgets, engage in trade liberalization, and stabilize their exchange rates (Eichengreen and Kenen 1994).

Just as the system was entering a stable period, convertibility controls were lowered in 1958 as major currencies became convertible on current account transactions (Meltzer 1991), and short-term capital flows and the eurodollar market began their rise. The eurodollar market allowed dollars to be borrowed and lent outside of the US. The large British support for the eurodollar market, resulting from exchange crises, allowed the British to finance trade outside the sterling bloc and resolved the British balance-of-payments imbalances, since dollars became more freely available to relieve the currency asymmetries (Helleiner 1994). American support for the eurodollar market allowed the US to skirt capital controls. The eurodollar market also allowed international lending and trade to occur on a much larger scale (Hirsch 1967). However, these solutions to relieve the binding constraints of Bretton Woods upset the system.

Systemic trouble started in 1959 when the US encountered balance-of-payments problems with mounting trade deficits, allegedly as a result of trade discrimination, and later seen as an outcome of extensive US military expenditures (Meltzer 1991). What is more, the US gold stock had fallen, while major currencies had become convertible for current transactions, threatening the US position as center of the Bretton Woods currency regime. Deficits and dollar accumulation abroad became a cause for concern. US domestic economic policy continued to be a priority despite the burgeoning balance-of-payments problem. Countries abroad were forced to compensate for this by devaluing their currencies relative to the dollar.

A series of balance-of-payments measures were enacted in the United States to reduce net dollar outflows, starting in 1960, with an expansion of Export–Import Bank lending to encourage US exports and also with a reduction in government purchases abroad. The most famous measure implemented by the US was known as "Operation Twist," and sought to drive up short-term interest rates to keep capital in the country, while keeping long-term interest rates low to maintain economic activity (Best 2004). These measures were not very effective, and were sometimes more onerous on the parties involved than beneficial.

Although the International Monetary Fund (IMF) provided standby funding to countries in need of reserve credit to defend their fixed exchange rate, IMF credit was insufficient to correct exchange rate imbalances (Eichengreen and Kenen 1994). Investors could withdraw capital from a country in anticipation of a devaluation. Other countries were forced to maintain or impose capital controls as a defensive move, as capital flowed more freely.

The threat to the Bretton Woods system intensified with increases in the London gold price as a result of increased demand for gold, due to a lack of confidence in the dollar. There were two prices of gold: that on the London market, and the official American price of $35 per ounce. A divergence favorable to speculators meant that central banks could potentially buy gold from the US and sell it on the London market. This arbitrage reflected the trend in increasing international speculation in the 1960s, which increased capital mobility in search of profit. The London price of gold increased to $40 per ounce in October 1960 upon fears that Kennedy's possible election to the US presidency would result in inflationary policies that would decrease the real value of the dollar. The London gold price increase forced the US to sell $350 million of gold to the Bank of England to maintain its set price of $35 per ounce.

The general fear of price deviations, as well as the immediate events of 1960, led to the creation of the Gold Pool in 1961, which sought to stabilize the London price of gold so as not to jeopardize the US parity. The Gold Pool allowed foreign governments to intervene in order to stabilize the price of gold (Eichengreen 2007).[3] Participants included Belgium, France, Germany, Italy, the Netherlands, Switzerland, the United Kingdom, and the United States (Eichengreen 2007). In addition, European central banks agreed not to buy gold on the London market if the price rose above the official rate. The Gold Pool broke down under growing demand for gold, and the London gold market was shut down for two weeks in March 1968 because of this.[4] The problem was that the supply of gold was fixed, and as countries increased dollar reserves, the ratio of dollars to gold increased, which meant that the dollar price of gold would have had to be increased over time in order to maintain the Bretton Woods exchange rate system. Because of this, Group of Ten (G-10) governments stopped trying to control the price of gold for private transactions, and foreign central banks agreed not to sell in the gold market for arbitrage gains.

The political economy that had focused on systemic economic cooperation and control had shifted since the beginning of the Bretton Woods period, with an increasing emphasis on free movement of capital in the US in the 1960s, and with the view that technical solutions, such as short-term capital controls, could resolve global imbalances. Keynesian policy as adapted by the Kennedy Administration allowed for capital flow controls through a mix of fiscal and monetary policies, urging surplus countries with expanding economies to increase taxes or decrease government spending while increasing money growth to lower interest rates in order to allow for capital outflows (Meltzer 1991). Deficit countries were encouraged to do the converse. It is doubtful that Keynes would have encouraged the loose policies that were devised in his name, but by this period of turmoil in the Bretton Woods system, Keynes was long gone. As Best (2004) emphasizes, Keynes understood that the economy could not be corrected through technical measures when underlying imbalances were in place.

The Germans insisted that these policy mixes were convoluted, and felt that domestically focused US monetary policy was to blame. Germany was concerned with the specter of inflation, and had worked hard to maintain economic stability through low inflation and large trade surpluses (Brenner 1976). The French were also highly critical of US policies and were opposed to the expansion of the US balance-of-payments deficit financed by foreign countries, particularly as France was subjected to speculative attacks in 1968. Britain, as a deficit country, faced a perpetual sterling crisis by the late 1960s and was in a position similar to that of the US.

Hence the economic powers engaged in talks to increase liquidity in the system. Devaluation of the dollar appeared to be out of the question, since it would erode confidence in the dollar for those holding dollar reserves. By the late 1960s, Western European governments grew less willing to finance expanding US deficits (Helleiner 1994). The US wanted to supplement gold reserves with an additional reserve asset (Meltzer 1991). A version of the US proposal was accepted, and in 1967, the Special Drawing Right (SDR) was created as an asset to supplement gold and dollars.[5] However, the SDR could only be held by official institutions such as central banks and international institutions, and was never very effective as a reserve asset. It was too weak to save the system.

Pressures on the dollar and an increasing unwillingness by the US to act as the center currency country resulted in the demise of the Bretton Woods system in 1971, described in the next section. While this demise has been viewed by some economists as inevitable, we do not take that view. The conflicting objectives between providing international liquidity and maintaining confidence in the convertibility of the dollar was dubbed the "Triffin dilemma." Triffin (1960) believed that the Bretton Woods exchange rate system was unsustainable, since the US would have to run a large current account deficit in order to provide liquidity to the rest of the world, while the same deficit would erode confidence in the dollar's convertibility into gold. This presumes that a large US current account deficit was beneficial to international liquidity, when it was, in and of itself, clearly not. The main complaint against the US current account deficit was that it pumped excess dollars into economies abroad, which could not be absorbed. A balanced US current account would have better promoted confidence in the dollar. Indeed, the President and other policy makers were increasingly concerned about the impact of the US deficit abroad, while at the same time justifying excessive spending through the necessity of war and domestic economic policy. At the end of the era, US domestic policy trumped its international concerns, and the Bretton Woods period was allowed to crumble.

Despite its ultimate failure, the Bretton Woods period was important in that it focused on maintaining economic stability that prevented large-scale crises. The policies required to maintain the system were extensive, but the effort proved worthwhile in allowing European countries to recover from the destruction of World War II and set up an international economic framework that bridged the gap between the gold standard and freely floating exchange rates. What could have been chaos in the currency and productive arenas was controlled and stabilized as countries played by the international "rules of the game."

AFTER BRETTON WOODS: THE 1970S

The 1970s were years of change and increasing volatility in the global financial architecture. The two most important changes were the collapse of the Bretton Woods fixed exchange rates regime in 1971, and the oil crises of 1973–74 and 1978–79.

By the early 1970s, the Bretton Woods system of fixed exchange rates was failing. Foreign governments had increasingly revalued their currencies to maintain ties to the dollar, which led to increased speculation against weakened currencies (Brenner 1976). The Germans had floated their currency in May 1971 due to speculation pressures. Major holders of foreign reserves understood that they were not to actually exchange dollars for gold, and most did not until the British requested a $3 billion conversion in 1971 (McCracken 1996).

At the same time, global inflation of dollar prices was on the rise due to currency revaluation (Galbraith 2008). Rather than tighten interest rates in order to control inflation, President Nixon lowered interest rates in order to reduce unemployment in anticipation of the 1972 presidential elections (Strange 1972). This led to a rapid outflow of eurodollars, which worsened the US deficit and caused European financial markets to anticipate a dollar crisis, leading to the unraveling of the Bretton Woods system.[6]

By 1971 the US supply of gold had dropped to dangerously low levels, just as inflation was rising. Liabilities to foreign central banks and governments skyrocketed.[7] Under pressure from a US balance-of-payments deficit, an excess of printed dollars, and foreign demands for gold, President Nixon closed the gold window by unilaterally declaring that the US dollar would no longer be convertible to gold. Nixon stated on television:

> We must protect the position of the American dollar as a pillar of monetary stability around the world . . . In the past 7 years, there has been an average of one international monetary crisis every year. Now who gains from these crises? Not the workingman; not the investor; not the real producers of wealth. The gainers are the international money speculators. Because they thrive on crises, they help to create them. In recent weeks, the speculators have been waging an all-out war on the American dollar. The strength of a nation's currency is based on the strength of that nation's economy – and the American economy is by far the strongest in the world. Accordingly, I have directed the Secretary of the Treasury to take the action necessary to defend the dollar against the speculators. I have directed Secretary Connally to suspend temporarily the convertibility of the dollar into gold or other reserve assets, except in amounts and conditions determined to be in the interest of monetary stability and in the best interests of the United States. (Nixon 1971)

This announcement stunned the global community. Currency values then increased in volatility, and the dollar's real exchange rate value plummeted.

World exchange rates were in limbo between 1971 and 1973. In December 1971, world leaders met at the Smithsonian Institute in Washington, DC to set new exchange rates. The US agreed to retain controls on capital exports to assist in maintaining new parities (Helleiner 1994). The price of gold was raised to $38 per ounce, while some countries agreed to appreciate their currencies relative to the dollar, resulting in a much-needed dollar devaluation. The French continued to blame the US for creating excess dollar liquidity in the international monetary system (Brenner 1976). The US went on the defensive, believing that the Bretton Woods system had been overly restrictive of US monetary policy, hampering domestic growth. The following year, many countries allowed their currencies to float, and the stable exchange rate system completely broke down in March 1973.[8]

Floating exchange rates brought with them currency risk, which became a feature of the global economy. Over this period, banks developed the ability to buy and sell currencies, developing new instruments to reduce currency risk. Financial instruments that were developed to hedge risk also gave rise to currency speculation and international interdependence in currency trading (Kapstein 1994). Banks and "market discipline" shaped the new global financial system (Galbraith 2008). The "originate to hold" method of banking also gave way to securitization and distribution of assets under a new "originate to distribute" approach (Paulson 2010).

Risk management of currency speculation and trading took time to design and implement, requiring offsetting increases in foreign exchange demand with limitations on foreign currency exposure. But the US was on the whole opposed to such controls of capital movements and underscored the notion that the international economy should espouse freedom of capital movements and freedom of trade in goods (Helleiner 1994). Western Europe and Japan were unable to convince the US to support a system of cooperative controls. This effectively ensured the protection of US financial interests, which sought increased profit that could be made at the expense of financial stability, and brought into existence a system of worldwide inflation and recession.[9]

Two large bank failures underlined the need for better risk control. Bankhaus I.D. Herstatt of Cologne in Germany failed in June 1974 due to large foreign exchange losses from speculation, in the absence of proper controls (Kapstein 1994). The failure of Herstatt led to a freeze-out of foreign exchange demands from smaller banks all over the world and a slowdown in international trade. Unlike the string of smaller banks that preceded it, Herstatt was a larger, more reputable bank that had engaged in eurocurrency speculation and lost, and by this time it was clear that eurocurrency markets were quite risky. As a result of this crisis, the Germans gave the Federal Banking Supervisory Office in Berlin new regulatory power with regard to foreign exchange trading. This began an international dialogue on foreign currency risk control. Many, including German Chancellor Schmidt, called for government supervision of eurocurrency markets (Hartland-Thunberg 1977).

The same year, a large American bank, the Franklin National Bank of New York, declared bankruptcy and was acquired by the German European–American Bank. Franklin National had engaged in risky lending and currency speculation. When the federal authorities discovered this, the bank lost access to financial markets. The Federal Reserve acted as lender of last resort to the bank's domestic and foreign branches to prevent contagion. However, in doing this, the Federal Reserve also acted as lender of last resort for an offshore American bank, thereby supporting its eurodollar operations (Spero 1999). This was the first case where a central bank stepped in and provided liquidity for a bank's foreign branches. Central banks were typically resistant to do this due to fears of potentially open-ended liability.

After these two bank failures, the G-10 central bankers met in July 1974 for a regular meeting in Basle, at the Bank for International Settlements (BIS). One of the primary concerns presented was the lack of information within governing agencies regarding the foreign operations of domestic firms. At the time it was nearly impossible to monitor the foreign activities of banks since the accounting and legal systems differed tremendously between each country. This allowed banks the opportunity to invest in risky practices that may have otherwise been prohibited within domestic operations. This type of investment carried with it the potential to disturb financial systems. In cases of banking crises, the US felt that central banks should act as lenders of last resort in euromarkets, while the Germans did not. Banks lost confidence in euromarket lending until the central bank governors made a statement vaguely supporting euromarket lending activities. The governments pledged to discount commercial paper, extend loans, or arrange currency swaps to prevent bank failures in such circumstances (Hartland-Thunberg 1977). The Federal Reserve was even prepared to bail out any large international commercial bank, regardless of its home country.

From this point onward, central bankers recognized that their policies were connected and that going forward, coordinated solutions, rather than purely national solutions, would be necessary. The UK felt particularly vulnerable since there were more than 200 foreign banks in the country, and the Bank of England's governor, Lord Richardson, felt that more extensive coordination among bank supervisors was necessary (Kapstein 1994). The G-10 in 1974 supported Lord Richardson's proposal to establish a committee of banking supervision, which is now known as the Basle Committee. Further specifications were laid out in the Bank Concordat, prepared in 1975, without explicit guidelines set out for the lender of last resort role,[10] but with the understanding that supervision would be based on consolidated reporting. Bank supervision was based ultimately on the idea of home country control, since the Basle Committee had no ability to enforce regulations, and since countries desired the freedom to create their own policies.

Petrodollar Recycling

Just after the Bretton Woods exchange rate system completely broke down, severe economic shocks struck. The Saudi Arabian Oil Minister, Zaki Yamai, had warned since 1967 that countries that directly or indirectly supported Israel would become the subject of oil embargoes (Shwadran 1986). In October 1973, Egypt and Syria attacked Israel, starting the Yom Kippur or October War, and the US was committed to intervene to provide Israelis with emergency arms. In response, ministers of the Organization of Arab Petroleum Exporting Countries (OAPEC), at the request of Saudi Arabia, met that same month to almost double oil prices and cut production, threatening to increase production cutbacks until Israel withdrew from what they considered to be Arab territories. These oil shocks created massive price increases for consumers and profits for oil producers.

Both developed and developing countries outside the oil producing nations suffered due to the oil price increases. Many oil importing nations felt that they were in no position to confront the OAPEC nations (not to be confused with OPEC, the Organization of Petroleum Exporting Countries), since they were afraid of being cut off from supplies (Levy 1980). The last British forces had been withdrawn from the Persian Gulf in 1972 (Prodi and Clo 1976). Hence oil producing countries were able to impose their own terms on importing countries.

The US had attempted to organize oil importing countries against the Middle East producers, but other countries, particularly France, and later Japan, did not want to be designated as enemies to Middle East producers. Neither were the producers aligned in opinion. Within OPEC, the worldwide organization for oil producing states, Saudi Arabia (ironically one of the more conservative states within OAPEC) clamored for higher prices, while other members disfavored this policy (Shwadran 1986). OPEC, for its part, attempted in 1974 to bring order to the oil pricing system and reduce instability passed on to the consuming countries (Penrose 1976).

US President Carter, in a move now called the Carter Doctrine, declared that any threat to the Persian Gulf region would be considered a threat to the US, requiring any defensive measures possible (Levy 1980).[11] The US, which produced about two-thirds of its own oil, passed on a reduction in oil supplies and the associated price increases to end users of gasoline, while maintaining oil consumption for industry and heating (Fried and Schultze 1975). Domestic demand and output fell as rising oil prices created a downward economic spiral into global recession.

High oil prices thus resulted in an international recession from which there was little recourse. Cost-push inflation could not be dampened by monetary policy without exacerbating recession. Monetary tightening in the US and Japan depressed these economies. Increases in oil prices led to higher costs of imported goods from oil importing nations, reduction in exports from OECD nations to oil importing nations, deepening trade deficits in developing nations, and a decline in real income in oil importing nations (Fried and Schultze 1975).

However, the oil producing nations had a much greater inflow of earnings (petrodollars) and the eurodollar market was growing. The oil profits, half of which were placed in US international banks, then went to developing countries through the international financial intermediaries, in the form of short-term eurodollar loans, since the underdeveloped economies of oil exporting countries had limited capacity in absorbing additional fund inflows (Wachtel 1980). The existence of international banks allowed OPEC states to refrain from direct bilateral lending to oil importing nations, which cushioned these countries from lending risk

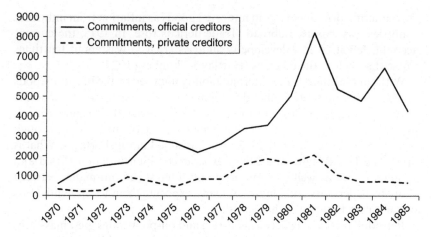

Source: World Bank.

Figure 3.3 Official and private commitments for low-income countries (millions of USD)

(Mikdashi 1981). Although international banks had been lending to developing countries before the oil crisis, after the crisis set in loans increased, and international banks were then able to pay interest on deposits to oil earning countries, as well as earn large profits for themselves. Figure 3.3 depicts official and private commitments for low-income countries.

For their part, Arab countries engaged in equity investments in or direct purchases of developed country firms. These included Iran's 25 percent purchase of Fred, Krupp Heuttenwerke in West Germany, Kuwait's purchase of St Martin's Property Corporation in the UK, and Libya's 9.6 percent share in Italy's Fiat Group (Mikdashi 1981). As Fouad (1978) points out, the absorptive capacity of the Arab nations themselves was underdeveloped due to limited technical, labor and population, and productive capacities. OPEC current account surpluses amounted to $7.2 billion in 1974, and between $20 and $40 billion per year from 1975 to 1979 (Wachtel 1980). OPEC invested to a large degree to reduce its own risk.

Oil importing nations not only had to borrow funds to pay for oil imports, but had to finance new trade deficits with an increase in exports. In the 1960s, developing countries had come to rely on export-led growth, increasing reliance on imports in step. Gradually, developing countries also became economically dependent on manufactured goods and luxury consumption goods. However, developing countries experienced falling export demand due to the global recession (Wachtel 1980), while simultaneously encountering price increases in imported goods as inflation from industrial countries was exported abroad. Trade deficits rose. In 1975, the current account deficit of less developed countries (LDCs) was about ten times worse than before the oil crisis (Hartland-Thunberg 1977).

Without the internal and external stability imposed by the Bretton Woods system, both developed and developing nations experienced economic fragility (Wachtel 1980). Oil price increases impacted consumers in oil importing states directly, through a higher cost of oil and gas, or through price controls, such as in the US, which resulted in oil shortages. What is more, the US, Britain, and Japan experienced high inflation (Fried and Schultze 1975) as well as a maturity and interest rate mismatch between short-term deposits and long-term loans, exposing them to a potential loss of capital and foreign exchange risk.

Petrodollar recycling between oil-rich and oil-poor states grew massively. Central bankers had in 1974 pledged to support a troubled eurocurrency system after the Bankhaus Herstatt and Franklin National crises, and this allowed petrodollar recycling to occur without much fear of financial failure (Kapstein 1994). Both banks and governments lent money to developing nations to offset the cost of rising oil prices, and this further reinforced bankers' comfort with petrodollar lending. An "oil facility" was even initiated by the managing director of the IMF to assist countries with deficits due to increases in oil prices. Much of the funding came from oil producing countries.[12]

Financing for oil deficits also came from the United States. In order to assist international lending, US capital controls were loosened to allow for expanded lending overseas, and export guarantees were issued by major industrial nations to developing nations, allowing these countries to borrow to purchase imported goods from the developed nations (Kapstein 1994). In the US, expected inflation increased, and real interest rates dropped to negative territory between 1974 and 1977, which assisted borrowers and consumers (but not lenders). Developing countries accumulated more debt as a result of negative interest rates, even as the debt service ratio began to rise sharply. The largest borrowers, such as Brazil and Mexico, had debt service ratios well above average, but high debt service ratios were rationalized by economists as being a poor indicator of debt servicing capacity (McDonald 1982). The situation worsened such that oil importing developing countries had exhausted their reserves by 1976 (Hartland-Thunberg 1977) and had little alternative but to borrow.

Just as economic stability was settling in after the large spike in oil prices, and banks were profiting, Iran in 1979 dropped out of the oil industry and instituted Islamic fundamentalism, which contributed to global uncertainty and unease. During the Iranian Revolution, Ayatollah Ruhollah

Khomeini overthrew the monarchy under Shah Mohammad Reza Pahlavi. Official OPEC oil prices again climbed, and this time the stoppage of oil was worse than the OAPEC 1973 embargo (Shwadran 1986). Anxiety felt by oil importing nations led them to stockpile oil at increasingly higher prices on the spot market, despite the absence of a true oil shortage (Levy 1980). Banks were forced to continue lending to Latin America so that the countries could service their debt. Several countries, including the US, feeling victimized by the oil cartel, called for the nationalization of oil companies in order to control imports of the strategic commodity from all private companies (Mikdashi 1981). Private oil companies, for their part, were profiting greatly from higher oil prices, charging top prices, and at times going above the OPEC ceiling price.

G-7 countries attempted to fuel real economic activity through Keynesian fiscal spending measures, but unfortunately for unemployed individuals, and for Keynesianism itself, increased demand did not stimulate increased supply since profitability had declined, causing instead rapidly rising prices and imports (Brenner 2006). Although Keynesian policies had softened the impact of the 1974–75 recession, the resulting inflation resulted in a general policy change in the US, Germany, Japan, and other advanced capitalist countries, which turned economic policy toward tight monetary policy and fiscal austerity.

In line with this thinking, US Federal Reserve Chairman Paul Volcker's fight against inflation and a rapidly depreciating dollar caused him to raise interest rates in 1979. Although this was a signal that the US was committed to restoring foreign and domestic confidence in the dollar through austerity and not through capital controls, this also meant that borrowers (including international borrowers) would have to reschedule loans. This caused difficulties that resulted in a series of debt crises in Latin America in the 1980s.

In retrospect, the IMF oil facility and the recycling of petrodollars as loans to Latin America were critical at the time in preventing economic collapse in developing countries. Since developing countries (particularly primary commodity producers) could not increase exports at a fast enough rate to compensate for increasing oil imports, additional funds were required. The initial cause of the debt crises that resulted in the 1980s was not overborrowing by developing countries,[13] but rather the oil shocks that removed liquidity from the global economy.

The overall impact of the 1970s oil shocks and the end of Bretton Woods was coupled with a sharp decline in the manufacturing profit rate through the 1970s and 1980s, which led to a decline in the rate of growth of investment and an increase in unemployment (Brenner 2006). Intercapitalist competition continued to increase with globalization, with lower-cost, lower-priced goods entering the market. As globalization spread, the global economic climate changed. The rise of US external deficits was paralleled by declining profits in other advanced capitalist countries such as Germany and Japan, coupled with the rise of financialization. Manufacturing in the US declined as the services sector rose. Wealth became concentrated in the financial sector across the developed world. Multilateral coordination retreated as developed nations, with the US at the center, became increasingly self-serving.

POLITICAL ECONOMY OF THE INTER-CRISIS PERIOD

The Marshall Plan was an American program designed to rehabilitate the economies of Western and Southern Europe, and has been viewed both as a way of containing Communism and implementing post-war political stability in Europe. Prices and exchange rates were stabilized, wartime controls and plans were dismantled, and markets were promoted (DeLong and Eichengreen 1991). The US contributed $13.2 billion to European recovery between 1948 and 1951.

Delong and Eichengreen (1991) make the case that while the Marshall Plan was significant, it did not alleviate resource shortages or bring about the total reconstruction of Europe. Rather, the plan fostered an economic environment that reduced product and factor controls and dampened the possibility that the citizenry would call for tight economic control in the form of a command economy. To some degree, it has been viewed as a strategic base for reinforcing Western power in the Cold War (Kunz 1997).[14]

Indeed, Cold War dynamics motivated many political actions. The Cold War also spanned the inter-crisis period, from 1947 to 1991. The war began with the Truman Doctrine of 1947, which sought to contain Soviet threats to Greece and Turkey. Communist takeovers in Czechoslovakia and China, as well as conflicts in Berlin, Korea, and Vietnam, spurred military and political action. The Korean war represented military action within the bounds of the Cold War, as American troops in South Korea fought Soviet-backed North Korea. The war lasted from 1950 to 1953. The Vietnam War (Figure 3.4) lasted for almost the entire inter-crisis period, from 1954 to 1975. In the Vietnam War, the South Vietnamese fought with Americans against the North Vietnamese, who were indirectly armed by the Union of Soviet Socialist Republics (USSR). US involvement in the war was justified by the threat of the spread of Communism in East Asia.

While not politically and militarily conflict-free, the inter-crisis period was economically more peaceful than other periods. Furthermore,

Source: Donn A. Starry, Department of the Army.

Figure 3.4   Tank and armored cavalry assault vehicle (ACAV) convoy securing supply route in Vietnam War

cooperation among Western powers under the North Atlantic Treaty Organization (NATO) against the threat of Communism reinforced political cooperation between North America and Europe. Bretton Woods institutions were controlled by NATO countries, underscoring the commitment to a global economic partnership.

CHANGING ECONOMIC THEORY OVER THE 1960S AND 1970S

Over the period under discussion, the international view of political economy of the 1960s gave way to national priorities in the 1970s. Keynesianism dominated the 1950s and 1960s with its emphasis on government economic intervention. Friedman's free-market economics dominated the 1970s.

Keynes believed that markets did not always run smoothly, and his ideas were altered and expanded by policy makers and intellectuals in the 1950s and 1960s to imply that the government should serve to stabilize the business cycle. Therefore, government played an important role in the domestic and international economy during this time. Keynes himself had supported the Bretton Woods exchange rate regime, albeit in a different version: he wanted to go even further than the practice of fixing exchange rates to the dollar and in turn to gold, using an international clearing union and an international currency. Still, the highly interventionist Bretton Woods system resulted in a long period of remarkable economic stability. Imbalances in the system caused by shifts in the US trade regime and domestic and international economic pressures led to criticism of the system and eventually to abandonment of the arrangement.

The pendulum of economic theory thus swung in the other direction, toward Milton Friedman, who believed that the government should play a small, rather than a large, role in the economy. Friedman believed that markets, left to their own devices, would stabilize themselves. Exchange rates, in his mind, moved to an equilibrium. Economic fluctuations were not due to private sector actions but rather due to changes in the money supply (Palley 2015) and other mistaken government activity. As Friedman stated in his Nobel Prize lecture in 1976:

> many countries around the world are today experiencing socially destructive inflation, abnormally high unemployment, misuse of economic resources, and, in some cases, the suppression of human freedom not because evil men deliberately sought to achieve these results, nor because of differences in values among their citizens, but because of erroneous judgments about the consequences of government measures: errors that at least in principle are capable of being corrected by the progress of positive economic science. (Friedman 1992 [1976])

Presidents Richard Nixon and Gerald Ford were both pro-free markets (although Nixon has been said to have abandoned his views out of political interest). President Ford stated that his economic goals included "less government intervention in the affairs of citizens and corporations, greater reliance on individual initiative and free market economy, and increased local responsibility for overcoming adversities" (Ford 1979).

Friedman's economic view laid the groundwork for the rise of neoliberalism, with its belief in free markets and containment of government intervention. The idea that an orchestrated environment of economic prosperity could be maintained by policy or international agreement faded away, and the consensus favored the individual pursuit of profit within a market framework. As markets gained more power, the specter of financial crisis again arose.

NOTES

1. The 1947 European crisis began with the British move to current account convertibility. Capital flight from Europe to the US exacerbated the crisis. Indeed, Helleiner (1994) attributes the 1947 European crisis in part to the instability created by the United States' lack of capital controls. The Marshall Plan assisted in promoting recovery by helping to resolve balance-of-payments crises.
2. This is despite the fact that Germany experienced a post-war boom, based on low wages and high rates of profit (Brenner 2006).
3. Eichengreen (2007) divides the Gold Pool into two periods: that between 1962 and 1965, in which the price of gold was low as new gold was discovered; and that between 1966 to 1968, in which the price of gold was high, with increased inflationary pressures and lagging confidence in the US dollar and pound sterling.
4. The Gold Pool could not help the British pound sterling from undergoing market pressure to devalue. This pressure began in 1964 and resulted in a devaluation of the pound by Britain and the rest of the sterling bloc in 1967 (Meltzer 1991).
5. The SDR could eliminate the problem of the Triffin dilemma, in which a national currency is appointed as international reserve currency, setting the stage for domestic versus global conflicts of interest.
6. Despres et al. (1966) do not view the US deficit as problematic, since US capital markets continued to provide liquidity both domestically and internationally.
7. These issues could be corrected by slowing down the economy, but since that was politically unpopular the government looked at other avenues. Import taxes imposed by Nixon did not change the dollar's valuation.
8. Floating exchange rates were legalized in 1976 at the IMF conference in Jamaica (Gilpin 1987).
9. Liberalization of capital controls has contributed to excessive increases in asset prices (creation of bubbles) and corresponding excessive declines in asset prices and associated recessions. Effectively, openness to financial flows has given way to damaging procyclical capital movements that have strongly impacted developing countries, resulting at times in financial crises.
10. These guidelines were rough and, due to a lack of explicit lender of last resort guidelines, led to a banking crisis when the Ambrosiano bank of Italy, in 1982, suffered a sharp liquidity crisis, and the Bank of Italy refused to provide lender of last resort support to its subsidiaries in Luxembourg (Kapstein 1994).
11. This was intended to deter the Soviet Union, during the Cold War, from seeking hegemony in the Persian Gulf.
12. Lending was not equally distributed, however. In 1975, four countries – Brazil, Indonesia, Mexico, and Spain – accounted for half of bank credits to LDCs (Hartland-Thunberg 1977).
13. Nevertheless, the result was unsustainable debt and an inability to service the debt. This is discussed in the next chapter.
14. The Marshall Plan was supplemented by the European Payments Union (EPU), established in 1950, which helped to clear trade payments and partly finance trade imbalances. Those in favor of freer currency markets viewed the EPU as a barrier to convertibility, while those opposed viewed the EPU as assisting in implementing an open system of payments (Helleiner 1994). The British at this time planned to achieve full currency convertibility, but the plan was dissolved by the Economic Cooperation Administration (ECA) which saw sterling convertibility as a threat to the EPU.

4.   1980s: emerging markets, debt default and savings and loan crises

As discussed in the last chapter, the economic shocks of the 1970s caused severe economic imbalances, leading to crises in the 1980s. Through the 1970s, oil importing nations were forced to accept higher oil prices and/or restricted supplies, and developed nations felt obligated to assist developing countries in financing their oil needs. Mounting debt in developing countries was a tremendous liability, particularly when interest rates ratcheted up in response to burgeoning inflation. This led to debt crises, particularly in Latin American countries.

In the United States, the savings and loan crisis, smaller in scale and scope than the debt crisis, sharply impacted the financial system as interest rates rose and real estate prices declined. Savings and loan institutions had engaged in excessively risky activities in the search for greater profitability. Many such institutions were shut down and the industry was put under stricter supervision. We now turn to the emerging market debt default crises.

EMERGING MARKET DEBT DEFAULT CRISES

The debt crisis refers to the subsequent financial problems in liquidity-squeezed debtor countries all over the world. Although the debt crisis in sub-Saharan Africa wrought disastrous effects on those economies, it was smaller in scale, especially in terms of private debt, than the crisis in Latin America. At the other end of the spectrum, Asia generally recovered more quickly due to higher growth rates (as in the case of Korea), targeted state intervention, and capital controls. Latin America, with large amounts of privately funded debt and a sudden slowdown in growth, bore the brunt of the crisis.

The instability of the 1970s paved the way for the rise of conservatism in the United States (US) and the United Kingdom (UK). Americans had struggled with recession in the 1970s and were interested in earning a better living on the free market. Monetarists such as Milton Friedman believed that control over the money supply was all that was necessary to control

the national economy, and promoted the free market ideals held by economists at the University of Chicago. Influential Western economists thus
became less focused on social welfare and more trained on individual gain.
This movement away from social needs toward the needs of the individual
was reflected in creditor nations' attitudes toward debtor nations.

Developing countries suffered not only as a result of the oil shocks, but
also as a consequence of declining aid. Official development assistance to
developing countries had already decreased in the early 1970s. There was
a gap not only in funds to finance oil imports, but also to finance development. Commercial banks involved in petrodollar recycling rushed in to fill
this gap, providing structured loans that extended risk to the developing
countries. The banks put the onus of currency and interest rate risk on
the borrowing countries by lending in dollars and using floating interest rates (Giddy 1994). Syndicated loans, put forth by a larger number
of eurobanks, spread default risk over several banks (Griffith-Jones and
Sunkel 1986). This, in combination with an expanding eurocurrency
market, meant that more money could be lent abroad.

As developing country debt burdens became larger, banks lent on increasingly shorter terms to reduce their exit risk. Short-term debt expanded
twice as fast as medium- and long-term debt in 1979 as Japanese and
European banks accelerated their participation in lending to developing
countries (Kahler 1985). As a result, external shocks from the oil crises gave
way to overlending to oil importing developing nations, many of which did
not have strong domestic policies. Banks, supported by Organisation for
Economic Co-operation and Development (OECD) governments, had lent
money to the developing nations without truly questioning it.

For their part, Latin American nations had turned from import
substitution industrialization policies to export-oriented production,
which generated foreign exchange, but in often sporadic flows. The export
sector stagnated when developed countries' demand for goods from Latin
America diminished, and tax collected from the sector lagged as well. Tax
reform to extend the tax base was necessary but difficult politically and
administratively, and the deficit grew as exports shrank (Griffith-Jones
and Sunkel 1986). Not only was the economic base, the export industry,
procyclical, but so were international credit flows. These factors together
exposed Latin American countries to external shocks. For these reasons,
trade liberalization often (as in Chile, Argentina, and Uruguay) had a
negative impact in the region in the 1980s.

Latin America was also dominated by authoritarian political regimes
by the mid-1970s, except for Costa Rica, Colombia, and Venezuela
(Dominguez 2008). These authoritarian governments made the decision to
go into debt rather than to undergo structural economic adjustment. These

governments also preserved institutions that created inequality, keeping much of the region poor and struggling to repay the sovereign debt.

In late 1979, and early 1980 and 1981, US Federal Reserve Chairman Paul Volker raised the federal funds rate to fight inflation in the US (Goodfriend 2005). The increase in interest rates caused recessions in the US in 1980 and 1981. The increase also strengthened the dollar and caused an increase in the London Interbank Offered Rate (LIBOR), to which most of the floating rate debt was tied. This made it extremely difficult for developing countries to repay and service their debts (Kahler 1985). In addition, the US recessions resulting from the Federal Reserve's policy hurt the exports of Latin American countries, leaving them with reduced income from which to pay their increasing debt service. As the debt-to-export ratio plunged starting in 1980, banks stopped lending to developing countries. Developing countries faced a sudden stop in economic growth and in access to foreign exchange (Meissner 1984). International banks, particularly US banks, faced potentially enormous losses from the outstanding loans.

The debt crisis came to a head on August 12, 1982, when Mexican Finance Minister Silva Herzog announced that Mexico could not meet its upcoming interest payments on foreign debt. Mexico's postponement of debt servicing was a surprise, since Mexico was an oil exporting, rather than an oil importing, nation. The debt, however, had been largely used for investment in infrastructure, economic development, and consumption. Reversals in oil earnings flowing into Mexico, triggered by a sharp drop in oil prices on the market just as Mexico tried to sell at higher prices (Trevino 1989), led to a sudden inability to service borrowings from abroad (da Costa 1991). In addition, interest rates that had been very low or negative in the 1970s suddenly increased and made debt servicing obligations for indebted countries unbearable.

The situation in other countries was similar: increasing interest rates, along with declines in commodity prices and a sharp reduction in foreign lending, produced shocks that rippled across the developing world (Sachs 1989b). Argentina, Brazil, and other countries soon followed with their own debt service moratoriums (Van Wijnbergen et al. 1991). Currencies were viewed as overvalued and a devaluation was expected to take place. Capital flight therefore represented not only the debt crisis but a speculative attack against local currencies, as domestic investors sought to move out of the local currency (Edwards 1989).

Economists had warned that this type of crisis could occur, as petrodollar recycling continued in the 1970s. The debt crisis as a phenomenon was not altogether a surprise, but the massive, systemic nature of the crisis was quite a shock. The Latin American debt crisis was viewed as a serious problem that could wreak havoc on the international financial system, and therefore developed nations' governments had a stake in maintaining liquidity in the system and enforcing debt repayment. This is because the debt crisis threatened to stop trade and finance between developed and developing nations, and to throw into question the solvency of many banks (Kapstein 1994). Although many banks in developed countries had lent to Latin America, American banks were particularly at risk, since they had an exposure of 177 percent of capital to the four largest Latin American less-developed country debtors (Ferraro and Rosser 1994). Should the largest debtors default, American banks would be left with no remaining capital.

Investors both abroad and at home had lost confidence in the financial systems in developing nations, and capital flight from Latin America grew. Several countries faced a debt crisis, in which they were forced to reschedule payments due to an inability to pay on time. However, even rescheduled payments faced the danger of becoming onerous with an increase in prime interest rates (Meissner 1984).

The four most highly indebted countries included Mexico, Venezuela, Argentina, and Brazil, which held 75 percent of commercial bank debt; and the larger debtors thereafter were located in Latin America (Bolivia, Chile, Colombia, Costa Rica, Ecuador, Peru, and Uruguay), in the Caribbean (Jamaica), in Asia (the Philippines), in North Africa (Morocco), in sub-Saharan Africa (Nigeria and Ivory Coast), and in Eastern Europe (Yugoslavia) (da Costa 1991). Countries in sub-Saharan Africa, which had relatively smaller levels of debt, faced severe debt servicing problems due to their relative impoverishment. Official development assistance to sub-Saharan Africa comprised the largest part of their debt, and this proved burdensome to debtor nations despite the adjustment efforts through the Paris Club, International Development Association (IDA) adjustment lending, and the Enhanced Structural Adjustment Facility (Humphreys and Underwood 1989).

Highly indebted countries had grown at a rapid pace due to increasing global trade between 1965 and 1973, but were forced to borrow during the oil crises in order to maintain growth, and hence suffered as a result of the subsequent interest rate increases. The collapse of commodity prices in 1980–82 due to the recession in developed countries worsened matters (Griffith-Jones and Sunkel 1986). These highly indebted countries, which had run average annual trade deficits of $2 billion between 1973 and 1982, turned the deficits into a surplus of $32.7 billion during the period 1983 to 1986, but this turnaround was also reflected in falling growth of gross domestic product (GDP) per capita, which fell from 2.6 percent between 1973 to 1980 to –2.6 percent between 1980 and 1985 (da Costa 1991).

Latin American financial sectors faced difficulties, and the governments of debtor countries often assumed the external liabilities of the private sector (Easterly 1989). Central banks made emergency loans to Mexico, Argentina, and Brazil. Extensive government intervention was required in the case of Chile's banking sector, in which foreign funds were suddenly reduced by more than 75 percent (Edwards 1989). Indebted countries such as South Korea, which cut budget deficits and devalued exchange rates, fared better than countries that did not implement these types of policy responses (Sachs 1989b).

In countries that performed worse during the debt crisis, fiscal conservatism was viewed as politically unpalatable. However, the type of spending was problematic. Although fiscal spending during a crisis can alleviate the impact of the downturn, fiscal spending in Latin America continued to favor social groups that were already better politically represented. Deficits increased. Deficits also grew as a result of reduced tax revenues (Edwards 1989). Government deficits were financed by printing money, which created inflation in the already weakened economies and subsequent devaluations. Hyperinflation resulted in Brazil and Mexico between 1980 and 1987 (da Costa 1991). Stabilizing the price level led to stabilizing the exchange rate by selling foreign exchange, running down central bank reserves.

Volatility of fiscal circumstances increased greatly in the 1980s throughout Latin America, as underlying macroeconomic indicators shifted (Gavin and Perotti 1997). This occurred both on the revenue and on the expenditure sides. Fiscal policy has been particularly procyclical during economic downturns. Monetary conditions were also volatile, with fluctuating currencies and high inflation. Argentina, Brazil, Peru, Uruguay, and Venezuela adopted several policies in attempts to stabilize their economies, with little to no success due to a lack of credibility arising from inconsistent policy mixes, lack of fiscal reform, and lack of structural reform. Attempts to improve economic stability by taxing financial and exchange transactions (as in Argentina and Brazil), instituting price and/or wage freezes (as in Brazil, Argentina, and Venezuela), and cutting public investment worked at times in the short run but not in the medium to long run. Countries with a more positive outcome were few, although Chile, Bolivia, and Mexico had some success in stabilizing their economies during the 1980s (Ter-Minassian and Schwartz 1997).

In response to the crisis, the US acted as lender of last resort to Mexico, providing $700 million at the beginning of 1982 (Kapstein 1994). Later that year, the Group of Ten (G-10) countries put together a $1.85 billion loan. The diagnosis of the crisis was that it was one of illiquidity rather than insolvency (Devlin 1989). Therefore, at the same time, banks were told that they had to continue lending to Mexico so that the country could make its interest payments. By contrast, increasing indebtedness was not viewed as a solution by the banks. Argentina and Brazil soon spiraled into crisis and received aid from the largest central banks. Rescheduling agreements were signed with the International Monetary Fund (IMF) and the banks.

Complicating matters was the fact that debt relief was not seen as sufficient unless it was linked to structural reform (Rotberg 1989). American political leaders insisted on austerity packages that would turn debtor countries away from what they viewed as bad economic management. Even given a commitment to structural reform, there was a view among some American bankers that political will would be key in determining whether countries could sustain long-term growth by giving up their "short-lived consumption-based policies" in favor of "job-creating investment-oriented policies" (Rhodes 1989).

These "new, improved" policies were later dubbed "Washington Consensus" policies. These included fiscal discipline, reprioritizing public expenditures, tax reform, liberalization of interest rates, liberalization exchange rates, liberalization of trade, liberalization of inward foreign direct investment (FDI), privatization, deregulation, and increase in property rights (Williamson 2004). Most of these policies were punitive toward the country undergoing them.

As long as countries did not default or impose a payment moratorium on their debt, they were forced to bear the brunt of the crisis. The US Congress was not in favor of bailing out banks with large exposure to developing countries' loans (Rotberg 1989). For the countries themselves, a current account deficit was no longer viable as foreign funds were unavailable to finance it. Even trade credit had evaporated. Hence, Latin American countries saw a sharp drop in imports, while exports fell somewhat (Edwards 1989). Countries were far from being able to increase exports to produce much-needed foreign exchange, dampening economic growth and worsening the ability of these nations to continue paying down debt. It was estimated that countries would require a 4 to 7 percent growth rate in order to repay debt without large net resource transfers, and this growth rate was, at least in the short run, unattainable (Meissner 1984).

There were real shocks as well, as income and employment in developing nations dropped and poverty soared. Real wages declined across Latin America (Edwards 1989). The lack of social security and unemployment benefits in developing countries translated into a shock, with no cushion, for developing country citizens (Griffith-Jones and Sunkel 1986). Many of those in developing countries were unable to pay for housing and public services such as water, sewage, and electricity. Loan repayment took precedence over economic well-being in developing countries. The time period in which indebted countries were expected to implement structural adjustment measures was about 18 months, a period too short to foment growth, especially when government officials who were supposed to oversee reforms were constantly in the process of negotiating with creditors (Collás-Monsod 1989). As a result of stringent loan repayment schedules, net resources did not remain in the country for the very investment required by the loans they repaid.

Devaluations occurred, varying by extent and timing from country to country, with most major debtors adopting some type of crawling peg regime as of July 1986 (Edwards 1989). Countries also adopted multiple exchange rate regimes, with different exchange rates on capital and current account transactions, to protect private sector repayment of foreign debt. In particular, a "preferential" exchange rate was provided for repayment of foreign debt. However, real devaluations were difficult to maintain for long periods of time due to the implementation of inconsistent macroeconomic policies, as domestic prices rose to combat the impact of devaluations.

The Reagan administration in 1983 obtained an $8.4 billion increase in funding to the IMF, on conditions, imposed by Congress, that international lending be improved in terms of risk evaluation, supervision, and regulation (Kapstein 1994). These agreements also required timely debt servicing of interest payments (an important element of international financial relations), rescheduling of existing bank claims, and co-lending by the IMF and commercial banks. The IMF began to require that debtor countries accept an adjustment package, in which fiscal spending had to be reduced, taxes raised, and money supply tightened (Kapstein 1994). In addition, the IMF required that IMF funding be accompanied by simultaneous lending from commercial banks. But IMF policies did not work to contain the chain of crises, in part because adjustment programs were never accompanied by robust investment that would catalyze growth (Serven and Solimano 1993). As Devlin (1989) points out, in order for an adjustment process to be effective, a trade surplus must be generated naturally through an increase in savings and production of export goods, rather than through a reduction in investment and output. The latter strategy is unsustainable since it is anti-growth. Crises were perpetuated because external financing was greatly reduced, placing a large burden for debt repayment on the private sector. A string of debt crises arose, and the international financial community sought to ameliorate each situation in turn (Cohen 1992).

IMF packages were problematic in their formation. The IMF reached an agreement with debtor countries that had already secured a loan commitment from the banks. In a bit of backwards policy making, the IMF used the estimate of committed external resources based on discussion with the banks to determine what the current account deficit should be (Collás-Monsod 1989). The focus was not on the sustainability of the debt or on the sustainability of economic activity in the face of the debt, but on what indebted countries could afford to pay, based on external funding.

Loan rescheduling fees and commissions were 2 to 3 percent of the loan value, and interest rate spreads for the rescheduled loans increased by about 1 percent. All of the debtor nations were forced to guarantee previously unguaranteed loans to the private sector (Mohanty 1992). After two years of efforts less than one-third of the outstanding debt had been rescheduled. By 1985, the lack of progress on debt reduction was evident. Lending to Latin America had all but stopped. Growth and capital formation suffered setbacks as indebtedness increased (Ffrench-Davis 1987).

The declaration by President Alan Garcia in Peru in 1985 that the country's responsibility to its citizens took precedence over its responsibility to creditors shocked the international community and prompted the implementation of the Baker Plan for debt relief (Collás-Monsod 1989). US Treasury Secretary James Baker further pushed "growth-oriented" structural adjustment, deregulation, and export promotion in developing nations. Mexico was the first to agree to a $12 billion rescue package under the Baker Plan, which included new loans and extended terms on existing loans (Bogdanowicz-Bindert 1986). As an alternative to participation in the restructuring cartel, commercial banks could trade their loans for an exit bond which paid a below-market interest rate, but allowed the banks to cap their losses and be released from calls for new loans (Mohanty 1992).

After two years, it was clear that the Baker Plan was not working, since the plan never abandoned the notion that all borrowing by the developing countries would ultimately be repaid in full. The economies continued to experience ongoing distress. The prices of non-tradeables in indebted countries collapsed and led to a profitability crisis in the production of non-traded goods. Banking systems in developing countries deteriorated and resulted in banking crises, resulting in government takeovers of banks (Sachs 1989a). The Baker Plan ultimately failed because commercial banks, which were to lend in tandem with the international organizations, failed to fulfill their end of the bargain since they had already suffered losses on previous loans (Mohanty 1992), and because the banks did not want debtor countries to repay other creditors before they were themselves repaid. (Collás-Monsod 1989). What is more, countries could not successfully marketize in time to "grow" out of their debt (Vasquez 1996).

In 1987, Brazil announced a suspension of interest payments in order to protect its diminishing supply of hard currency, while attempting to renegotiate its debt with commercial banks (Riding 1987). Banks did not want to continue making loans so that debtor nations could pay their debt interest. In response, Citicorp, the largest commercial bank at the time, added $3 billion to its loan loss reserves, signaling that it was willing to write off a large amount of its developing nation debt and stop making new loans (Kapstein 1994). Banks followed Citicorp's lead and lending to the indebted nations dried up.

During this period, developing nations' debt was sold on a secondary market at a discount, which allowed the banks to hold their loans on the books at full value while the loans themselves were actually worth less (Kapstein 1994). This period has been dubbed the "market-based menu approach" (Mohanty 1992). The logic was to provide options to the individual banks for restructuring and let each optimize their selection based on individual needs. Brazil's 1988 financial package was the first specifically based on the market-based menu approach (Husain and Diwan 1989). The Brazilian creditor claims were consolidated in the hands of a multiyear deposit facility, with installments paid at close to the six-month LIBOR rate and deposits eligible for debt–equity conversions (Lamdany 1989). Brazil and Mexico accounted for more than 72 percent of reduced external debt transactions. Through mixed measures, banks did astonishingly well in terms of recovering debt. Innovative debt reduction structures began to be employed more frequently. Until this time, assets, much less distressed assets, had rarely been traded among banks (Newman 1989). Chile retired nearly 15 percent of its medium- and long-term liabilities to commercial banks through debt–equity swaps (Larrain and Velasco 1990). Bolivia used debt buy-backs to reduce its debt, buying its debt back at the market rate of 6 cents on the dollar (Mohanty 1992). Mexico used securitization to offer creditors the opportunity to exchange Mexican debt for a smaller amount of debt that would be backed by zero-coupon US Treasury bonds and carry a higher spread, thus canceling $1.1 billion of its debt (Newman 1989). By 1989, many banks had recovered up to 40 percent of their original loans in a very short period of time (Cohen 1992).

US Treasury Secretary Nicholas Brady then tried a new approach through debt reduction. In 1989, as part of the Brady Plan, Mexico then offered its creditors three options: to reduce the face value of the debt by 35 percent, to reduce the interest rate to 6.25 percent, or to keep both the face value and interest rate and to lend an additional 25 percent of the face value over the next three years (Cohen 1992). Most creditors chose the first or second option. Other nations, including Costa Rica, Venezuela, Uruguay, Argentina, and Brazil, followed suit (Vasquez 1996). The Brady Plan used the IMF and World Bank to collateralize debt-for-bond exchanges at large discounts, to replenish reserves after cash buy-backs of debt took place, and to underwrite payment of new and modified debt contracts (Mohanty

1992). Although some bankers loathed the Brady Plan for "forcing" debt forgiveness on banks, the secondary market responded well to the loan securitization offered by the plan.

Under Mexico's plan for debt relief, Mexico worked on its official debt with the Paris Club, the IMF, the World Bank, and the EXIM Bank of Japan, then worked with a Bank Advisory Committee which represented the more than 600 banks involved in Mexico's debt. The commercial creditors agreed to a $48.9 billion debt restructuring. The Brady Plan worked in Mexico since most of the debt was with commercial banks rather than official lenders (Van Wijnbergen et al. 1991).

Ultimately, neither the Baker Plan nor the Brady Plan was able to prevent a net transfer of resources from developing to developed nations (da Costa 1991). The 1980s have been referred to as the "lost decade" for Latin America. The impacts on the debtor countries were severe. Between 1981 and 1988 per capita income declined in almost every country in South America. Living standards fell and triple- and quadruple-digit inflation raged in many countries as seignorage was used to replace capital inflows (Sachs 1989b).

Monetary and fiscal policy over the 1980s was mostly unsuccessful, and it was not until the end of the decade that policies were able to bring about some stability. Monetary stabilization policies were implemented in the late 1980s and early 1990s to dampen monetary and exchange rate volatility. Some examples included Mexico's *pacto* of 1988 and Argentina's currency board of 1991. According to Belaisch et al. (2005), countries that had high inflation rates before taking stabilization measures focused on exchange rate-based stabilization plans, while those with moderate inflation rates adopted inflation objectives. Explicit exchange rate-based stabilization policies were more effective in bringing down inflation than inflation-targeting policies. While these latter-day policies experienced some success, it can generally be said that crisis resolution in Latin America over the 1980s may be used not as an example, but as a counterexample of best practices.

POLITICAL ECONOMY OF THE DEBT CRISIS

The debt crisis played a role in ushering in a democratic transition in Latin America. Previously authoritarian regimes in Argentina, Bolivia, Brazil, the Dominican Republic, Colombia, Ecuador, Peru, and Uruguay became democratic in the 1980s and 1990s (Mainwaring et al. 2001). This Third Wave of democratization was accompanied by macroeconomic liberalization to combat the crisis.

In addition, Latin American populism under a variety of political regimes, which emphasized expansion of domestic demand and income redistribution, faced challenges to predominance during the 1980s crisis. In particular, neoliberal policies weakened labor movements, which were important components of populism in some countries as a result of working class or multiclass supporting coalitions. Public sector workers were laid off and business groups lost state subsidies; both groups, closely tied to the state, were disadvantaged by the debt crisis (Kaufman and Stallings 1991). The state increasingly became market-friendly rather than socially proactive.

The turn toward markets was not uniform, however, and the response to IMF policies was mixed. Governments with right-leaning political ideologies tended to embrace IMF-style reforms, while those with left-leaning views questioned them. Political resistance to IMF policies arose in pre-1985 Bolivia and post-1985 Peru, for example. Similarly, Pop-Eliches (2008) shows that when international forces favoring cooperation rose, neoliberal reforms were preferred, whereas when international incentives were weak, neoliberal reforms might have exacerbated domestic tensions between democracy and the inequality generated by neoliberalism. The sociopolitical response to the debt crisis was therefore complex, and this can explain to some extent the rather slow recovery experienced through the 1980s.

US SAVINGS AND LOAN CRISIS

Crisis arose in the United States as emerging markets were experiencing debt defaults. The Federal Home Loan Bank Board (FHLBB) regulated the savings and loan institutions separately from commercial banks.[1] The Federal Savings and Loan Insurance Corporation (FSLIC) also guaranteed deposits in thrift institutions separately. Regulation of savings and loan institutions was relatively lax compared to that of banks, particularly as the savings and loan industry transformed in the early 1980s. Savings and loan institutions were originally chartered in order to provide mortgage loans and were mainly created to provide a public service. In the 1980s, much of this changed. Mortgages as a percentage of financial assets fell from 73 percent in 1960 to 51 percent in 1986 (Brumbaugh and Carron 1987).

Historically high interest rates led to insolvencies in the savings and loan industry in the United States. Savings and loan deposit interest rates were capped in the 1960s and 1970s, and these institutions could not compete in attracting depositor funds, particularly against new money market funds. When the cap on deposits was relaxed through the Depository

Institutions Deregulation and Monetary Control Act of 1980 and the Garn–St Germain Depository Institutions Act of 1982, savings and loan institutions offered higher interest rates to depositors, but maintained lower fixed-interest assets or invested in highly risky assets, neither of which produced a constant stream of funding at high, stable returns. The cost of funding rose from 7 percent in 1978 to more than 11 percent in 1982 (Brumbaugh and Carron 1987). Between 1980 and 1982, 118 savings and loan institutions with $43 billion in assets failed (FDIC 1997).

Deterioration in these institutions was hidden or ignored due to regulatory changes and insufficient supervision. Savings and loan insolvencies were viewed as stemming from the interest rate hike, so little action was taken to improve the underlying financial issues. Instead, more funding was provided. In 1983, thrifts were permitted to extend the maturities on liabilities by borrowing from Federal Home Loan Banks for 20 rather than ten years. Changes in accounting treatment of goodwill in 1982 allowed thrifts that acquired weaker institutions to appear stronger than they were. Accounting standards used lenient rules, selecting the easiest sections from the regulatory accounting principles (RAP) or generally accepted accounting procedures (GAAP). Ownership restrictions on stock-held institutions were relaxed in 1982, allowing new owners to take part in the industry. An increase in deposit insurance provided depositors with a sense of security, no matter how weak the institution in which they placed their funds. The FHLBB did not strongly enforce regulations in the savings and loan thrifts, and relied on the states or on voluntary supervisory agreements for enforcement.

Although interest rates declined in 1982, restoring some measure of profitability, real estate lost its value, especially in the Southwest. Balance sheets deteriorated as a result. The FSLIC ran low on funds necessary to close flagging institutions, so that many insolvent thrifts remained open. By 1982, 1824 FSLIC-insured institutions were failing the RAP net worth requirement used in 1980 (Brumbaugh and Carron 1987). This opened the door to even greater risk-taking, as institutions desperately attempted to stay afloat. Analysts have pointed out the looming presence of moral hazard, as thrift operators could take large risks, while the FSLIC would remain responsible for repaying depositor funds.

Risky investment activities of near-insolvent banks were reduced near the end of 1984 through FHLBB enforcement, and three regulations were adopted in March 1985 by the Bank Board to limit risk. These regulations limited direct investments to 10 percent of assets or twice the net worth, whichever was larger; required additional net worth for thrifts growing at greater than 15 percent per year; and eliminated loose rules that allowed some thrifts to maintain minimum net worth below the 3 percent level.

These regulations, however, were insufficient to prevent large losses in the industry. Between 1986 and 1989, the Federal Savings and Loan Insurance Corporation closed or resolved 296 institutions with assets of $125 billion.

The Financial Institutions Competitive Equality Act of 1987 allowed the Federal Home Loan Bank System to create an institution to borrow funds on behalf of the FSLIC in order to close down insolvent thrifts. The Financial Institutions Reform, Recovery and Enforcement Act of 1989 (FIRREA), announced by President George H.W. Bush, substantially altered US financial industry regulation. Under FIRREA, the FHLBB was replaced with the Office of Thrift Supervision. The FSLIC was replaced by the Savings Association Insurance Fund. Financial institution regulators were given more powers of enforcement, and reformed the Federal Home Loan Bank System.

The Resolution Trust Corporation (RTC) was created under FIRREA to further wind down thrift institutions between 1989 and 1992 (Curry and Shibut 2000). The RTC was to have no employees of its own, but rather to utilize employees from other federal departments or agencies (Davison 2005). The RTC was to be responsible to the public, managed by the FDIC, and overseen by a board of directors. Rules governing the RTC were stringent, incorporating those governing conflict of interest, ethical responsibilities, and post-employment restrictions. The RTC was further required to obtain the maximum net present value from assets it controlled. The RTC closed or resolved 747 institutions between 1989 and 1995.

POLITICAL ECONOMY OF THE SAVINGS AND LOAN CRISIS

The US savings and loan crisis was highly politicized. Little attention was given to industry troubles politically or in the media until 1988, when news broke nationwide about the savings and loan crisis. The crisis became known as people who took advantage of the crisis situation, particularly Charles Keating, rose to notoriety. It turns out that white-collar crimes were rampant throughout the thrift industry. For example, the Chief Executive Officer (CEO) of Centennial Savings and Loan in northern California, Erwin Hansen, in 1980 used company funds to throw an expensive Christmas party and traveled around the world in the company's private airplanes. Hansen also purchased antique furniture and expensive art, and renovated a home at the company's expense (Calavita et al. 1997).

Charles Keating, an even more infamous character than Hansen, had purchased a savings and loan firm in the 1980s and invested in highly risky assets. Keating was associated with the "Keating Five," US Senators who propagated fraud stemming from the savings and loan industry. US Senators Alan Cranston, Dennis DeConcini, John Glenn, John McCain, and Donald Riegle, Jr blocked a regulatory investigation into Charles Keating's dealings in the Lincoln Savings and Loan by the Federal Home Loan Bank Board in exchange for political contributions. In fact, between 1983 and 1988, more than 160 political action committees representing savings and loan companies contributed almost $4.5 million into US House and Senate campaigns (Calavita et al. 1997).

Congressman Fernand St Germain, who sponsored the Garn–St Germain Depository Institutions Act of 1982 to deregulate savings and loan institutions and allow banks to offer adjustable rate mortgage loans, was himself investigated by the US Department of Justice for conflict of interest, due to frequent dinners with lobbyists for the US League of Savings Institutions. He was found guilty of misconduct by both the Justice Department and the House Ethics Committee, but remained in office.

While fraud accounts for a relatively small percentage of losses, the savings and loan crisis has been surrounded by the stench of cronyism and political back-scratching due to highly visible investigations. Perhaps worse than fraud, moral hazard was rampant, as thrift institutions used deposit funds to invest in risky assets, and regulation was insufficient to curb this behavior. The cost to US taxpayers was high, with a direct cost of $124 billion (Curry and Shibut 2000).

THE IMPOTENCE OF ECONOMIC THEORY

Economic theory at this time had shifted away from Keynesianism back into the hold of neoliberalism. President Ronald Reagan in the United States and Prime Minister Margaret Thatcher in the UK stressed the superiority of markets and attempted to reduce the size of government. They promoted supply-side economics, which focused on tax reform for the purposes of increasing tax revenues and reducing inflation. Tax rates for the wealthy were cut in order to induce greater output, and less government intervention was called for.

Robert Mundell and Arthur Laffer both favored tax cuts. Mundell had recommended in 1974, in the face of stagflation, that taxes should be reduced rather than raised in order to reduce economic stagnation. Arthur Laffer emphasized the importance of lowering tax rates for the wealthy in boosting government revenue. Tax cuts and tight monetary policy were implemented under Ronald Reagan's Economic Recovery Tax Act of 1981, exacerbating the debt crisis of the 1980s as interest rates soared.

Abroad, the "job-creating investment-oriented policies" implemented in debtor nations emphasized less government and more forceful markets in line with neoliberal tenets. Burdensome structural adjustment policies and pressure for repayment may have prolonged rather than relieved the crisis, as debtors were unable to declare default before the Brady Plan but instead limped along under fluctuating fiscal and monetary circumstances, frequently defaulting temporarily on debt service payments (Bertola and Ocampo 2012). Without alternative ideologies attractive and powerful enough to challenge neoliberalism, debt-ridden countries were forced to accept deep structural reforms oriented toward fiscal conservatism.

CONCLUSION

The debt crisis was caused by the high levels of external debt held by developing countries, coupled with the sudden strangulation of foreign lending. Unsurprisingly, Eichengreen and Rose (1998) find that developed country interest rates, more than any other factor, were highly related to banking crises in developing countries over this period. This underscores the assertion by some economists that the underlying cause of the debt crisis was not the ratio of external debt to GDP at the time, but rather the sudden credit squeeze (see da Costa 1991; Mohanty 1992).

The debt crisis left behind debtor countries unhappy, even angry, about the austerity measures they were required to impose for IMF loans. IMF measures, designed to stimulate export production and increase foreign exchange reserves of governments, required dramatic cuts in public spending, restraints on imports, and elimination of protectionism (Walton and Ragin 1990). Demonstrations occurred in 26 of the 80 debtor countries. Protests against austerity measures were not taken seriously in the 1980s debt crisis, and the IMF did not reform its conditionality measures until they became a laughing-stock during the Asian financial crisis. In the meantime, Latin America struggled to regain economic vitality.

NOTE

1. Savings and loan institutions, along with mutual savings banks and sometimes credit unions, are referred to in the US as "thrifts."

5. Early 1990s: advanced countries crises

In the early 1990s, several crises occurred: the Western European Exchange Rate Mechanism crisis of 1992, the Nordic country crises, and the Japanese crisis that spanned the decade. Crises in Western Europe and the Nordic countries in the early 1990s were not, unlike the debt crisis of the 1980s, calamitous. The Western European Exchange Rate Mechanism crisis of 1992 resulted from an unforeseen politico-economic shock – the reunification of Germany – while the Nordic country crises resulted from premature financial liberalization. Although Japan's crisis was directly associated with financial deregulation, the roots of the crisis were embedded in structural problems in the economy, extending Japan's financial distress for years after its real estate bubble burst in 1992. In this chapter, we first examine the Western European Exchange Rate Mechanism crisis of 1992, then discuss crises in the Nordic countries of Norway, Sweden, and Finland. Afterward, we turn to the long-lasting Japanese crisis.

WESTERN EUROPEAN EXCHANGE RATE MECHANISM CRISIS, 1992

For some time, European currency coordination was a primary goal in Western Europe. As international currency coordination became increasingly fragile, heads of European states met in 1969 at The Hague, agreeing on a plan to create a European economic and monetary union. The European Community had, in the previous decade, completed a transition period toward a full customs union, laid out a common agricultural policy, and created a system of own resources (Committee for the Study of Economic and Monetary Union 1989). Plans to fix intra-European exchange rates were implemented in 1972 to maintain exchange rate stability, even before the Bretton Woods system collapsed. "Snake-in-the-tunnel" and "floating snake" exchange rate policies were adopted with the dollar at the center, but fell short of providing sufficient financing for weak-currency countries (Klein 1998). By 1979, only a handful of countries remained within the "snake" arrangement; these included Germany, Luxembourg, the Netherlands, Denmark, Norway, Sweden, and Belgium.

The Western European Exchange Rate Mechanism was created in 1979, when the European Monetary System (EMS) was created to reduce exchange rate shocks in the wake of Bretton Woods. The EMS consisted of the European Currency Unit (ECU) and the managed float exchange rate system, the Exchange Rate Mechanism (ERM) (BBC 2003). These were created in anticipation of setting up a greater European economic union. Efforts to coordinate European currencies resulted in the Western European ERM crisis in 1992.

The ERM was brought about by the desire on the part of European political leaders to create an orderly internal market for goods and assets without barriers to trade. The ERM would ease the movement of goods, capital, and people by stabilizing exchange rates between countries. The ERM was also supported by the European aversion to flexible exchange rates due to hardship experienced from exchange rate instability in the 1920s and 1930s (Higgins 1993). Destabilizing speculation, competitive devaluations, short-term capital flows, and the deflationary impact of the gold exchange standard plagued Europe in the interwar period (Bordo and James 2001).

The ERM was adjusted to suit countries' individual macroeconomic fundamentals, and exchange rates were satisfactorily realigned 11 times to 1987. A country could put in a request for realignment, and terms could be negotiated in Monetary Committee meetings, and the final decision on implementation required approval by all members (Buiter et al. 1998). Unilateral realignments were not allowed. Still, even by 1987, a large divergence in economic policy prevailed in ERM countries, as inflation ran high in the peripheral countries of Spain and Italy.

Commitment to creation of the European Monetary Union (EMU) was maintained, however, and was carried out in stages. Stage one of the EMU began in 1990 with narrowing exchange rate bands and more tightly coordinated economic and banking policy. Capital and exchange controls were removed, creating increased openness across participating European nations. The German Mark, a very low-inflation currency, became the unofficial reserve currency, since the Bundesbank was strongly committed to setting anti-inflationary policy (Buiter et al. 1998). Other countries were forced to mimic German monetary policy to ensure alignment with the Deutschemark. Furthermore, both an ECU currency parity and a bilateral parity grid (focusing on exchange rates between pairs of countries) were maintained, putting pressure on weak-currency countries to maintain their exchange rates. As capital controls were removed, the ERM became at once less flexible and even more subject to exchange rate pressures. The two critical safety valves of capital and exchange rate controls were gone.

Removal of the safety valves needed to be undertaken during a period of economic stability. However, just as stage one of European Monetary Union was carried out, Germany reunified, and West Germany worked to raise the living standards of East Germany. East Germany was unified with West Germany under the assurance that wages, pensions, and savings would be preserved on a 1:1 currency ratio. This caused the ERM crisis, since net transfers of public funds from West to East Germany were exorbitant, and West Germany's public sector became increasingly indebted because the budget deficit was financed by loans (Buiter et al. 1998). The trade surplus became a trade deficit. Increases in consumption created demand-driven inflation and increased interest rates in Germany. Ironically, the same currency that was chosen to maintain low inflation in coordinating countries was at fault for transmitting inflation to its partner countries at this time. Germany's insistence on fiscal expansion translated into a "beggar thy neighbor" policy that transmitted high interest rates to the rest of the EMS region.

Germany, as the center of the ERM system, was willing to accommodate increased inflation within its domestic economy only up to a point, and proceeded to tighten its money supply and raise interest rates. High interest rates were transmitted to other European countries through the ERM. The Deutschemark became even more attractive due to high interest rates, inducing dollar holders to switch to Deutschemarks, and further appreciating the currency. Macroeconomic fundamentals, in terms of unemployment, output gaps, inflation, and debt, in France, Spain, Italy, Sweden, and the United Kingdom (UK) therefore deteriorated, providing cause for later devaluation and flotation (Krugman 1996). The ERM was in turn weakened by poor macroeconomic fundamentals in participating countries, revealing governments' willingness to allow systemic deterioration in the ERM rather than use alternative fiscal policies (Knot et al. 1998).

Periphery countries (that is, countries other than Germany) did not want to undergo a nominal realignment, but neither did they want to bear the cost of deflation (Buiter et al. 1998). As it were, loss of competitiveness according to price and cost indicators had been occurring in Spain, Portugal, and Italy. In addition, the UK entered its worst recession since World War II, but could not use expansionary monetary policy to revive the economy due to its commitment to the ERM. UK interest rates were floating and therefore vulnerable to rate changes, reducing credibility of the Bank of England to defend the pound. The Bank of England had to use reserves to defend its currency.

After the collapse of the Finnish peg in 1991 due to the Nordic crisis, the markka depreciated against the Deutschemark by 15 percent. This was one indication that there were intra-European exchange rate disequilibria. Denmark's rejection of the Maastricht Treaty was a negative market signal that began a downward spiral in the ERM in 1992. The Maastricht Treaty was meant to lead to further European monetary and economic integration, and Denmark's rejection increased volatility in the foreign exchange market as devaluation expectations increased, particularly with regard to the Italian lira (Eichengreen 2000). The lira was endangered due to increasing lack of competitiveness of the Italian economy and a positive inflation differential toward Germany. As the Deutschmark appreciated relative to other currencies, the British pound was precariously set just above its ERM floor. To defend the pound and maintain the exchange rate, the Bank of England replenished its international reserves to purchase pounds and raised the base interest rate. Britain's exchange rate stability came at a cost, however. The appreciation of the Mark, and therefore of the pound, resulted in a fall in net exports, and higher interest rates in Germany and other areas of the world resulted in an outflow of capital.

The appreciation of the pound and the lira, the latter within its new band, were insufficient. Buiter et al. (1998) even posit that the realignment of the lira led to a sharp decline in market sentiment. Speculative attacks against the pound and other non-German ERM currencies occurred. As a result, Italy, Spain, the UK, Norway, and Sweden were forced to abandon the ERM. France, Germany, and the Netherlands remained (Hénin and Podevin 2002). Germany's monetary policy remained shaped to domestic concerns about inflation, despite calls from European central banks to lower interest rates (Higgins 1993). France came under increased speculative pressure in June 1993, as the country experienced continuing unemployment, which put pressure on the French government not to raise interest rates, while being pressured externally not to lower interest rates to defend the franc (Eichengreen 2000). The Bank of France was unable to sterilize capital inflows.

On July 30, 1993, almost all currencies were at the bottom of their bands against the Deutschmark, and on August 1, under persistent pressure, the "hard" ERM was replaced with a much softer ERM policy (Buiter et al. 1998). The softer ERM policy was far more similar to a floating exchange rate policy than it was to a target band. Speculative attacks subsided, as Europe's clear commitment to monetary unification allowed member countries to recover exchange rate credibility.

One may make the argument that the ERM crisis was not caused directly by high debt, liberalization, or even currency deterioration (although this did result), but rather by a crisis of monetary union and the import of destructive monetary policies. Supporting this claim is the idea that, had countries not been tied to Germany's monetary policy, they would have been able to improve their own economic circumstances. This type of crisis of monetary rigidity had occurred as a result of the gold standard during the Great Depression and later in the Great Recession within the eurozone.

Because the crisis stemmed from the adherence to the ERM, it was easily resolved by changing the ERM to which affected countries had committed. After the crisis, in contrast to what has happened after crises in developing nations, output did not fall and access to international capital markets was not lost (Calvo and Reinhart 2000). Calvo's "sudden stop," or economic paralysis, was not experienced. Overcoming the crisis was a critical step in Europe's monetary unification that reinforced its unique, decades-old commitment to political and economic integration (Eichengreen 2000).[1] The European Union continued to evolve in terms of both economic and political unification. Membership of the European Union was extended to almost the whole of Western Europe by 1995. Reforms were carried out that continued to work toward a unified European market with the reduction of barriers to trade between countries. The euro, which replaced individual country currencies, was brought into being in 1999, and was one of the most important stages in carrying out the Maastricht Treaty, which was approved in 1993.

Political Economy of the ERM Crisis

The Delors Report, written in 1989 (Committee for the Study of Economic and Monetary Union 1989), proposed a three-step process in moving toward a European monetary union. The first stage was undertaken in July 1990, and was to be implemented gradually. However, due to revolutions in Eastern Europe and the fall of the Berlin Wall, Germany's Chancellor Helmut Kohl identified German reunification as part of a greater European union (Sevilla 1995). French President Francois Mitterand pushed forward the concept of a European monetary union, visiting 11 European capitals to discuss the issue. By the end of 1990, Germany was reunited and revisions to the original European Community treaty were under way.

The details of the Delors Report garnered some criticism, particularly for Stage II, which required there to be some transfer of monetary authority to a central institution. France and Italy wanted to move toward monetary convergence rapidly, and supported the proposition that a European Central Bank be set up in Stage II. Germany and the Netherlands emphasized the necessity of nominal and real convergence before making the transition to a monetary union. Britain also wished to draw out the first stage before committing to a deeper integration. The Maastricht Treaty was a compromise plan drawn up by French President Mitterand and Italian Prime Minister Giulio Andreotti, which proposed that the EMU would become obligatory in 1999 for all European Community countries that fulfilled the following conditions, put forth in a proposal drawn up by the Netherlands:

1. Implementation of strong price stability measured with respect to the average inflation rate, over a period of one year prior to the examination.
2. Maintenance of government debt at less than 60 percent of gross domestic product (GDP) and a budget deficit less than 3 percent of GDP.
3. Adherence of the exchange rate to within the narrow ERM margins, with no devaluations for at least two years before the examination.
4. Adherence to interest rates of no more than 2 percent higher than the three members with the lowest inflation, for one year prior to the examination (European Council and European Commission 1992).

President Mitterand was committed to maintaining the value of the franc under the *"franc fort"* policy, and this meant that he was required to impose economic austerity and market liberalization. Voter satisfaction dwindled by 1992, as slow economic growth and high unemployment resulted from the *franc fort* policies. The public endured an increase in short-term interest rates to 13 percent on September 23, 1992 to defend the franc (Sevilla 1995).

In the UK, Prime Minister Margaret Thatcher was a proponent of the Single European Act for the promotion of free markets, but not of ERM requirements of complex managed exchange rates. Chancellor of the Exchequer Nigel Lawson ordered the Treasury and the Bank of England to informally link the pound to the Deutschemark. Over time, Prime Minister Thatcher was pressured into joining the ERM during the first stage of implementation. Thatcher's reluctance to join the ERM rendered the British commitment to the pact questionable and subject to speculation. Prime Minister John Major, Thatcher's successor, viewed a single European currency as a long-term objective. Major lacked a domestic coalition that supported sterling's position, since economic conditions were poor. Eventually, Britain could not defend its commitment to the ERM, and the pound was forced to withdraw from the ERM in September 1992.

September 1992 resulted in a number of troubles. European Ministers of Finance and central bank Governors failed to come to an agreement on realignment at a meeting in Bath (Sevilla 1995). Finland abandoned its peg to the ECU. The lira devalued by 7 percent, only to face further downward pressure and then be withdrawn from the ERM. The only highlight of the month was a successful defense of the franc by the Bundesbank and Banque de France. The former spent 160 billion francs to defend the currency, while the latter committed between 10 and 30 billion Marks. Ultimately, it was only the franc that was successfully defended against speculation. The crisis was finally resolved in 1993 with adherence to a softer peg, and commitment to the monetary union continued. We now turn to the crises in the Nordic countries of Norway, Sweden, and Finland.

NORDIC COUNTRIES

Norway, Sweden, and Finland had been known for their extensive welfare states after World War II. Economies were growing, unemployment was low, and welfare benefits were generous. This changed beginning in the 1970s as the oil crises struck. Sweden used countercyclical fiscal policies to address the economic slowdown, but built up public deficits as a result. Unemployment rose in Finland, remaining above 5 percent for most of the 1980s. Still, the welfare state persisted even as financial liberalization arose.

The three largest Nordic countries experienced a large boom-and-bust period in the 1980s and early 1990s. Norway, Sweden, and Finland had relatively tight control of their banking systems until the 1980s. These included capital controls, quantitative banking restrictions, and interest rate regulations (Drees and Pazarbaşıoğlu 1998). Bank profitability was stable and price competition was non-existent. The banking system was conservative and lending was relationship based. Government-owned banks originated a large percentage of loans in Norway and a significant percentage of loans in Finland.

The system, however, was shielded from market forces and in many ways inefficient, as lenders found ways to circumvent interest rate restrictions (Drees and Pazarbaşıoğlu 1998). Rising inflation and nominal interest rate restrictions put further constraints on the financial system. Circumvention of the rules became increasingly popular, and did not correct distortions. Regulators therefore decided to deregulate the financial market to increase efficiency in preparation for the development of a European-wide financial market.

Deregulation began with the removal of interest rate restrictions, and ended, in Norway and Sweden, with the opening up of the financial market to foreign competition. Finland took a more radical path and started with opening to foreign banks and liberalizing the capital account even to the extent that private households were allowed to raise foreign currency-denominated loans. Credit demand climbed in step with liberalization, which coincided with economic growth. Some of this was due to pent-up credit demand, while additional demand resulted from procyclical forces that gave rise to higher asset, particularly real estate, values.

Household and corporate borrowers were willing to incur debt to purchase assets because they were unable to foresee the new downside risks introduced by liberalization. Borrowing in foreign currency increased greatly, especially in Finland. Whereas lenders might have controlled the inflating bubble, they were uncertain in the new competitive environment, and responded by competing for loans. Government involvement in banking, particularly in Norway, declined dramatically. Hence no party was sure how to respond to deregulation, and each acted in their own self-interest to maximize perceived profitability.

Housing and equity prices increased in the late 1980s, and expansionary fiscal policy in Sweden and Norway exacerbated the situation. House price volatility was highest in Sweden and Finland (Jaffee 1994). These rapid expansions of credit, with riskier engagements, were doomed at the downside of the business cycle. When the business cycle turned and asset prices leveled out, it became clear that the boom was in fact a bubble, which subsequently burst in the late 1980s and early 1990s (Mai 2008). Tightening of monetary policy in all three countries in response to inflationary pressures from Germany through the ERM, and of fiscal policy in Sweden and Norway, led to a decline in asset prices and a credit crunch (Mai 2008). Monetary policy was tied to keeping exchange rates stable, while fiscal policy was overly lax (Sandal 2004). In response to the crises, capital was injected into banks on a growing scale, and government takeovers of banks soon occurred (Mai 2008). Creditor guarantees were issued in both Sweden and Finland.

Unlike other crises, the Nordic crisis was relatively straightforward in its problem and resolution. A combination of financial deregulation without sufficient risk provision, along with external shocks, affected Norway, Sweden, and Finland. The problem did not stem from problems embedded in the past, nor were they, particularly in Norway and Sweden, real economic structural problems. The resolution was swift, as the government was able to inject sufficient liquidity into the banking system to suffocate the flames.

Norway

The crisis in Norway was least severe, even though it preceded crises in Sweden and Finland. Consider the following: in Norway, real GDP dropped cumulatively by 0.1 percent, while in Sweden GDP dropped by 5.3 percent and in Finland GDP dropped by 10.4 percent; Norway's cumulative fall in bank lending amounted to 4.9 percent, while in Sweden it was 26.4 percent, and in Finland it was 35.5 percent (Sandal 2004). In part, this was because financial liberalization in both Norway and Sweden was less radical than in Finland. Unlike Sweden, however, Norway was not under economic pressure from other sources during the deregulation period. Sweden suffered from lack of exchange rate credibility due to recurring devaluations, high inflation, and a costly, expanding public sector (Ergungor 2007). Norway was lucky to be free from such problems.

The case of Norway is therefore the cleanest to examine first. Financial deregulation in the form of lifting interest rate ceilings and quantitative restrictions occurred in Norway beginning in 1984 (Vale 2004). This was followed by a bank lending and real estate boom, as borrowers who had previously been unable to obtain loans were able to borrow at very low interest rates, particularly between 1984 and 1986. Much of the lending was funded from abroad (Steigum 2004).

As consumption increased, the savings rate dropped. Prices of real estate, particularly non-residential real estate in Oslo, increased greatly until 1986 and then fell through 1992, indicating a real estate bubble (Steigum 2004). Borrowing for real estate loans and other purposes was encouraged by the government's policy of favorable tax treatment of interest payments. Deregulation also allowed new banks to enter the market, while supervision was reduced from on-site inspection to document inspection (Vale 2004). This led to excessive risk taking and poor managerial control.

External shocks then set in. First, a decline in the price of oil, a major export commodity, led to a fall in asset prices. Bank loan growth subsequently slowed by 1989 (Ongena et al. 2000). Second, in 1990, Norway's banded peg to the Deutschemark and Germany's increase in interest rates after unification forced Norway to raise interest rates despite the slow economy (Vale 2004).

During the first part of the crisis, between 1988 and 1990, there were many small bank failures. The first bank to encounter losses was Sunnmørsbanken, a medium-sized bank that was troubled by loan losses (Sandal 2004). The small banks, backed by government guarantees, were merged with larger banks. Deposit insurance was managed by the banking industry itself, which first injected capital into troubled banks (Ongena et al. 2000). At the same time, guarantee funds were depleted due to a worsening position in the large banks, including Fokus Bank, Christiania Bank, and Den norske Bank.

In all three Nordic countries, the government offered assistance and engaged in takeovers. When it was found that Norway's banking industry facilities had run out of funds to make up for bank losses, the Government Bank Insurance Fund (GBIF) was set up to extend loans to distressed banks. By October 1991, the Norwegian banking crisis became systemic when the second-largest bank lost its equity capital and the fourth-largest bank lost its shareholder capital (Vale 2004). The GBIF was depleted, and the government stepped in and took control of the large failing banks (Ongena et al. 2000). The government was left as the dominant owner of Den norske Bank and the sole owner of Christiania and Fokus Bank. During the Norwegian banking crisis, 13 banks representing more than 95 percent of the total commercial bank assets in Norway either failed or were seriously impaired.

The ERM crisis worsened the Nordic crisis, forcing Norway, Sweden, and Finland to import Germany's high interest rates and suffer currency attacks. After attempts to defend the currency, in late 1992, Norway abandoned the ERM and the krone was allowed to float. As Norges Bank, Norway's central bank, brought down interest rates, the economy began to grow again, bringing down loan losses (Vale 2004). The government gradually sold back its bank shares over the following decade and economic recovery was rather swift.

Sweden

Sweden experienced a similar downward trajectory, but its macroeconomy was not robust even before deregulation. Sweden's currency was weak and inflation was relatively high. Labor unions, anticipating continuing devaluations and hence increasing inflation, lobbied for higher wages (Ergungor 2007). Bank deregulation occurred simultaneously, starting in 1983 with the elimination of liquidity ratios for banks, and continuing with the lifting of interest rate and lending ceilings, and placement requirements for insurance companies in 1985. Financial markets were rapidly diversified to include certificates of deposit (CDs) and Treasury bills.

As in Norway, new lending surged in the late 1980s, particularly from banks and mortgage institutions (Englund 1999). Banks also issued guaranteed investment certificates (*marknadsbevis*) to finance companies that were not allowed to accept deposits, which exposed banks to high-risk transactions. Banks and other financial institutions lent increasingly in foreign currency through the late 1980s. The stock market, as well as real estate prices, increased rapidly after deregulation, creating asset price bubbles. Unemployment declined as the economy verged on overheating.

In the fall of 1989, it appeared that the commercial property market had peaked, and real estate managers were having difficulty finding tenants (Ergungor 2007). The stock market reacted and fell, just as interest rates were rising in step with German reunification, imported as a result of Sweden's fixed exchange rate. The ERM crisis was affecting Sweden, resulting in interest rate increases and the endangerment of foreign-denominated debt. Reforms in the tax system and high interest rates caused asset prices to fall (Jackson 2008). The value of commercial paper also dropped suddenly.

The first financial firm affected by declining real estate prices was Nyckeln, a financial firm that had specialized in commercial real estate financing (Jackson 2008). Nyckeln's fall then affected Sweden's banking system. Credit losses surged between the end of 1990 and 1993, accounting for 17 percent of lending (Englund 1999). The first bank to enter difficulties was Första Sparbanken, the largest savings bank (Sandal 2004). The Swedish government stepped in to guarantee bank debt. Then the third-largest bank, Nordbanken, suffered loan losses. At the time, the state owned most of the bank equity, and the state purchased more bank equity and later restructured the bank.

Bad loans were transferred to the new government-owned bank, Securum, which was to recoup losses from non-performing loans. This restored confidence in existing banks by ensuring good loans were separated from bad loans, which were subsequently transferred away.

In 1992, the Riksbank was forced to defend the krona with drastic measures after the UK and Italy left the ERM (Englund 1999). After a series of speculative attacks, the Riksbank allowed the krona to float on November 19. Foreign withdrawal of loans resulted in heavy credit losses in all seven of the largest banks, although Riksbank provided foreign currency liquidity support (Sandal 2004). A crisis resolution bank, Bankstödsnämnden, was instituted in May 1993 to provide capital support to crisis banks upon their application. Most state capital support ended up going to Nordbanken and Gota Bank.

Interest rates fell with the flotation of the krona. The flotation of the krona was important in alleviating the macroeconomic pressures experienced both before and after financial liberalization, since it allowed Sweden to regain control over monetary policy.

Because 40 percent of bank lending was in foreign currency, with mounting signs of distress, loans became increasingly short term. The state guaranteed bank obligations in September 1992, and the guarantee was maintained until 1996 (Sandal 2004). Both the banking and currency crises dampened aggregate demand and exacerbated the economic downturn, but, as in Norway, actions taken by the government were successful in restoring confidence in the economy.

Finland

Finland's story is the most dramatic. Here, financial deregulation was most pronounced, since unlike Norway and Sweden, Finland allowed foreign banks to enter its financial market earlier, in 1982 (Drees and Pazarbaşıoğlu 1998). In the late 1980s, securities markets developed rapidly and interest rates were liberalized. Abolition of exchange controls resulted in a large increase in borrowing from abroad (Brunila and Takala 1993). Capital movement liberalization in 1986 and 1987 allowed unrestricted long-term borrowing from abroad for particular sectors at the same time that interest rate deregulation was completed. The share of foreign liabilities on commercial bank balance sheets increased from 17 percent in 1980 to 41 percent in 1990 (Koskeynkylä and Vesala 1994).

At the time, households were able to deduct interest expenses from taxable income, which encouraged increased borrowing. The expansionary period was amplified, as in Norway and Sweden, by increasing asset prices. Credit rationing was viewed as less important in the booming economy, even though banks had significant holdings in large corporations (Brunila and Takala 1993). Bank loans ballooned much further than in Norway and Sweden. However, in this new, liberalized environment, banks were unused to controlling for risks. Macroeconomic policy was not used to cool credit overheating. Terms of trade improved due to falling oil prices and rising export prices, driving demand even higher (Nyberg and Vihriälä 1993).

Monetary policy was tightened in early 1989, but not by enough to make an immediate difference (Nyberg and Vihriälä 1993). Borrowing in foreign currencies continued to increase until the end of the year, when debt servicing occupied an increasing percentage of private sector income. Then the real estate sector experienced falling demand, and a large external shock occurred. With the collapse of the Soviet Union in 1991, exports to the USSR, a major trading partner, disintegrated.

Output fell sharply and resulted in declining incomes and thus an increase in households' indebtedness, along with overleveraging in the corporate sector (Brunila and Takala 1993). Bank profitability plummeted, much lower than in Norway and Sweden. A rapid output decline led to a balance-of-payments problem, weakening confidence in the economy and in the fixed exchange rate (Nyberg and Vihriälä 1993). A speculative attack on the markka forced the Bank of Finland to tighten monetary policy further to defend the currency, but this resulted in a severe economic contraction. In November 1991, the markka was devalued by 12.3 percent. Newly high interest rates, accompanied by a devalued markka, led to an inability in the private sector to service debt.

Skopbank, a commercial bank used as a central bank for savings bank, was the first bank to encounter large losses (Nyberg and Vihriälä 1993). The bank came under a restructuring program at the end of 1990, by which the savings banks each provided capital to their central bank. In 1991, Skopbank faced a severe liquidity shortage and the Bank of Finland subsequently took control of the bank, even injecting equity capital into the bank so that shareholders would not face losses. Skopbank's bad assets were transferred to two asset management companies ("bad banks") that were capitalized by the central bank (Sandal 2004). Non-performing loans throughout the banking sector grew, most of which were linked to real estate and retail trade (Nyberg and Vihriälä 1993). Savings banks accounted for half of the losses.

In March 1992, the government provided banks with capital in the form of purchases of preferred capital certificates (Sandal 2004). In August 1992, the government announced that stability would be provided to the Finnish banking system under all conditions. In September 1993, the markka was floated.

Recovery came in late 1993, and was concentrated in the capital-intensive export sector (Honkapohja et al. 1999). Recovery in the domestic sector came later, and unemployment persisted even after recovery began. This has been attributed to the presence of structural problems in the Finnish economy.

As in Sweden and Norway, prudent financial practices were under-developed when financial liberalization took place, opening the door to excessive and risky lending. In the lead-up to the crisis, fiscal policy was not used as a countercyclical instrument. Moral hazard was also an issue, since institutions were regarded as too big to fail (Koskeynkylä and Vesala 1994). This led to the creation and fomentation of the crisis.

In all three countries, after speculative attacks on their respective currencies, Norway, Sweden, and Finland devalued and were at last able to regain some control over monetary policy. All three countries pursued an inflation-targeting policy. Flotation of the currency also helped these economies to regain competitiveness. Government guarantees of stability and intervention in the banking sector helped to re-establish confidence among all three countries as well, so that the crisis could be overcome successfully.

Political Economy of the Nordic Country Crises

All political parties within the Finnish government were committed to resolving the crisis, although exactly which policies to implement were a matter of debate. Policy makers were surprised by the depth of the crisis, particularly as policies to balance the budget by raising taxes and reducing expenditure exacerbated matters. The Finnish government, however, was committed to ensuring stability of the banking system, confirming this policy formally within the parliament in January 1993 (Sandal 2004). This policy was set in place through 1998.

Swedish authorities also held broad political support for crisis resolution measures, even though the Social Democratic government of 1982–91 had laid the groundwork for crisis through deregulation in the 1980s, and the center-right government of 1991 basically inherited the resulting problems. The state guaranteed that all banks would meet their obligations as required. This blanket guarantee was held from 1992 through 1996. The bank support agency, the Bankstödsnämnd, was set up as an independent body and made transparent to the Social Democratic opposition. The body worked closely with the Riksbank, the Finansinspektion (financial supervisory authority) and the National Debt Office (Jonung 2009).

While Norway did not announce blanket guarantees, as did Finland and Sweden, the state maintained political support for emergency measures. Norway provided emergency liquidity support to individual banks. The Financial Supervisory Authority of Norway (FSAN) had been created before the crisis arose, and had yielded to pressure to maintain low levels of bank supervision (Steigum 2011). After the crisis, the FSAN was given more resources for expansion and set up a new program for macroeconomic surveillance. Thus began Norway's program of "active risk-based supervision," with cooperation among the FSAN, Ministry of Finance, and Norges Bank.

Conclusion

The Nordic crisis was not inevitable, since proper mechanisms for reducing market risk were not put in place before liberalization. However, the crises did not have deep roots in the economies, and the policy response was swift. The currency crises were associated with the ERM crisis and were not, by contrast to the Asian financial crisis at the end of the decade, caused by sudden capital outflows.

Honkapohja (2014) writes that in response to the Nordic crises, the Nordic countries introduced crisis resolution agencies to manage the crises. Private solutions, such as mergers and takeovers of banks, were attempted before public takeovers. The government injected funds and engaged in takeovers as needed. As Stefan Ingves (2002) noted:

> it must be strongly stressed that the Nordic countries are unusually orderly at the micro level. Hence they represented an almost ideal environment for crisis management and bank resolution. This was the case even in the absence of a systemic resolution framework or a clear regulatory framework for dealing with problem banks – a lot was improvised, but it was done very well because

the microeconomic structures were in place (it was relatively easy for the public sector to take over and recapitalize a bank, lend or guarantee funds to a private bank, set up limited liability companies for dealing with problem assets, etc. – transactions that have proven extraordinarily difficult in many other countries).

The resolutions were both speedy and transparent, and losses to creditors were minimized. Prudential regulations were put in place to prevent further loan losses.

JAPAN

As in Sweden, Norway, and Finland, Japan's financial crisis began after the bursting of the real estate bubble that had developed over the 1980s after a period of financial deregulation (Nakaso 2001). However, the crisis was structurally grounded in the real economy rather than just policy based. The crisis began in the early 1990s and culminated in 1997 to 1998, depressing growth for years and earning the period the name, "the lost decade."

The crisis had roots in the institutions of the economy. After very rapid growth in the 1950s and 1960s due to historically large rates of investment and major government involvement in the funding of large firms and infrastructure creation, Japan was presented with a slowdown in the 1970s due to the oil shocks. The oil shocks strongly affected the US economy and drove down the value of the dollar as the country became increasingly indebted. Japan's export-oriented economy suffered from a rising yen in relation to the dollar (Brenner 2006). What is more, in Japan, the same institutions that had allowed for unprecedented growth through coordinated competition before the first oil shock, and which embraced the concept of total employment (that is, no unemployment) became a liability as productivity declined and large corporations were forced to continue a policy of guaranteed employment (Gao 2001). A lack of innovation reduced the demand for Japanese goods and therefore profits, and companies looked to reduce costs in order to increase efficiency. Starting in the mid-1970s, companies engaged in the practice of *zai'tech*, investing in stocks and bonds to increase profits. This, coupled with the liberalization of finance encouraged by the United States (US), drove a period of speculation in real estate, overseas investment, stocks and bonds, and even golf club memberships, that created a growing bubble through the 1980s (Gao 2001).

An increase in US current account deficits and a rise in Japanese current account deficits was rebalanced after the Plaza Accord, which allowed for dollar devaluation (Brenner 2006). Yen appreciation was a shock to the export-oriented economy and set the stage for economic decline in the Japanese economy. Financial deregulation allowed investors to seek other methods of profit generation.

Financial deregulation in the late 1980s consisted of loosening of interest rate controls, lifting of prohibition on short-term euro–yen loans, deregulation of the corporate bond market, creation of commercial paper, and increases in lending ceilings to particular institutions (Kanaya and Woo 2000). Increasing competition in the environment of deregulation led to an expansion of risk-taking activities with poor ongoing risk evaluation. Banks had less monitoring control over loans as they faced decreasing demand from traditional, larger companies and increasing demand from less-known, smaller companies (Gao 2001).

At the same time, Japan continued to lose its comparative advantage in technological innovation. Japan had relatively far fewer computers and websites than the US throughout the late 1980s and 1990s (Gao 2001). Social welfare, once covered by the policy of total employment through both large and small companies, had declined markedly, and the social programs moved into the domain of the government sector. Government spending grew and, in conjunction with loose monetary policy, created an overheated economy.

The Ministry of Finance recognized, at least by 1990, that the lending boom at the end of the 1980s had led to overlending to the real estate sector, and imposed temporary lending restrictions for the real estate sector (Kanaya and Woo 2000). This officially deflated the real estate bubble and led to a decline in economic growth but, as Bernanke (2000) points out, also led to an immediate asset-price crash. The tightening thereafter, until 1994, created continued asset price declines.

The Nikkei 225 stock index plunged at the end of 1989, and economic indicators worsened. GDP contracted over the decade. Over this period, the presence of "zombie" firms crowded out more efficient firms (Caballero et al. 2008). Non-performing loans became a monstrous issue in 1992 through 2000, cumulatively forming 17 percent of GDP (Nakaso 2001).

The safety of the banking system, particularly of large banks, was implicitly guaranteed by the Ministry of Finance. Because of this, and due to the absence of bank failures since World War II, the deposit insurance system was underdeveloped for large financial institutions. Smaller financial institutions began to fail in 1991, but the financial authorities remained optimistic that the fallout of the bursting of the asset price bubble would be contained (Nakaso 2001). In 1992 and afterward, banks restructured failing loans by extending credit lines to imperiled borrowers and reducing loans to new borrowers (Kanaya and Woo 2000).

There were attempts to encourage banks to write off non-performing loans in order to obtain a tax deduction for the loan loss. Few companies wanted to do this, since large write-offs might encourage borrowers to stop repaying loans. The Cooperative Credit Purchasing Company was created to purchase bad assets from banks, but with funds backed by the banks themselves. Therefore cleaning up balance sheets was a slow process in which there was little bank cooperation.

Banks faced a lack of strong corporate governance, and the crisis began to strike harder in 1994. At this time, the Governor of the Bank of Japan, Yasushi Mieno, stated that the government would not save all failing financial institutions (Nakaso 2001). Shortly thereafter, two urban credit co-operatives, Tokyo Kyowa and Anzen, failed. The Ministry of Finance tried to find a buyer for the institutions, but there was none to be had. A new bank, therefore, had to be established to take over the failed banks, and capital was injected from both the public and private sectors. After this move, the Bank of Japan was heavily criticized for bailing out the credit co-operatives.

After 1994, the overnight call rate was lowered by the Bank of Japan and finally reached zero in 1999 in attempts to revive the economy (Hoshi and Kashyap 2004). Fiscal deficits of close to 6 percent per year were used to finance countercyclical measures. However, a lack of aggregate demand continued to produce economic stagnation, as deflation wracked the economy (Bernanke 2000). Lack of aggregate demand resulted in the lay-offs of employees, many of whom were middle-aged women with lower tenure (few years at the same job) (Kato 2001).

Deflation, which started in 1994, continued for years. Yen appreciation was coupled with continuing attempts to stimulate the domestic economy by lowering interest rates, which failed to increase demand or correct for deflation. The deflation problem is illustrated in Figure 5.1.

Deflation caused decreased investment in local industry due to falling prices for goods and services. Consumers held cash due to uncertainty about the future.

During the crisis, there was little time to resolve the proper method of unwinding failed institutions. Several bank failures followed in 1995: Cosmo Credit Cooperative, Kizu Credit Cooperative, and Hyogo Bank, resulting in liquidity transfers from the Bank of Japan and business transfers to other banks (Nakaso 2001). There was no denying, by the mid-1990s, that the economy would not recover on its own and restore viability to non-performing loans and flagging businesses.

Jusen (real estate) loans to the real estate sector had been established in the 1970s to extend home mortgage loans, but had become large real estate lenders in the 1980s and 1990s (Kanaya and Woo 2000). Concern over the

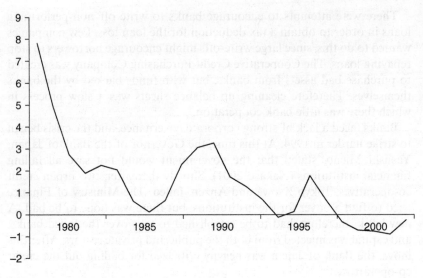

Source: World Bank.

Figure 5.1   Japan's deflation problem (CPI)

viability of these institutions incited investigations in the early 1990s, and
accumulated losses were uncovered in 1995 (Nakaso 2001). The government had to bail out these banks with taxpayer money. This move was
deeply resented by the public, and taxpayer funds were not used to assist
failing banks until 1997, when the situation was quite dire.

The financial safety net was enhanced in 1996, with a better plan for
unwinding failed institutions. Authorities were then able to assist failed
banks without depending on the private sector for additional support.
Deposit insurance was extended to fully insure depositors until March
2001 (Fukao 2003). This occurred just in time for the serious banking
troubles that were about to hit.

In 1997, major financial companies faced solvency issues. Nissan Life
Insurance was suspended by the Ministry of Finance (Kanaya and Woo
2000). Nippon Credit Bank suffered many loan losses from real estate
loans (Nakaso 2001). The Ministry of Finance organized a bailout from
private financial institutions which were financially interconnected to the
bank, and a second bailout from both private and public sources. Despite
these efforts, the bank failed in 1998 and was subsequently nationalized.
Hokkaido Takushoku Bank attempted a merger with Hokkaido Bank, but
this attempt was thwarted by historical rivalry that ended in the collapse
of the former.

The crisis then spread in the fall of 1997 to securities houses, resulting in the failures of Sanyo Securities, Yamaichi Securities, and Tokuyo City Bank (Nakaso 2001). Sanyo's default on unsecured call money resulted in a freeze of the entire interbank market. The Bank of Japan injected large amounts of liquidity into the interbank market, thereby acting as market maker of last resort. Yamaichi Securities failed three weeks after Sanyo's collapse. Yamaichi was closed down slowly, settling existing contracts, while the Bank of Japan acted as lender of last resort. The firm was declared bankrupt in 1999, with the Bank of Japan as the single largest creditor. At the end of 1997, Tokuyo City Bank failed and bank runs began. The notion of "too big to fail" became a thing of the past, and confidence weakened even more as the Asian financial crisis hit in Southeast Asia.

Major steps were taken in 1997 and 1998 to curb the crisis, as part of a "Big Bang" financial system liberalization and reform. These included expanding methods of asset investment by liberalizing securities derivatives and expanding the use of stock options; facilitating corporate fundraising by revising listing and initial public offering (IPO) standards and introducing new corporate bond products; providing a wider variety of services by reforming market-entry regulations and reducing restrictions on the range of business open to securities companies; creating efficient markets by deregulating unlisted companies and strengthening the over-the-counter securities market; assuring fair trading by enhancing fair trading and the dispute settlements system; and ensuring soundness of intermediaries by enhancing financial disclosure and creating investor and policyholder protection rules (Okubo 2003).

The Financial Crisis Management Committee was created in 1998 to direct newly legislated public funds to handle the crisis. All major bank received capital injections in two rounds (Kanaya and Woo 2000). This improved confidence in the market for two months, until the failure of Long Term Credit Bank of Japan. The Long Term Credit Bank was subsequently nationalized months later. After the crisis of the Long Term Credit Bank, legislation was passed under the Financial Reconstruction Law to deal with failed financial institutions. Economic measures were implemented in April 2001 to resolve corporate debt and deal with non-performing loans (Okubo 2003).[2]

There are several reasons for Japan's financial meltdown. Due to deep economic structural problems stressed by Gao (2001) and touched on by Bernanke (2000), Japan's economy had become relatively unproductive, and a lack of profitability led to an increasing interest by firms and individuals in speculation. Loans were extended to unprofitable businesses and ventures, and finance was liberalized in several directions. To make things worse, Japan had insufficient provisions against loan losses and an antiquated financial system (Hoshi and Kashyap 2004). Banks were grossly under-reserved, even against recognized bad loans. Banks disguised large loan losses during the 1990s by realizing capital gains. But banking accounted for most of the financial sector, and banks lacked measures sufficient to deal with risk. The final burden was to be borne by the taxpayer, estimated at 4 percent of GDP.

There was also an optimistic expectation that the financial problems that began in the early 1990s would diminish on their own, that asset prices would once again increase (Sato 2003). Reflecting this hope, extensive policy measures were not implemented until the late 1990s. The policy changed from preventing failure in the early 1990s, to accepting inevitable failures while limiting their repercussions. Risk management became critical.

Monetary policy strained to find a fix for the crisis, to combat the "three excesses" of debt, capacity, and employment, and later to eliminate deflation (Takahashi 2013). The discount rate was lowered nine times between 1991 and 1995, going from 6.0 percent to 0.5 percent. This proved ineffective. At the same time, fiscal policy was carried out with little impact. Tax cuts and government spending were unable to stimulate the economy, because they fell short of what was needed either qualitatively or quantitatively. Recovery after the crisis was quite slow, and economic troubles, including deflation, continued into the 2000s, even to the extent that both the 1990s and 2000s are sometimes included in the "lost decade."

Political Economy of the Japanese Crisis

While the 1990s in Japan have often been viewed in a negative light, due to sharply declining financial and economic conditions, from a political perspective they were somewhat more successful. A particular focus is on the electoral reform of 1994, which introduced single-member districts in order to end the decades-long one-party dominance. Japan had been governed by the Liberal Democratic Party (LDP) from 1955 to 1993, but governed less securely under coalitions (with the New Party Sakigake and the Japan Socialist Party) starting in 1994. Under the new system, truly competitive parties had to garner more widespread support than under the old system, in which they could align with and appeal to special interest groups.

As a result of this change, electorally popular reform measures, rather than those catering to financial industry constituents, were promoted by the LDP in 1996. The LDP's coalition partners also called for reorganization of the Ministry of Finance, which was attacked for ineffectiveness and corruption. The financial industry was not consulted over reforms during this period, and did not benefit greatly from the outcome, losing competition to foreign financial firms that were positioned to enter the market. Concentrated power declined, as informal relations between politicians, bureaucrats, and businessmen were weakened (Kushida and Shimizu 2014). Large *keiretsu* firms morphed into relationships between banks and weaker firms, and into *keiretsu* groups with different functions.

Conclusion

The Japanese crisis and its lack of a robust recovery has puzzled many economists. Although Japan is a highly developed country in terms of both standard of living and innovation, true economic vibrance has failed to return, as it usually does after the crisis fades away. This may be one of the most important conundrums in the modern history of financial crisis: why has the economy failed to rebound to its pre-crisis rate of growth? Some posit that it is due to the aging of the population, or to Japan's reaching the end of its development curve and increased concentration in the services sector. Still, it is not clear why this is so, or what implications this might have for the future of other developed countries that are currently trying to emerge from crisis (that is, the US and Europe).

ECONOMIC THEORIES OF THE EARLY 1990S

Robert Mundell laid out important theoretical grounds for the single currency which would later become the euro. Mundell (1973a) made a strong case for a single currency and economic unity (in what is called the "second" Mundell model), showing that countries with a unified currency could dampen impacts of asymmetric shocks by diversifying income sources to other countries. He has been referred to as the "intellectual father of the euro." Mundell made the case that Europe should move to a single currency. He stated in his chapter entitled, "A Plan for a European Currency":

> the only way to establish a unified money market is to kill the sporadic and unsettling speculation over currency prices that ravaged the European markets between 1967 and 1969, and permitted discounts and premia to develop on currency futures. The exchange rate should be taken out of both national and international politics within Europe. Rather than moving toward more flexibility in exchange rates within Europe the economic arguments suggest less flexibility and a closer integration of capital markets. (Mundell 1973b)

Hence Mundell paved the way for the ERM and later for the euro.

Neoliberalism remained *en vogue* through the 1990s, prompting finan-cial deregulation that was a major cause of the Nordic crisis. Even in the wake of the Nordic crisis, policy makers refused to believe that deregula-tion posed potential economic threats. Therefore, the theory-cum-ideology continued to prevail, leading to crises further down the line.

CONCLUSION

The crises of the early 1990s shocked those involved, but were mild in comparison to what was to come. At the time, it seemed that policy was more or less successful in containing the ERM crisis and the Nordic crisis. The impacts of an external shock (German reunification in the case of the ERM crisis) and financial deregulation (in the case of the Nordic crisis) were severe but swiftly and effectively dealt with. The Japanese crisis, on the other hand, did not elicit an immediate response and dragged on for some time. But it would not prove as devastating in impact and virulence as the crises to come. Next, we turn to the crises of the mid-1990s, the Mexican and Asian crises, which were significantly more difficult to untangle.

NOTES

1. However, there were losses. The final cost to taxpayers in the United Kingdom was estimated at £3.4 billion, due to devaluation of the pound sterling on Black Wednesday (September 16, 1992) (Eichengreen 2000).
2. In 2002, deposit insurance was scaled back to an upper limit of 10 million yen to reduce moral hazard and public responsibility for bank failures (Sato 2003).

6. Mid-1990s: Mexican crisis and Asian financial crisis

The political economic climate had changed dramatically by the mid-1990s, as the United States asserted itself as the world's only superpower. The fall of Communism at the end of the 1980s and the beginning of the 1990s ended the decades-long Cold War and marked the triumph of democracy and free markets. In the United States, the Clinton administration, which came into office in 1993 and remained for two terms, focused less on security and more on economics than previous governments. Globalization became a major focus. Neoliberalism and its tenets were upheld, including in Latin America, and East Asian newly industrialized countries were viewed as shining examples of neoliberal policy reforms.

As a result, starting in the mid-1990s, financial crises worsened. With the continuing trend of liberalization, countries had opened themselves up to volatile capital flows. Mexico, which had suffered like other Latin American countries in the 1980s from the debt crisis and its accompanying slow growth, had been eager to regain its foothold in development through liberalization. What was not well understood at the time was that liberalization could create dangerous instability, and this is indeed what occurred as foreign capital flows reversed.

The newly industrializing economies in Asia had also followed the path of liberalization. At the time, it seemed to work miracles; economic growth was as high as 11 percent in the early 1990s in Singapore and Thailand. James Riedel (1988) wrote that:

> the policy lessons that derive from the experiences of the East Asian countries are simple and clear-cut . . . that neo-classical principles are alive and well, and working particularly effectively in the East Asian countries. Once public goods are provided for and the most obvious distortions corrected, markets seem to do the job of allocating resources reasonably well.

As in Mexico, growth in the Asian countries did not last, and capital flows rapidly switched course and fled the Asian nations. The capital outflows caused both currency and banking crises, and threatened to spread to other countries.

Both crises threatened global financial stability. For this reason, the

International Monetary Fund (IMF) became the global lender of last resort, embarking on a controversial role that it would play on the world stage. At the time, its wisdom was accepted. The crisis-ridden countries were viewed as culpable for the crises, and neoliberal policies were not greatly questioned, even though crises had become both more substantial and more globalized. In what follows, we examine the historical context of these two crises and describe how events unfolded.

MEXICAN CRISIS

Mexico faced a financial crisis in 1994 stemming from a balance of payments of crisis and political events. This led to a dramatic currency devaluation at the year end, and a crisis of confidence both in Mexico and abroad. Mexico was already undergoing severe political turmoil and economic change, with a guerilla uprising in Chiapas, the assassination of two important political leaders, economic liberalization, and additional political reforms (Springer and Molina 1995).

To some degree, the financial crisis of 1994 can be viewed as a product of its debt crisis in the 1980s. Policies implemented in the late 1980s strove to increase competitiveness of the economy through liberalization, and were known as "El Pacto." El Pacto was a pact between government, private industry, and labor organizations to liberalize trade and investment (Gallagher 2007). To control inflation, the peso was pegged to the United States (US) dollar, and later was allowed to float within a band.

As intended, Mexico's economic liberalization led to increased direct and portfolio investment, particularly since Mexico's formal international economic participation was expanding. Mexico had negotiated the North American Free Trade Agreement (NAFTA), become a full member of the Organisation for Economic Co-operation and Development (OECD) and the forum for Asian-Pacific Economic Cooperation (APEC), and become an active participant in the Uruguay Round of the General Agreement on Tariffs and Trade (Springer and Molina 1995).

But short-term investment was insufficiently checked. The average amount of capital that flowed into the country between 1991 and 1993 was about 15 times the total amount of capital inflows of the previous decade (World Bank 2012). Capital mobility, which worked in Mexico's favor for the first half of the 1990s, changed course with the rise of adverse conditions.

In addition, banks had engaged in poor lending practices, implementing few safeguards against lending risks. Mexican commercial banks owed a great deal of short-term debt to foreign creditors (Cypher 1996). In

1991–92, President Salinas had re-privatized the 18 banks that had been nationalized in 1982, and profit in the expanding private financial sector grew by 70 percent between 1992 and 1993. According to the OECD, one-third of loans extended in Mexico in 1994 were in foreign currencies, in part to borrowers with no foreign currency income (OECD 1995). The growth of loans between 1988 and 1994 was mainly for consumer credit and hence did not generate growth. Foreign capital inflows also required a rising interest rate, even in the face of falling inflation. Unemployment increased as maintenance of the nominal exchange rate was sought at the cost of economic growth, opening up the possibility that a devaluation might occur (Ramirez de la O 1996).

While the Salinas administration was credible in its commitment to defending the peso, instability set in when the political arena degenerated. Political trouble began when the Zapatista movement declared war against the Salinas administration and seized several cities in the state of Chiapas. This uprising led to severe criticism of the security policies of the Salinas administration (Springer and Molina 1995). The assassinations of Luis Donaldo Colosiò, the Partido Revolucionario Institucional (PRI) presidential candidate, and José Francisco Ruiz Massieu, who would have become the congressional leader of the PRI, led to political upheaval.

As 1994 set in, the Salinas government began to loosen monetary policy, and foreign investors began to grow wary of the situation. Mexican *tesobonos*, short-term bonds issued by the government and indexed to the dollar, increased foreign currency exposure. Foreign capital did not generate growth as expected. These were initially created to allow investors to decrease their peso risk without losing their position in Mexico (Ramirez de la O 1996). However, the *tesobonos* essentially shielded foreign investors from the risk they took. The burden of the *tesobono* problem became clear as the prospect of devaluation rose.

Further, President Zedillo did not bring about confidence in the continuity of economic reform. Neither did the Zedillo administration recognize that the ballooning current account deficit was partly financed out of international reserves during the second half of 1994. Over the early 1990s, the current account deficit was growing, moving from $6 billion in 1989 to more than $20 billion in 1993 (Whitt 1996). The current account deficit was not viewed as problematic, since it was seen as the result of foreign capital inflows. There was a disjoint with reality as the Bank of Mexico had assumed that a developing country could carry large external deficits over a long period of time. What is more, newly privatized banks were sold at overvalued prices and led bankers to undertake riskier practices to recoup these costs in a slow-growth environment. Bankers increased their exposure to inflation-indexed, and later dollar-indexed, financial instruments.

It became clear in November that the government would not continue to raise interest rates in order to defend the peso, reducing international reserves yet again. This spurred a large amount of capital flight. US interest rates had begun to increase in March 1994 and were attracting international investment; therefore, foreign funds had a safer and still profitable haven in the US economy. Mexican Secretary of Finance, Jaime Serra Puche, had signaled a strong commitment against devaluing the peso, even though the economy faced significant structural problems. But after international panic ensued on December 19, 1995 and foreign investors withdrew more than $3 billion, Serra Puche proposed the following day to float the peso by 15 percent (Springer and Molina 1995). On December 22, the peso was floated and immediately depreciated. The Zedillo administration's decision to float the peso has been referred to as the "December Mistake," after which the Mexican economy spiraled into crisis. Serra Puche was unable to convince top New York bankers to remain confident in Mexico. Serra Puche was replaced on December 29 by Guillermo Ortiz.

Policy makers were faced with three serious challenges after the peso was floated: these were to stabilize the macroeconomy after a sharp decline in capital inflows, to refinance the dollar-denominated public debt, and to ensure that the banking sector remained solvent (Carstens and Werner 1999). Tight monetary and fiscal policy and provision of liquidity to the banking system were implemented.

These emergency relief measures announced on January 3, 1995 were debated both domestically and internationally, as the Mexican government was perceived as indecisive and not particularly committed to the policies, further eroding confidence in the market (Springer and Molina 1995). The measures touted the importance of fiscal austerity, including wage and price increases that were slowed more than inflation, sell-off of public enterprises, and cuts in government spending (*Rural Migration News* 1995). These measures were viewed as slow in coming, since the peso had already lost 50 percent of its value (Smith 1996). An international relief package was put forward at the end of January 1995, after confidence was sharply diminished.

The US, Canada, and European central banks, through the Bank for International Settlements (BIS), increased credit to Mexico at the end of January 1995 to alleviate the crisis. Mexico then asked the IMF for an additional loan to shore up resources. The total amount extended to Mexico was $50 billion. In Washington, the crisis was seen as one of short-term liquidity, and US funding of a bailout was unpopular (Roett 1996). But the trouble was not over. Mexico then proceeded to suffer a banking crisis through September 1995, with the number of non-performing loans almost doubling from the previous year (Cypher 1996). Bank losses were socialized in following policies under Fobaproa and Procapte.

The United States government had a strong interest to mitigate the crisis, since America was now a strong commercial partner of Mexico in NAFTA. But the Mexican financial crisis jeopardized a major precondition of NAFTA: that financial markets undergo liberalization (Morales 1997). Even as NAFTA promoted foreign direct investment (FDI) inflows, in the years preceding the crisis, portfolio investment and money markets increased even more, creating a speculative bubble. NAFTA itself was also viewed as becoming subject to reassessment. US representatives who had originally been opposed to NAFTA considered forcing a US withdrawal from the agreement (Roett 1996). The devaluation of the peso made Mexico's exports highly competitive with respect to American products, generating fear of unemployment in the US.

The devaluation of the Mexican peso indeed increased Mexican exports to the US, but pressures on the peso owing to large current account deficits made it necessary to do so (Whitt 1996). These current account deficits were a by-product of El Pacto, which strove to maintain low inflation through limitations on wage and price increases. The government attempted to lower inflation in import prices by keeping exchange rate depreciation lower than the rate of inflation. Inflation slowed, but not by enough to prevent real appreciation of the peso that encouraged imports and widened the current account deficit. Much of the investment that had entered the country between 1990 and 1994 was short term (about 75 percent). These capital flows were invested in stocks and bonds, both of which experienced a large degree of volatility (Whitt 1996).

What is more, during the political turmoil of 1994, the authoritative structure of the political system broke down and was unable to continue to strictly control Mexico's transition to a financially liberalized economy (Morales 1997). The immediate impact of the crisis was painful: numerous firms failed and overall production fell drastically; unemployment rose, along with the inflation rate. Yet the policies implemented to overcome the crisis at last yielded a recovery. The gross domestic product (GDP) growth rate fell by more than 6 percent in 1995 but increased to 5.6 percent in 1996. The unemployment rate decreased from 7 percent in 1995 to 3.5 percent in 1998. The inflation rate skyrocketed right after the crisis (52 percent in 1995) but decreased in subsequent years (15.7 percent in 1997). The current account deficit benefited from the abandonment of the exchange rate regime and dropped down to 1 percent in 1997. Finally, the public debt declined and international reserves increased.

The Mexican crisis lightly brushed Brazil, but severely impacted Argentina, reversing foreign capital inflows (Bouzas 1996). Bank deposits and the central bank's international reserves fell dramatically. There were speculative attacks against the dollar-convertible Argentine peso, and the situation was dire by February 1995. In response, the monetary base was dollarized, and monetary authorities were allowed to use excess reserves to aid institutions with liquidity problems. The IMF extended a loan to the troubled country in 1995, and fiscal adjustments cut spending and extended the tax base. Crisis was curtailed with these measures. Argentina's predicament was resolved more easily than that of Mexico, since the country had more consistent monetary and exchange rate policies and a lower external imbalance (Bouzas 1996). Government response in Argentina, in contrast to that in Mexico, was swifter and more stabilizing.

Two models arose to explain Mexico's financial crisis. The first model, the real disequilibria hypothesis, states that an overvalued exchange rate and unsustainable current account deficit set the stage for Mexico to enter a financial crisis. In the second model, the speculative attack hypothesis, Mexico's balance-of-payments crisis led to a speculative attack on the currency. Sachs et al. (1996) dismiss both models for their assumption that the crisis was more or less inevitable, and point out that Mexico was doing well by following conservative fiscal policy and maintaining relatively low debt ratios. Although the real exchange rate had appreciated by up to 25 percent, inflation had declined with the net effect of stabilizing the overvaluation. In addition, although the current account deficit had increased to 7.9 percent in 1994, public debt levels were much lower than the OECD average, so currency overvaluation again was not as bad as had been described elsewhere. And, although loose monetary policies ran down gross reserves by around 80 percent between year start and year end 1994, Mexico's risk premium as measured by the spread between *tesobonos* and US Treasuries did not fall until after the December devaluation. Hence the authors find that the real crisis began in December 1994 after the announcement of a 15 percent currency devaluation; the December Mistake was a mistake that kicked off the crisis.

Without knowing what the counterfactual, without devaluation, would have been, we cannot say for certain that the December devaluation caused the crisis. Certainly, capital flight had already begun, and it is possible that the December devaluation simply accelerated an inevitable process. As discussed above, pressures on the exchange rate were mounting due to growing current account deficits, and the maintenance of the status quo became increasingly hard to hold. Financial liberalization had opened the door to potential crisis. Bankers were engaging in risky lending practices, particularly with the re-privatization of the banking sector in 1991 (Hernández-Murillo 2007). Banks were being allowed to participate in a variety of new businesses, including leasing, factoring, currency exchange, mutual fund management, and asset-based warehousing. It is therefore not a simple matter to state that Mexico was or was not headed for one type of crisis or another.

The Mexican bailout maintained the country's market-oriented trajectory, while tacitly approving the costs imposed on the Mexican people (Vasquez 2002). The people experienced a long period of unemployment, falling wages, and a sudden contraction of consumer spending. Small farmers and small and medium-sized enterprises in particular suffered from liberalization policies. Costs imposed on the populace, which was not responsible for the crisis per se, were viewed as acceptable. The Mexican crisis caused a sharp fall-off in total factor productivity, as modeled by Pratap and Urrutia (2012). The December devaluation, the authors find, accounts for a 3.5 percent decline in total factor productivity, accounting for about half the decline in productivity.

The Mexican bailout began a period of IMF bailouts, which changed the nature of the IMF. The IMF became reliant on policy requirements (including Washington Consensus policies) to change countries' means of operation. It has also been argued that the Mexican bailout encouraged moral hazard in other countries, which would rely on IMF bailouts in response to crises created by excess borrowing and spending.

Political Economy of the Mexican Crisis

The Mexican crisis turned a short-lived period of optimism into one of panic. The so-called "Tequila Crisis" was brought about by the combination of financial liberalization and excessive debt. Mexico was coming from a long period of import substitution industrialization, which had led to economic stagnation for some time, as well as from a decade-long debt crisis, which resulted in bailouts contingent on liberalization measures. Mexico had just negotiated on NAFTA with the United States and Canada. NAFTA lowered or eliminated tariffs.

Presidents de la Madrid and Salinas privatized Mexico's commercial banks over the 1980s and early 1990s, which resulted in a credit boom. The new bank owners often lacked proper experience in running banks and faced little competition, while adoption of international banking standards was delayed (Musacchio 2012). Optimism created a financial bubble within a poorly managed banking system. The optimism ran out when political conditions deteriorated.

On January 1, 1994, the Zapatista National Liberation Army took control of some of the largest towns in Chiapas. More than 3000 indigenous people participated and denounced NAFTA for harming small producers. The Zapatistas called for mobilization against President Carlos Salinas de

Gortari. Violence in Chiapas ensued. In March, the presidential candidate of the ruling party, Luis Donaldo Colosio, was assassinated, shaking political and economic confidence as suspicions of conspiracy churned. The ruling party, the PRI, then held another election, and Ernesto Zedillo won the election. One of the highest officials of the PRI, José Francisco Ruiz Massieu, was assassinated in September of the same year. Allegations that Raul Salinas, brother of the previous President, was responsible for this assassination, further marred perceptions of Mexico's political stability. Additional Zapatista violence in December shook Mexican markets.

The December Mistake, in which the Mexican peso was suddenly devalued, led to capital flight and has been viewed by many as the immediate cause of the crisis. The term "December Mistake" was political, however, dubbed by former Mexican President Carlos Salinas de Gortari to divorce himself from his administration's responsibility for the crisis. The devaluation of the peso had been discussed in the months leading up to December, and was supported by some foreign economists and the Mexican Deputy Finance Minister, Guillermo Ortiz Martinez, but was opposed by Finance Minister Pedro Aspe, central bank governor Miguel Mancera, and President Zedillo (Boughton 2012). In the end, El Pacto, was adjusted according to the wishes of the business and labor partners, and the peso was devalued by 15 percent. A second decision, to float the peso, followed on the heels of the devaluation as capital poured out of the country.

Foreign investors became incredibly wary of the Mexican economy, withdrawing funds en masse. Mexican officials reached out to the US Treasury, the IMF, and commercial bank creditors. The US intervened by lending to Mexico in order to avoid the "Tequila Effect," or contagion to other emerging markets. Mexico was loath to accept assistance from the IMF, and Larry Summers, Under Secretary for International Affairs at the Treasury, underscored the view that Mexico faced a temporary liquidity problem that could be addressed by assistance from the US alone.

President Zedillo replaced his Finance Minister with a former member of the IMF Executive Board, Guillermo Ortiz Martinez (Boughton 2012). The IMF discussed with Ortiz the importance of using the IMF to stabilize the currency and the economy. Ortiz finally agreed to formally request assistance two weeks after the start of the crisis. Extensive negotiations occurred between the Mexican government and the IMF, with the IMF urging Mexico to involve them fully and Mexican officials attempting to gain some latitude in fiscal adjustment and language of the agreement. The agreement was finally resolved, yet the outcome was controversial: a sizeable portion of the funds went to repaying Wall Street investors in Mexican securities.

The Mexican bailout was the largest IMF program to date, and was unique in making large-scale use of the US Exchange Stabilization Fund at the Treasury. Many US Congressional leaders railed against lending so much to Mexico. Within Mexico itself, Mexican debtors protested the bailout of banks, since domestic debtors were provided no debt relief and were charged heavy penalties for late payments.

Despite the criticisms, the bailout enabled Mexico to re-establish its creditworthiness. In light of later financial crises, providing ample liquidity to Mexico appeared to be justified. We next turn to the Asian financial crisis, which in itself changed the way in which crises were perceived: not as stemming from poor fundamentals per se, but from other forces, including fear.

ASIAN FINANCIAL CRISIS

The Asian financial crisis was seen by some as a failure of Asian economies due to poor domestic institutional structures, and it is still portrayed that way in some channels. But its quick succession by the Russian financial crisis, the Brazilian financial crisis, and the Argentine crisis dispelled that view for many leading scholars who viewed the crisis as a combination of institutional weaknesses, external shocks, and poor IMF intervention.

Like many crises, the Asian financial crisis was unexpected; first, in its arrival; and second, in its scale and scope. The Asian financial crisis that began in 1997 was both a banking and a currency crisis, essentially caused by large-scale short-term yen and dollar capital inflows into Thailand, Indonesia, South Korea, and Malaysia, and to a lesser extent into Singapore, the Philippines, and Hong Kong, coupled with fixed, overvalued exchange rates. Asset price bubbles were created in all of these countries as investment demand increased. The crisis was sparked by the floating of the Thai baht on July 2, 1997, followed through year-end by the floating of the Indonesian rupiah, the Korean won, the Malaysian ringgit, and the Philippines peso as the asset price bubbles burst. These events incited panic among international investors who, previously, had blithely poured capital into the region. Ultimately, IMF loans had to be extended to Indonesia, Korea, and Thailand.

How did the crisis come about? Initially, capital flows from abroad increased with the financial liberalization in each of these countries. Before liberalization, domestic and international capital controls imposed ceilings on domestic interest rates, limits on repatriation of foreign direct and portfolio investments, limitations to borrowing abroad, and restrictions on foreign investors for acquiring ownership of particular types of firms

(Desai 2003). Liberalization lifted these controls and resulted in current account convertibility of currencies. Financial liberalization allowed the Asian nations to increase leverage themselves using foreign debt.

In Indonesia, liberalization took place through a variety of banking reforms, resulting in a threefold increase in the number of private (rather than state-owned) banks between 1988 and 1996, making it difficult for the government to adequately supervise them (Haggard 2000). Foreign investors were allowed to invest in the stock market up to 49 percent of the ownership of listed stocks (Desai 2003). Foreign direct investment was allowed in additional sectors.

Thailand also underwent bank deregulation, beginning in 1989 with the removal of interest rate controls, as well as additional capital account liberalization with the initiation of the Bangkok International Banking Facility (BIBF) that allowed banks to borrow abroad and lend domestically. The goal of BIBF was to advance Bangkok as a regional financial center. This was undertaken during a period of political strife, which left little room to monitor the newly deregulated banking sector (Wade and Veneroso 1998). BIBF greatly expanded the access of Thai firms to foreign loans, accounting for two-thirds of the increase in external debt between 1992 and 1996 (Hanna 2000).

Malaysia's financial sector was liberalized in the early 1990s, allowing foreign investors to buy shares in Malaysian corporations up to 30 percent. Controls on interest rates were removed in 1991; and in 1995, capital controls were liberalized. Banks lent aggressively to the real estate market. Malaysia wanted to transform Kuala Lumpur into Asia's leading financial center (Desai 2003). Privatization took place not only for reasons of efficiency, but also for political reasons to increase *bumiputra* ownership of firms (Perkins and Woo 2000).

In South Korea, interest rates were decontrolled, and controls on foreign borrowing by domestic institutions, and on foreign investment in commercial and financial securities, were lifted. *Chaebols*, large business conglomerates, were to focus on core industries and in return were exempted from credit controls and barriers to investment and entry. The South Korean government also allowed investment and finance companies to become merchant banks in the mid-1990s, while the government continued liberalization of the capital account. Prudential regulations and supervision were not implemented.

The countries thus became more attractive to foreign investors, particularly as the growth phenomenon was overenthusiastically dubbed the "East Asian Miracle," in which capital account and financial market liberalization could spark a growth frenzy. The World Bank (1993) made famous (now notorious) the moniker and characterized the "high-performing Asian economies" as operating in an environment of good macroeconomic management with limited fiscal deficits, increased saving and investment, growth of human capital, and export promotion policies. Growth rates ranged from 7 to 9 percent between 1991 and 1996 and there was very little inflation (Desai 2003). Government participation was viewed as "high-quality civil service" and judged to be impartial. Foreign borrowing was used for investment rather than consumption, and current account deficits were perceived as relatively low (Goldstein 1998). For these reasons, many investors, including privately managed mutual (retirement) funds, looked to East Asia as a relatively safe source of profit (Pempel 1999). Contrary views, such as that of Paul Krugman (1994), who questioned the sustainability of East Asian growth without real gains in efficiency, were scarcely heard amidst the investment mania. None of the Southeast Asian tigers remotely suspected that they would enter a financial crisis after such a glorious boom.

Japanese and European banks lent heavily to Southeast Asia. Japanese banks were able to borrow both domestically and abroad at low rates, and extend short-term loans to Southeast Asian banks and firms at higher rates, seeking aggressive returns (Wade 2001). Berg (1999) summarizes the lead-up to the crisis concisely:

> The Asian crisis countries experienced tremendous capital inflows in the 1990s . . . Most of these capital inflows, and associated investment booms, were intermediated through weak domestic financial institutions that were often undercapitalized and poorly regulated. Long periods of macroeconomic stability and high growth led to complacency on the part of foreign creditor banks, borrowers, and the authorities. Liberalization of domestic financial markets was not accompanied by appropriate supervision and regulation of financial institutions . . . The combination of weak financial sectors with strong capital inflows and credit booms created two related but distinct sets of potential problems: potential inefficiency of the resulting investments, and financial fragility of an overleveraged corporate sector.

Short-term capital inflows into the region, including both portfolio flows into the stock market and other financial flows, grew so quickly that the task on the part of bank and non-bank financial institutions of monitoring the hundreds of new borrowers and projects put a severe strain on the risk assessment abilities of institutions from the start (Alba et al. 1999). There is evidence that firm-level weaknesses before the crisis contributed to the deterioration of the corporate sector (Claessens et al. 2000). What is more, leverage skyrocketed in Thailand, Korea, and Malaysia to 200 percent of GDP in 1997 (Hanna 2000). The level of bank credit as compared to GDP can be viewed in Figure 6.1.

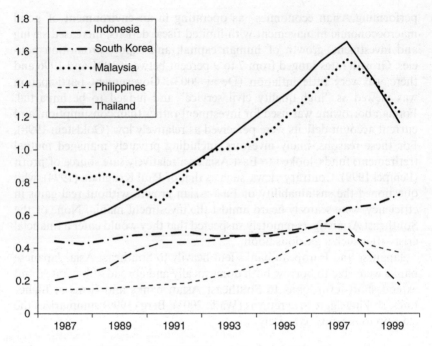

Source: Beck and Demirgüç-Kunt (2009).

Figure 6.1   Private credit by deposit money banks to GDP

Bank credit to GDP reached its pinnacle in all countries but South Korea, dropping off sharply thereafter. Much of the capital that flowed into Thailand and Indonesia went into the real estate sector. Ries (2000) writes that foreign investment was easy to spot in Bangkok, with the building of office complexes and luxury hotels, as well as high-end residences, apparent to all. The level of spending on construction greatly increased. The supply of available office buildings in Southeast Asia had increased greatly by 1996, and the size of the real estate sector was large compared to GDP (Quigley 2001). By 1995 an increasing amount of bank non-performing loans could be attributed to real estate loans.

But danger signs were not obvious to all investors. From previous experience with financial crises, such as those of the 1980s debt default crises, the Asian tigers were seen to be low risk since macroeconomic fundamentals such as inflation and budget deficits were low, while foreign exchange reserves were high (Wade and Veneroso 1998). Neftci (2002) discusses the overpricing of sovereign credits; for example, in October 1997, Korea was rated AA– by Standard & Poors, and downgraded to B+ six months later, a difference of nine steps. Asset overpricing led to an increase in risky positions, since potential financial vulnerabilities were not perceived. To make matters worse, country assets may have been overrated to begin with, but were later underrated after the start of the crisis. Ferri et al. (1999) show that the extent of sudden downgrading of crisis countries was unjustified by the fundamentals, exacerbating the difficulty countries faced in borrowing abroad and worsening the crisis situation.

One cause leading to the mispricing of risk was that the prior crisis models ("first" and "second generation" models) did not account for private debt. "First generation" models describe crises as the product of budget deficits (Krugman 1979), while "second generation" models describe crises as a conflict between supporting a fixed exchange rate while attempting to expand monetary policy (Obstfeld 1994). Therefore, the type of crisis that occurred was not even on the radar.

Looking back, there were warning signs that a reversal was in the works. The currencies were all fixed or, as Tobin (1998) dubs them, "adjustable pegs." In 1996, the appreciation of the US dollar and, therefore, Asian currencies, led to a decline in export growth in Thailand and Korea.[1] This put pressure on the Asian currencies and began to worry investors. Fixed currencies presented a large, unforeseen vulnerability since domestic currencies had what was seen as an implicit guarantee of stable convertibility. This was easy to achieve before the crisis, when the countries were flush with foreign currency, despite the fact that there was a gradual real exchange rate appreciation for the export-oriented economies and increasing current account imbalances (Goldstein 1998). Export growth declined as cost competitiveness was eroded due to the increase in prices of non-traded goods and services, such as property, and to the appreciation of the dollar against the yen (Hussain and Radelet 2000). This contributed to the appreciation of the real exchange rate. But a fixed exchange rate was difficult or impossible to maintain post-crisis, when foreign currency suddenly exited the region. The cyclical correlation between each country's economies created regional multiplier effects that amplified the difficulties (Wade 2001). Figure 6.2 illustrates the sharp decline in the real effective exchange rate that took place between 1997 and 1998.

In addition, over time, residential real estate prices in Thailand, Indonesia, and Malaysia began to fall, indicating that the real estate bubble in these countries was beginning to burst (Berg 1999). In Thailand and Indonesia, the percentage of bank loans that went to real estate was more than 18 percent, and by 1996 the vacancy rates were around 14 percent (Alba et al. 1999). The percentage of profits going to pay interest expenses had increased to between 30 percent in Indonesia, Malaysia, and the Philippines, and 85 percent in Korea.

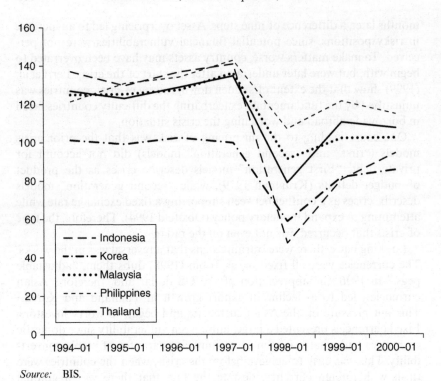

Source: BIS.

Figure 6.2   BIS real effective exchange rate

In January 1997, Hanbo, a South Korean *chaebol*, declared bankruptcy; while Somprasong Land, a Thai company, became delinquent on foreign debt in February. Sammi Steel and Kia Motors, South Korean companies, then failed. The central banks of Malaysia and Thailand limited lending with exposure to the stock and real estate sectors, respectively.

Indonesia's growth reversal of 18 percent was dramatic (Radelet and Woo 2000). The stock market and bank lending had remained strong until mid-1997, when they suddenly reversed. As the outflow of foreign exchange in Southeast Asia increased, both Thailand and Korea made great attempts to defend their currency pegs (Berg 1999), but the attempts were soon thwarted. Thailand was whipped into a frenzy by the threat of devaluation, and went through four Finance Ministers in the 14 months before the baht was floated (Ries 2000). In May 1997, the Thai baht underwent a speculative attack, and its defense caused the depletion of reserves. The central bank suspended operations of 16 finance companies and tightened currency controls to stabilize the baht, but two days after signaling that the baht would not be devalued, the currency was forced to float. After this day on July 2, 1997, when Thailand devalued its currency, other countries in the region felt the pressure to devalue or face a speculative attack on their own currencies. Thailand, Korea, and Indonesia were most strongly affected by the crisis.

The currency crises experienced by the Southeast Asian "Miracle" countries were tantamount to "runs" on both the currencies and on the banks. Thus fixed exchange rates posed a threat to financial stability in the region from the start. In hindsight, this is clear; for future reference, as several leading economists have noted, exchange rate overvaluation has been among the best early-warning indicators of crises (Kaminsky and Reinhart 1999; Reinhart et al. 2000). Not to be ignored, too, was that the real economy in Southeast Asia was facing challenges in terms of exports starting in 1996, and increasing competition from China (Goldstein 1998).

Initial IMF support packages were insufficient to cover debt service, leaving countries to convince some investors to roll over their debt (Berg 1999). Agreement by some foreign creditors to roll over short-term debt in Korea into medium-term debt helped the situation somewhat. Thailand, Korea, and Indonesia closed down insolvent institutions, and created specific institutions to take over, manage, and strengthen the banking system. Fiscal discipline had been exercised in all countries but the Philippines until the crisis hit; after the crisis began, fiscal policy was initially contractionary as funds were reserved for private sector firms. The IMF itself recommended fiscal stringency in the crisis, and this quite arguably worsened the crisis. Monetary policy was tightened to prevent the cycle of currency depreciation from spiraling into inflation and further depreciation.

It became clear that moral hazard had been a problem in these countries in the build-up to the crisis, although downplayed during the "Miracle" period. Politicians were closely connected to financial institutions and/ or firms in these countries, and there was an underlying assumption that financial institutions would be bailed out if they got into trouble. For example, Thailand's central bank spent 53.7 billion baht on bailing out troubled institutions and 62.4 billion baht on bailing out holders of commercial paper issued by finance companies (Ries 2000). In Indonesia, the Suharto family owned major shares in 1247 companies. Indonesia's interest in stabilizing its economy was seen as motivated by the Suharto family's interest in preserving its fortune, and attempts by the Finance Minister to close down insolvent banks resulted in his prosecution (Ries 2000). And in Korea, close ties between the government, banks, and *chaebols* resulted in bad, presumably guaranteed, loans to the *chaebols* (Ries 2000).[2]

Moral hazard is viewed as playing a role in creating the crisis, but is not the whole explanation. In general, liberalization and fixed currencies, paired with poor regulatory and institutional environments, made control of capital inflows much more difficult. The extent to which institutional interrelatedness exacerbated or initiated the crisis has been a matter of vigorous debate. Some leading economists, including Alan Greenspan, Chairman of the US Federal Reserve; Larry Summers, Deputy Secretary of the US Treasury Department; and Michel Camdessus, Managing Director of the IMF, attacked the countries for engaging in "crony capitalism," and maintaining ties between government, finance, and business (Sundaram 2007; Corsetti et al. 1998), while other economists have pointed out that these types of relationships had been ongoing, even during decades of growth and stability (e.g., Tobin 1998; Chang 2000), and that they were often beneficial to growth (Wade and Veneroso 1998), or at least not the underlying cause of the crisis (Singh 2002).

In the aftermath of the crisis, poorly performing institutions often did little to alleviate the economic suffering. Suharto's government in Indonesia used IMF funds for pet projects, and Suharto was replaced after the May Revolution resulted in bloody protests and rioting throughout Jakarta (Ries 2000). The economic outcome of the crisis varied greatly depending on the strength of the bank regulatory system, even though most Southeast Asian countries had some type of asset price bubble in the 1990s (Collyns and Senhadji 2002) and may or may not have suffered from "crony capitalism."

Countries suffered most when and where they were weak (Collyns and Senhadji 2002). Because Malaysia had better regulated and capitalized institutions, the economy fared better than those of Thailand, which experienced sharp losses on loans in the relatively unregulated financial sector, and Indonesia and Korea, which had allowed highly leveraged firms to obtain dollar-denominated loans. Korea in particular had very high levels of corporate debt, with a corporate debt to GDP ratio up to 50 percent higher than that of the US (Wade and Veneroso 1998). This created a greater vulnerability to interest and exchange rate shocks. The Asian financial crisis itself also increased financing costs for firms. Asian firms with a 10 percent rise in leverage experienced a 1.41 percent increase in the credit spread for corporate bonds during the Asian financial crisis (Mizen and Tsoukas 2012). Korea was also affected strongly since exports were concentrated in a few main sectors, and prices of exports fell (Hong and Lee 2000). High interest rates, part of the IMF adjustment program, aggravated the indebtedness of firms.

Drilling down to an even lower level than the banking industry, the quality of individual investments was relatively poor. Much of the investment went to speculative activities, industries already burdened with overcapacity, and inefficient government projects and monopolies (Goldstein 1998).

The breakdown of the banking sector occurred as follows: the deterioration of bank balance sheets before the crisis, due to excessive lending and low capital returns, coupled with the assumption that governments would back lending institutions, created an environment ripe for banking crisis (Haggard 2000). Lending rose rapidly as GDP grew slowly. As the currency crisis ensued and the currency was devalued, banks' balance sheets deteriorated. A simultaneous deterioration in firms' balance sheets also led them to take on greater financial risk since they had less to lose if bank loans fail (Mishkin 1999). Financial firms that had poor capital adequacy, asset quality, management, earnings, liquidity, and sensitivity to market risk (CAMELS) were more likely to be distressed or closed, although large institutions were less likely to be allowed to fail (Bongini et al. 2001). The banking crisis in turn exacerbated the currency crisis, and a vicious downward spiral ensued (Kaminsky and Reinhart 1999).

Krugman's (1999) "third generation" crisis model exemplified some of these features, including the role of firms' balance sheets in determining their ability to invest, and the role of capital flows in affecting the real exchange rate. Krugman de-emphasized the role of banks[3] or moral hazard as primary causes of the crisis and the important role of balance sheet difficulties in constraining investment, underscored by a deterioration in the real exchange rate. A loss of confidence created a downward spiral by putting pressure on the exchange rate, leading to a real depreciation that worsened balance sheets of firms, spreading the loss of confidence.[4]

The interconnectedness of these Asian economies, and the speed at which cross-national capital movements operated, also served to amplify the crisis (Pempel 1999). Contagion between the financial markets of Thailand, Malaysia, Indonesia, Korea, and the Philippines was evident in currency and sovereign spreads (Baig and Goldfajn 1999). By contrast, China, which had capital account controls and trade restrictions at the time, weathered the crisis well. The contagion aspect of the Asian crisis was confirmed by Baig and Goldfajn (1999), who find a significant increase in correlation between currency and equity markets in Thailand, Korea, Malaysia, and the Philippines during the crisis, after controlling for own-country effects. Contagion was also verified by Kaminsky and Schmukler (1999), who found that daily changes in stock prices between 1997 and 1998 in Hong Kong, Indonesia, Japan, Korea, Malaysia, Philippines, Singapore, Taiwan, and Thailand were due to local and neighboring-country news regarding, in particular, international organizations and credit rating agencies. Relatively inconsequential news also carried weight as herd behavior took over. This climate of fear overtook the region.

The yen carry trade, in which US and European banks borrowed yen and lent funds throughout Asia, contributed to the volume of short-term capital inflows into East Asia. By mid-1997, Japanese funds comprised more than one-third of total outstanding commercial debt in the Association of Southeast Asian Nations (ASEAN) countries (Pempel 1999). Japan's economy was, at the same time, continuing to suffer from the crisis that began earlier in the decade.

Adverse real impacts on each economy ensued. Living standards fell, unemployment rose, and import prices increased. The poor within these developing countries, who were already vulnerable to small changes in the business cycle, fell into even more crushing poverty, and the middle class felt robbed of their savings and financial security (Wade and Veneroso 1998). In some areas, the recession was the worst since World War II (Berg 1999). Social conditions also deteriorated. The region, which had experienced a large amount of poverty reduction two decades before the crisis hit, underwent declines in social services such as health and education, increasing unemployment, and increasing psychological stress and crime. Pre-crisis vulnerabilities, such as poverty and inequality, lack of labor rights, and household insecurity became serious problems after the crisis hit (Atinc and Walton 1998).

The resolution of the crisis at the policy making level was grueling. Indonesia faced political and economic volatility, with dissension between the IMF and government about appropriate recovery-oriented policies. President Suharto was reviled due to his inability to stem the crisis, and protests against his administration began in May 1998. Suharto resigned and his successor, B.J. Habibie, attempted to gain credibility. Policy making independence was granted to Bank Indonesia (Desai 2003). Indonesia also established the Indonesian Bank Restructuring Agency (IBRA) in 1998 to recover liquidity credits that Bank Indonesia had lent to ailing banks (Radelet and Woo 2000). The government closed 38 domestic private banks, nationalized seven domestic banks, and recapitalized nine banks, and banks were to repay all overdue trade credits. Bank closures in Indonesia, required by the IMF, caused bank runs and nearly dissolved the entire banking sector (Djiwandono 2007). Due to political uncertainty, Indonesia's recovery was long in coming.

Korea's economy was affected by the inadequacy of the IMF rescue packages and by massive debt owed by the private sector to foreign banks (Desai 2003). The $57 billion IMF rescue package failed to restore confidence, and the economic turmoil faced by *chaebols* such as Halla and Coryo Investment & Securities worsened the country rating. Debt restructuring was essential. Korea set out to reduce non-performing loans, which by March 1999 amounted to 143.9 trillion won (Hong and Lee 2000). The

Korea Asset Management Company (KAMC), used to purchase non-performing loans, was supported by the government through bond issues. Korean recovery arrived quickly thereafter, mainly due to expansionary monetary and fiscal policy.

IMF-induced structural reforms in Korea led to mass lay-offs in the Korean automobile industries, which brought about strikes and riots (Weisbrot 2007). Financial reforms culled by the IMF also failed to account for the close relationship between banks, corporations, and governments and the systemic character of the banking crisis. The IMF was later called out for implementing these policies along with promoting tight fiscal policy stances particularly at the outset of the crisis.

As an immediate response to the crisis, Malaysia tightened monetary and fiscal policy. Malaysia implemented capital controls in September 1998, fixed the exchange rate, reduced interest rates, and later expanded fiscal policy. Current account transactions were regulated such that imports must be paid for in foreign exchange, and export earnings must be brought back within six months and converted to local currencies. The movement of FDI was also temporarily limited.

Thailand faced problems with non-performing loans through 1999, and the government introduced a voluntary debt restructuring program and implemented fiscal stimulus programs in attempts to repair the financial and real economic damage (Flatters 2000). Fiscal stimulus programs throughout East Asia reflected a change in IMF stance toward fiscal deficits.

The Philippines were somewhat better able to weather the crisis since the country had completed an IMF-supported program of macroeconomic adjustment and structural reform in the late 1980s and early 1990s. Monetary policy was tightened and the banking system was strengthened just after the crisis hit. Monetary and fiscal policy was relaxed in mid-1998.

The countries gradually recovered through 1999 and 2000, even as investment ratios and stock market prices fell (Barro 2001). On the whole, when the panic ended, the exchange rates and interest rates recovered, and banking sector repair ensued (Sachs and Woo 2000). Economic recovery was V-shaped, due to countercyclical fiscal measures and recovery, particularly in Malaysia and South Korea, in the electronics sector in anticipation of Y2K (Sundaram 2007). A good portion of banks in Indonesia, Thailand, and Korea were closed, merged, or nationalized. The main remaining problem left over from the crisis was the large amount of non-performing loans remaining on the books of financial institutions.

The lender of last resort, the IMF, has been blamed for worsening the crisis. IMF policies tied to loans to the beleaguered nations resembled to some extent failed policies employed by President Hoover during the

Great Depression. Radelet and Sachs (1998) detail the policies that exacerbated the crisis, noting that IMF requirements to close banks, enforce capital adequacy requirements, and tighten credit greatly worsened the banking panics in the region. Other destructive measures included IMF requirements to tighten fiscal spending, impose structural changes on the non-financial sector, and increase central bank discount rates.

The IMF program for Korea went beyond measures needed to resolve the crisis, calling for structural and institutional reform, and, destructively, called for even wider opening of Korea's capital and current accounts (Wade and Veneroso 1998). IMF programs for other countries required similar institutional reforms and capital account liberalization. Kissinger (1998) emphasizes the importance of reevaluating the IMF rescue program package, particularly since, "as the chief economist of the Deutsche Bank in Tokyo pointed out, the IMF acts like a doctor specializing in measles and tries to cure every illness with one remedy."

It was proposed that a market-driven reward and punishment system would create financial stability. In response to this, the IMF produced Reports on the Observance of Standards and Codes and launched a Financial Sector Assessment Program, which were to help provide information on economic situations. These measures were unsuccessful in providing external stability, and amounted to a list of structural issues rather than a true monitoring system (Wade 2007). The crisis led to many suggestions to remake the international financial architecture to prevent another meltdown. These suggestions are discussed in the final chapter.

For some time during and after, many top officials in Western nations perceived the Asian crisis as fundamentally rooted in the structure of those economies themselves. Singh (2002) makes the case that this is not so, since Asian economies, under government intervention, had been growing rapidly since 1980, while financial liberalization, the source of asset price bubbles that led to the crisis, was more recent. After the US crisis of 2008, these beliefs have been revised, as both developing and developed nations found themselves in peril.

The crisis led to a number of institutional reforms at the international and regional levels, including creation of the Group of Twenty (G-20), the Financial Stability Forum, the IMF/World Bank Financial Sector Assessment Program, and the Chiang-Mai Initiative for currency swaps (Takagi 2007). The G-20 is a group of finance ministers and central bank governors from 20 countries. Two financial surveillance institutions include the Financial Stability Forum, which is a group of major national financial bodies that promote international financial stability, managed by the Bank for International Settlements; and the IMF/World Bank

Financial Sector Assessment Program, which provides in-depth analysis of countries' financial sectors.

Other institutions were left unchanged, including the IMF, credit rating agencies, and hedge funds (Prakash 2001). The IMF remained unaccountable to stakeholders who are forced to implement liberalization and privatization policies. Ratings agencies continued to rate in a procyclical fashion, while hedge funds continued to engage in excessively risky activity which influenced the financial industry.

The Asian financial crisis led to a general crisis of confidence in the region after the economies returned to normal rates of growth. Institutions were founded in the region to improve corporate governance and fight corruption, which sent positive messages to investors, but investment, needless to say, has not returned to pre-crisis levels.

Political Economy of the Asian Financial Crisis

Some views regarding the political economy of the Asian financial crisis are now outdated, particularly after the Great Recession struck. As the Asian crisis took hold, many analysts at the time viewed the crisis as a product of "crony capitalism," in which close ties between the business and government sectors created conditions for moral hazard, in which the business community was able to sway the government toward working in its favor. Political leaders were viewed as corrupt and self-interested, opposed to reform. This view was tempered over time, as the "Asian" aspect of the crisis was stripped away to better understand the causes of the crisis. In addition, a diversity of political regimes meant that Asian nations dealt with the crisis politically in different ways, and the stereotype of Asian corruption diminished.

In South Korea, President Kim Dae Jung faced a divided government, but worked with the outgoing government to implement some reforms before taking office in 1998. President Kim had looser ties to the business community than his predecessors, but maintained popularity with labor and was viewed as a populist (Haggard 2000). President Kim turned out to be more in favor of market liberalization than expected, assessing the crisis as stemming from insufficient market regulation and management. Kim was able to successfully foster negotiation between business and labor. Referenda held in June 1998 on the reform process resulted in victory for President Kim, particularly in Seoul, and the President continued his reform path.

In Thailand, the coalition government, which held weak ties to the Democrat Party, was not unified in the response to the crisis. Economic policy making was scattered by October 1997, but a proposal for media censorship and a curfew was blocked by the military. Prime Minister Chuan Leekpai, installed in office in November 1997, faced challenges in maintaining a government coalition and in quelling social unrest from diverse groups. Business opposed the government's macroeconomic policy position, which was in line with IMF policy. Although the government later reached an agreement with the IMF to relax fiscal policy, the pro-business wing of the cabinet demanded further focus on the financial sector and exchange rate instead of concentration on the real economy (Haggard 2000). Post-crisis policy making in Thailand remained relatively slow-moving as a result.

In Indonesia, Mohamed Suharto was President when the crisis hit. As civil unrest grew, protesters demanded that Suharto step down and a democratic government be installed. Escalating violence and political alienation eventually induced Suharto to step down and B.J. Habibie to take office. Under President Habibie in Indonesia, the government faced challenges to reform in the vested interests of the ruling party and private sector. The *reformasi* movement that opposed abuses under Suharto created a backlash against the government, resulting in social violence and political confrontations. Habibie instituted political and economic reforms, including those required by the IMF, but was ultimately constrained in reforms instituted due to severe administrative restrictions.

The financial crisis did not produce political crisis in Malaysia, but did result in increased concentration of power in the hands of Prime Minister Mahathir. The government quashed dissent that arose to challenge the Prime Minister's leadership. Reform was limited.

The Asian financial crisis produced a great deal of economic and political uncertainty, and generated political opposition to varying extents in the affected nations. Next, we briefly examine the Turkish crisis, which was brought about in part as a result of the Asian crisis.

TURKISH CRISIS

Turkey also experienced financial crisis starting in January 1998, resulting from an inadequate recovery from a previous recession and the effects of the Asian crisis of 1997. Economic liberalization occurring in the 1990s resulted in a surge in public debt between 1991 and 1994 and boom–bust cycles. Current account deficits and interest rates increased. A stabilization program announced on April 5, 1994 was insufficient to counter the impact of the recession, and as the Asian financial crisis produced negative international economic effects, debt levels were rendered unsustainable (Yurdakul 2014). Troubles escalated by 1999, and programs for fighting inflation were implemented. The exchange rate stabilization program functioned for a short time, but thereafter got off course. The IMF stepped in during the fall of 2000 with a large bailout package. Attacks on the currency led to abandonment of the currency peg in February 2001 (Akyuz and Boratov 2003).

Fiscal austerity and monetary tightening measures in response to the crisis worsened the recession and dampened growth. The global economic environments did not help matters, since the Asian financial crisis and later, the events of September 11, 2001, led to slowing growth worldwide. The Turkish financial crisis required four IMF bailout packages. Deregulation of interest rates, and liberalization of the capital accounts, had the impact of increasing the cost of public sector financing, as the government was forced to pay higher interest rates relative to safer dollar assets and the rate of inflation.

ECONOMIC THEORIES OF THE MID-1990S

Neoliberal theory was in full effect by the mid-1990s, encouraging liberalization in trade and capital flows. The "Washington Consensus," discussed briefly above, emphasized fiscal discipline, tax reform, trade liberalization, deregulation, and liberalization of foreign direct investment. The list was expanded by some policy makers and scholars to encompass financial and exchange rate liberalization. The liberalization of credit flows was often not accompanied by prudential supervision and adequate regulation, leading to financial crises through the 1990s and beyond.

The application of Washington Consensus policies varied; when first applied by the Bretton Woods institutions, little thought was given to issues of income distribution until after the Asian financial crisis played out (Williamson 2004). The IMF in particular encouraged liberalization of the capital account in the mid-1990s. The policies were simple enough to be widely understood by policy makers around the globe. It was not until the early 2000s that growth-oriented policies were reframed from a more equitable perspective. Around this time, Asian nations such as South Korea, Taiwan, and later China, were increasingly perceived as exceptions to the Washington Consensus view that state retrenchment and privatization were key to fostering economic growth. In the wake of the Asian financial crisis, economists shifted away from neoliberalism to some extent toward more inclusive theories of growth.

CONCLUSION

At the time, the Asian financial crisis was arguably the worst since the Great Depression, affecting much of Asia. It rapidly spread to other countries and threw the population into hardship, albeit in the short run. The Asian crisis showed that crisis could spread like wildfire if not contained, and at the same time, that containing it through austere fiscal measures was not the best answer. After the Asian financial crisis, much worse was to come. Immediately following the crisis, other countries caught the "Asian flu" and faced rapidly deteriorating circumstances. These included Russia, Brazil, and Argentina, which we turn to next.

NOTES

1. Additional forces put pressure on exports, such as competition from China, Vietnam, and Mexico, and the decline in world semiconductor prices (Berg 1999).
2. These countries were certainly operating within different political and economic paradigms. Malaysian Prime Minister Mahathir blamed the crisis on rich Western countries, and sought to ban currency trading. Mahathir made wild accusations toward others for engineering the crisis, isolating George Soros as a major culprit. Soros later responded that Mahathir was a "menace to his own country" (Ries 2000). But despite the invective, Mahathir was a strong political figure who promoted anti-recessionary policies and immediately imposed barriers to capital outflows (Desai 2003).

    Mishkin (1999) notes that risk was inadequately managed, and moral hazard through implicit bank government bailouts in the event of financial distress created barriers to financial efficiency. He finds that an international lender of last resort is critical for emerging markets in crisis, since they do not have adequate domestic lenders of last resort themselves. However, the lender of last resort must impose appropriate conditionality to restore investor confidence in the economy which will reduce moral hazard and ensure that creditors and debtors alike do not engage in excessive risk-taking.
3. Like Krugman, Mishkin (1999) emphasized the impact of the crisis on firms' balance sheets. By contrast, however, Mishkin emphasizes the role that banks' risky behavior played in causing the crisis.
4. Irwin and Vines (1999) build on the Krugman model, following Dooley (2000) and Sachs (1996), with a unique long-run equilibrium with overinvestment, but multiple equilibrium in the short run with a fixed capital stock but a variety of possible risk premia.

    Sachs and Woo (2000) generalize the theoretical model in a three-stage process. The first stage witnesses the overvaluation of the exchange rate as a result of internal or external events. The second stage requires central bank use of foreign exchange reserves to defend the currency. And the third stage, occurring after the depletion of foreign reserves, results in a massive outflow of short-term foreign capital. The crisis is created when the currency is defended, sending signs of weakness to investors. Sachs and Woo believe that the currency should be allowed to weaken before a strong defense of reserves is undertaken, and that the central bank should provide banks with liquidity to meet withdrawal of deposits while allowing the currency to float.

7. Late 1990s and early 2000s: Russian financial crisis, Brazilian financial crisis, Argentine crisis

INTRODUCTION

The world became more closely intertwined in the late 1990s and beyond, as production processes and finance became increasingly global. However, the global institutional infrastructure did not change dramatically, and financial contagion followed on the heels of foreign indebtedness and declining economic conditions.

Several crises followed the Asian financial crisis in rapid succession. These were impacted by contagion from the Asian crisis and from one another to different degrees. A loss of foreign investor confidence added fuel to the fire in these countries, which were overindebted to foreign investors to begin with. The Russian financial crisis began in 1998, and was caused by serious vulnerabilities associated with economic restructuring due to the privatization process. The Brazilian financial crisis also began in 1998 and was less serious than the Russian crisis, brought about by overspending during its privatization process. The Argentine financial crisis was the least expected, since Argentina had been working closely with the International Monetary Fund (IMF) to prevent crisis. The crisis began in 2000 as Argentina became increasingly indebted and descended into recession. The country was unable to use monetary policy to revive its economy, and its fiscal policy suffered from structural shortcomings. We examine each of these crises in turn, starting with the Russian financial crisis.

RUSSIAN FINANCIAL CRISIS

The Russian financial crisis, which began in 1998, was caused by both internal and external economic weaknesses. The crisis made underlying economic problems more evident. Pre-existing vulnerabilities included exposure to exchange rate volatility through issuance of United States (US) dollar-denominated bonds, and dependence on an export-oriented economy. During the crisis, halting of foreign demand for Russian metals and energy led to a severe downturn and a sudden liquidation of Russian assets. External shocks from the Asian financial crisis exacerbated the crisis and eventually necessitated an IMF bailout.

Causes of the Crisis

The Russian financial crisis was one in a series of crises after Asia, but was also rooted in fiscal shortcomings that began prior to 1998. The Soviet Union had disintegrated in large part due to bankruptcy of the Soviet state, and Russia continued to struggle with the debt crisis that this created (Vavilov 2010). Without fiscal reform, the government struggled to operate effectively. The cash tax collection of September 1996 was disastrous and hence government wages and social expenditures could not be paid, resulting in a vicious cycle of non-payments (Gilman 2010). Government expenditures meanwhile only increased through 1996. Tax arrears were essentially subsidies to the debtor institutions. Weak fiscal performance contributed to high interest rates and political uncertainty. The inability to collect sufficient taxes to fund government spending repressed further economic reform. Poorly designed tax rules and tax administration, and the pervasiveness of criminal gangs who both collected "taxes" and provided protection, led to severe fiscal shortfalls. Government budgetary expenditure was also undisclosed, preventing external advisors from helping matters. Tax revenues in 1997 were again disappointing, leaving the government in a quandary over its budgeted expenditures.

Financial liberalization did not help matters. Current account convertibility was introduced in 1996, while capital controls were easily averted. A large amount of foreign money flowed into the stock market in 1996 as investors expected high returns. The formal granting of permission to foreigners to purchase Russian government bonds prompted a surge in foreign investment in 1996 and 1997 (Buchs 1999). GKO[1] government bonds were purchased in large amounts, at $1.6 billion in 1996, and more than $4 billion in both Q1 1997 and Q2 1997. Banks, weak institutions that lacked true independence, acted as a conduit for government debt investment (Pinto and Ulatov 2010). Banking liabilities accumulated (Perotti 2002).

What is more, through 1997, political instabilities mounted as President Boris Yeltsin's health deteriorated and many government officials were sacked (Gilman 2010). President Yeltsin's ratings were low to begin with, as Communists and Nationalists opposed Reformers. Most observers were aware that decisions were made (funds and projects appointed, state assets distributed) according to insider preference rather than economic or political efficiency. In addition, corporate governance was very poor due to the privatization process, and firms were still in a process of adjustment to the new economic circumstances. These destabilizing events occurred even though macroeconomic fundamentals improved: the trade surplus was moving toward balance, the IMF and World Bank continued to provide aid (after rigorous negotiations) to stabilize the economy and prevent ruble devaluation, inflation had fallen, and output was rising (Chiodo and Owyang 2002). As the Asian crisis had shown, macroeconomic fundamentals were no longer sufficient for economic growth or even stability. Hence the domestic conditions were ripe for crisis.

In addition, the Russian financial crisis of 1998 was triggered in part by contagion from Southeast Asia. Contagion from the Asian financial crisis threw the country into a downturn. In late September 1997, Korean and Brazilian investors, experiencing crisis at home, withdrew from Russian assets to cover their positions at home (Gilman 2010). By October 1997, investors nervous about contagion from the Asian crisis began to pull out of the stock and bond (GKO) markets. Foreign bondholders began to abandon GKOs. Most owners of the GKOs were foreign investors and the large Russian domestic banks (Sutela 1999). At the end of 1997, yields began to rise on Russian debt as the government significantly increased the amount auctioned.

Events of the Crisis

In November 1997, the Russian central bank had lost 25 percent of its foreign reserves. Investors started pulling their investments out of the Russian stock market, which depressed equity prices and put further downward pressure on the currency. Due to concerns about emerging markets caused by the Asian financial crisis, the ruble went under a speculative attack at the end of 1997 and the beginning of 1998, and a net outflow of funds from the government bond market occurred, causing rating agencies to downgrade Russia's outlook.

In response, the Russian Central Bank (CBR) raised interest rates to boost investor confidence and help defend the ruble against external pressure, but bankers opposed this tightening of monetary policy. The stock of government securities became larger than the ruble money stock by 1998. Sberbank held up to 40 percent of the GKO stock and most household ruble savings, which were used to pay the public deficit. The outflow of funds from the bond market continued after President Yeltsin limited foreign ownership in the national electricity company in May 1998, and after the anti-crisis plan was opposed in the State Duma (Buchs 1999).

To make matters worse, falling oil prices reduced Russia's oil revenue

(Chiodo and Owyang 2002). Through 1998, some large banks were undertaking extensive risks, borrowing large amounts in foreign exchange from abroad to make profits from high-yielding GKOs and purchase the foreign exchange on maturity to repay the loan (Gilman 2010). The current account balance fell and then turned negative in the first half of 1998 (Desai 2003).

The political situation within Russia continued to deteriorate, with the Duma rejecting policies that would conform to IMF loan covenants. Government churning brought in Sergey Kiriyenko as Prime Minister with an inexperienced new team. Fiscal imbalances continued, and the government attempted to collect more taxes in cash, reducing banks' and firms' liquidity. The central bank attempted to stave off a potential devaluation crisis by raising the lending rate to banks and decreasing the growth of the money supply, both of which had unintended adverse consequences on government revenues and liquidity.

Without a concrete solution to Russia's financial troubles, investors started to grow impatient and withdraw their funds. This led yields on three-month GKOs to rise to 50 percent in 1998, and to 90 percent later that same month. New Russian debt was issued at successively higher interest rates, which further undermined investor confidence. Banks came under scrutiny after Tokobank found itself unable to meet margin calls against collateral held to secure foreign credits. Interbank loan defaults ensued as several large banks, including Tokobank and SBS-Agro, became insolvent (Perotti 2002).

The large-scale loss of confidence in Russia's economy put the ruble under serious pressure. In response, the exchange rate had to be fiercely defended, and the Russian stock market fell 20 percent. Soon after, Russia and the IMF were able to reach an agreement to release $670 million to bolster the economy. In July 1998, facing a weighted average interest rate on GKOs of 126 percent, Kirienko canceled GKO auctions and offered to convert outstanding bonds into medium- and long-term notes denominated in dollars. The conversion had the following features: it was to be voluntary and market-based, allowing swaps only on GKOs maturing before July 1, 1999. Those wanting to convert their bonds could receive an equal amount in terms of market value of 7- and 20-year dollar eurobonds (Pinto and Ulatov 2010).

The conversion restored a degree of confidence in the economy and prompted the IMF, the World Bank, and the Japanese government to offer $22.6 billion in assistance. The weighted average yield of outstanding GKOs fell to 53 percent. The reforms agreed to as conditions for the IMF loan were again stalled by the Duma, leading the IMF to scale back assistance. The failure to push reforms through the Duma demonstrated Russia's political weakness.

The Russian economy then had to deal with a liquidity crisis. Russian banks received loans from abroad, and in exchange posted GKOs as collateral. As Russian banks began to sell off the government debt to exchange for foreign currency to meet the margin calls, global markets became nervous. Sberbank itself redeemed all of its GKO holdings falling due in July for 12.4 billion rubles ($1.28 billion) (Gilman 2010). Foreign currency reserves continued falling, from $19.5 billion in July 1998 to $16.3 billion in August 1998. The ruble was still imperiled from loss of foreign investor confidence (Buchs 1999), and Russian-era external debt had increased by more than $16 billion between June 1 and July 24, 1998 (Pinto and Ulatov 2010).

On August 13, George Soros wrote in the *Financial Times* that Russia's crisis was in the "terminal" stage and called for a devaluation of the currency and the creation of a currency board to keep the ruble pegged to the dollar or a European currency (Gilman 2010). This caused panic among global investors and Russia's sovereign foreign debt was downgraded to junk bond status. Despite the fact that the central bank extended emergency credits to banks, the stock exchange and the ruble collapsed. The ruble, which had remained relatively stable for three years beforehand, lost most of its value. On August 23, the Russian cabinet resigned, effectively annulling any outstanding agreements with the IMF. This frightened markets, and the sell-off continued. On August 31, 1998, $1 could be exchanged for 7.905 rubles. On September 9, 1998, $1 could be exchanged for 20.825 rubles. In 1998, the Russian stock market lost 89 percent of its value. Figure 7.1 shows the sharp increase in the ruble–dollar exchange rate.

The sharp ruble devaluation exacerbated the banking crisis and household deposits were frozen to prevent further bank runs. The Central Bank shifted private deposits to Sberbank. The lack of bank transparency contributed to a liquidity crisis (Sutela 1999). To exacerbate matters, the collapse of the GKO assets wiped out bank assets, which caused a solvency crisis. Insolvent banks were not declared bankrupt, and bank owners engaged in asset-stripping (Perotti 2002). As costs rose, imports of consumer goods came to a halt. Consumers hoarded food as Russians panicked.

Outcomes of the Crisis

The crisis lowered living standards even further and added to the personal woes of the population. Although exporters gained from the currency devaluation, there was a further sharp decline in real wages. In real terms, household income fell by 20 percent due to the crisis, while the average

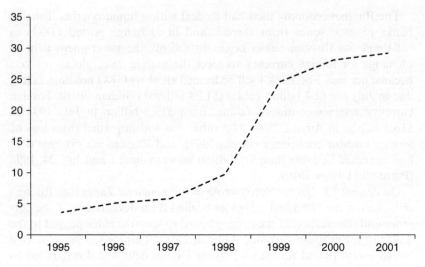

Source: World Bank data.

Figure 7.1   Ruble–dollar exchange rate

amount of government transfers fell by 18 percent, and help from relatives declined by 40 percent. The poverty rate increased from 22 percent to 33 percent. Using household survey data,[2] Lokshin and Ravallion (2000) confirm that welfare declined as a result of the crisis. Problems with wage and other payments remained.

Russia quickly recovered from the crisis as world oil prices rose in 1999 and 2000. In addition, the new administration under Yevgeny Primakov used monetary financing and currency controls to restore basic financial services (Süppel 2003). The administration also engaged in aggressive fiscal tightening. Rapid import substitution occurred as domestic costs fell in comparison to those of international competitors. This shifted up the merchandise trade surplus. Output rebounded, inflation slowed, inter-bank payments were restored, and federal government revenue collection quickly rebounded.

As a result of the crisis, Russia's privatization process was stalled and the need for tax reform was highlighted. Some viewed the economic liberaliza-tion process as a mistake, while most agreed that better reform practices were in order. Clearly, Russia's difficult transition from a planned to a market economy was made even more difficult by weaknesses imposed due to financial globalization, in which the economy was exposed to external capital flows and global contagion (Pinto and Ulatov 2010). The Russian crisis also underscored the premise that sound macroeconomic fundamentals were insufficient for a positive investment climate; microeconomic and structural economic conditions also matter.

Political Economy of the Russian Crisis

The Russian crisis was seen as a turning point in Russia's development after the break-up of the Union of Soviet Socialist Republics (USSR). Some believed, at the time, that Russia would enter a longer period of crisis due to severe economic fragilities, although this did not come about (Robinson 2007). The economy was moving away from outright dysfunction, with negative value-added production, to a market-based system. Economic churning occurred alongside political churning. The political elite was increasingly divided, especially between center and local leaders, as some reforms failed.

Indeed, the Russian crisis was exacerbated by the sharp turnover in the Russian government in 1998, when President Boris Yeltsin fired the entire government and appointed Sergey Kiriyenko Prime Minister. Kiriyenko was in office for only a short period, from March 1998 until August 1998, when he was fired. Prime Minister Kiriyenko was known as a reformer, and was necessarily at odds with the oligarchs in power. Yet it was the oligarchs who supported President Yeltsin, and their presence in the parliament halted legislation. President Yeltsin in return began to legislate by decree.

Within this period of conflict, the executive branch, the Duma, and the Central Bank of Russia were all at odds. The Duma was forced to confirm Kiriyenko as Prime Minister in April 1998, the Central Bank Chair Sergei Dubinin signaled a potential debt crisis which was read as impending devaluation, Kiriyenko claimed that the government was "quite poor now," and Lawrence Summers, Deputy Treasury Secretary, was turned away from meeting with Kiriyenko by his aide in a political gaffe (Chiodo and Owyang 2002). By the time the IMF left Russia without reaching an agreement on an austerity plan in May 1998, investor sentiment had taken a sharp blow.

Prime Minister Viktor Chernomyrdin was reappointed by President Yeltsin after Kiriyenko was dismissed, but the parliament rejected him and nominated their own candidate, Yevgeny Primakov. This defeat for the President exacerbated the political crisis, especially because Primakov lacked experience in managing economic affairs. However, young reformers continued to comprise about half of the ministries, maintaining the path of reform. Political volatility continued even as the crisis subsided. We now turn to the Brazilian financial crisis, which was triggered by contagion from the Asian and Russian financial crises.

BRAZILIAN FINANCIAL CRISIS

The Asian crisis spread to Brazil at the end of 1997. Foreign investors began to flee, putting pressure on the real. The real was temporarily stabilized by President Fernando Henrique Cardoso's administration, which raised the lending rate and reduced government outlays (Desai 2003).

Trouble resurfaced in August 1998 when the Russian crisis peaked, and at the same time a large Brazilian state, Minas Gerais, declared a debt moratorium. Brazil had been spending excessively and owed a large amount of debt to foreign creditors. Persistent accumulation of debts worried foreign investors. When the Asian crisis and the Russian crisis struck, Brazil raised interest rates. At the same time, it put forth a fiscal reform package. These policies reduced Brazil's credibility as a debtor nation. The increased interest rates had the effect of forcing up nominal deficits. Speculative attacks on the currency ensued as investors predicted currency devaluation (Gruben and Welch 2001). Foreign exchange reserves fell as the government tried to support the real, but by December 1998, the government was forced to turn to the IMF. The real was floated on January 18, 1999.

Although growth was present, the budget and current account deficits were considered unsustainable. IMF requirements brought budget deficits under control, but slow exports and increasing current account deficits put the currency under pressure again in 2001. The IMF again injected funds to prevent a debt default and promote investor confidence (Desai 2003).

Causes of the Crisis

Brazil's currency, the real, was initially introduced in 1994 as part of a plan to combat inflation and was successful. The Real Plan used indexation tied, through the exchange rate, to the number of dollars used to purchase goods, and the real was allowed to fluctuate within a band (Gruben and Welch 2001). Brazil also liberalized trade and foreign investment restrictions in order to increase competitive forces, decreased funds distributed to its states, and increased federal income tax rates. Indeed, capital flows into the country through 1997 increased greatly, particularly in the form of foreign direct investment, allowing expenditure to be increased (Palma 2000). Although foreign debt increased, Brazil's transition from state-led to private sector-led growth appeared to be taking off.

Unemployment and current account deficits rose in 1997. Fiscal spending at the state and central levels over this period was out of control, and translated into the current account deficits that depended on net foreign inflows for balance. Fiscal revenues were increasing, but fiscal government expenditures grew significantly. Government payroll expenses, social secu-

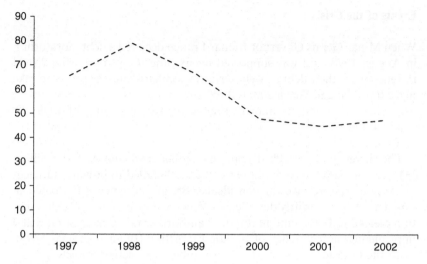

Source: World Bank data (2012).

Figure 7.2 Brazil's real interest rate

rity expenditures, and transfers to states continued to rise over the period (Giambiagi and Ronci 2004).

Brazil encountered several external shocks – the Mexican, Asian, and Russian crises – after each of which the Brazilian government raised interest rates (Figure 7.2), in order to prevent capital flight (Palma 2000). Once capital outflows began as a result of the Asian crisis, trouble began. Interest rates were doubled on October 31, 1997 to combat the crisis, but higher interest payments on government debt and a widening fiscal deficit perpetuated the crisis (Bulmer-Thomas 1999). As a result of interest rate increases, industrial production declined.

In addition, despite increases in interest rates, it became clear that the real was increasingly overvalued and foreign investors expected devaluation. To make matters worse, foreign investors were aware that the Brazilian government lacked consensus on deficit reduction policies. The Parliament was notoriously slow in approving the budget, which did not improve confidence in Brazil's mounting external and internal public debts. President Cardoso, attempting to push through Congress an amendment to the constitution which would allow him to run for a second term, made many concessions to Congress on fiscal reform (Amann and Baer 2000).

Events of the Crisis

When Minas Gerais Governor Itamar Franco declared a debt moratorium in August 1998, and was supported by six other Governors who wished to renegotiate their debt as well, serious speculative attacks began to take place (Gruben and Welch 2001). Brazil's commitment to fiscal adjustment was called into question. Shortly after, at the very beginning of 1999, the head of the central bank, Gustavo Franco, resigned, and capital flight increased.

The currency was attacked again in October 1998, and the $41.5 billion IMF rescue package issued in December 1998 failed to provide sufficient reserves to restore investor confidence. Brazil's currency was floated in January 1999 and swiftly devalued to 45 percent of its value. The devaluation created inflation, and in response authorities raised interest rates and implemented a new policy of inflation targeting (Bulmer-Thomas 1999). With the flotation of the currency, an inflation targeting framework as a nominal anchor was chosen to create a more transparent monetary commitment, in the hopes that market uncertainty would decline (Fraga 2000). Exports became more competitive with the devaluation. The exchange rate continued to float with little central bank intervention.

Brazil's IMF package totaled $41.5 billion, and included more than $18 billion in loans from the IMF, $4.5 each billion from the World Bank and Inter-American Development Bank, and $14.5 in bilateral credits from 20 governments (Flynn 1999). The size of the package was intended to assure markets, but because there were no policy requirements to engage with the private sector or to change the exchange rate regime, the package did not produce the confidence that was expected. According to the IMF requirements, Brazil was to achieve a primary budget surplus of 3.1 percent of GDP (Amann and Baer 2000). This was obtained by collecting more taxes from wealthier individuals. Attempts to increase taxes on public workers to add to the fiscal surplus were declared unconstitutional by the Supreme Court. IMF requirements also required reforms of social security, public administration, public expenditures, and revenue sharing (IMF 1998).

In February 1999, the central bank President, Francisco Lopes, was sacked after only three weeks in office, due to his failure to prop up the real on January 29 (Flynn 1999). Reserves declined rapidly, from US$75 billion in August 1998 to less than US$35 billion in January 1999 (Amann and Baer 2000).

Export and gross domestic product (GDP) growth picked up in the aftermath of the crisis, with exports increasing steadily as a percentage of GDP for several years thereafter (see Figure 7.3). Foreign direct investment

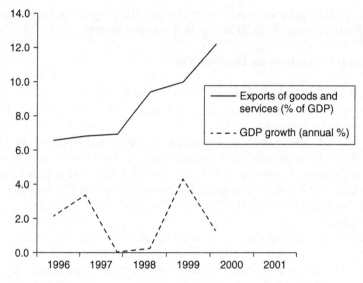

Source: World Bank (2012).

Figure 7.3 Export and GDP ratios, Brazil, 1996–2001

continued to flow into the country (Palma 2000). Recovery after the crisis was quite fast, due to Brazil's low dependence on imports, its political stability at the time, its largess of reserves after the crisis, and the promise of an IMF package before the crisis took place.

Outcomes of the Crisis

The banking sector suffered due to events of the crisis. As a result of increasing interest rates, many individuals and firms were unable to repay their loans, which resulted in a large increase in non-performing loans (Amann and Baer 2000). Maturity mismatches between liabilities and assets created additional problems for banks. State banks in particular faced difficulties, since they had little experience managing risk and insufficient autonomy, with non-performing loans. For private banks, the government set up a Credit Guarantee Fund, to which all financial institutions were required to contribute 0.024 percent of all balances in accounts covered. Forty-three financial institutions were put under a Temporary Special Administrative Regime to shore up resources. Banking mergers and acquisitions were also made easier through the Program of Incentives for the Restructuring and Strengthening of the National Financial System, while privatization was made easier through the Program of Incentives for the Restructuring of the State Public Financial System.

Political Economy of the Brazilian Crisis

Brazil was governed, over the crisis period, by President Fernando Henrique Cardoso. Cardoso was a scholar who believed that Brazil followed the dependency theory, which meant it had been caught in a low state of development due to vested interests on the part of the bourgeoisie and foreign powers. Cardoso believed development was possible where domestic ownership of industry was significant. He later became an advocate, in his role of President, for business interests. Cardoso was one of the main architects of the "Real Plan" which was formulated to stabilize the economy.

Brazil was entering a pre-crisis phase in 1998, and Cardoso made a speech underscoring the fact that major fiscal adjustment was to take place. Government scandal involving wiretapping of privatization deals further weakened political capital. A bailout package, centered around a crawling rate exchange rate regime, was approved by the IMF in December.

Cardoso had just been re-elected when Brazilian state Minas Gerais declared a debt moratorium. Cardoso was accused of postponing new economic policies in the run-up to his re-election, and his government was later blamed by the Group of Seven (G-7) and IMF for failing to preserve the crawling peg, which had been a requirement of the December bailout package (de Paiva Abreu and Werneck 2005). A new central bank board was appointed to uphold the conditions of the IMF package. The government proved successful in carrying out fiscal adjustment, reducing the inflationary shock from devaluation, and improving exchange rate conditions.

Brazil recovered rapidly from its crisis, as Argentina's economy became increasingly vulnerable. Mounting external debt, coupled with a number of external shocks, from the Asian, Russian, and Brazilian crises, weakened the Argentine economy. We next turn to the crisis in Argentina that began in 2000, and examine the causes, events, and outcomes of the crisis.

ARGENTINE CRISIS

Argentina had grown at an average rate of 6.7 percent per year between 1991 and 1997 (Hausmann and Velasco 2002). During the period of 1991–97 the Argentine economy experienced high growth and low inflation levels. This high growth was only interrupted in 1995, when the country experienced a recession due to the Mexican peso crisis. This rapid growth disguised vulnerability in the fiscal and banking systems, which, coupled with poor policy responses, worsened economic circumstances (Perry and Servén 2004). In addition, rigidity imposed by the currency board created a vulnerability in the exchange rate regime. As the dot-com boom in the US unraveled, Argentina entered crisis.

A series of external shocks hit the Argentine economy at the end of the 1990s (Chudnovsky and Lopez 2007). In 1997, the Asian crisis resulted in a temporary increase in risk spreads and a decrease in the terms of trade for Argentina. In 1998, the Russian crisis followed causing a tightening of credit and Brazil, Argentina's main trading partner, was in recession. Still, Argentina was perceived to be under control as it faced these negative shocks (Hausmann and Velasco 2002). During 1998, Argentina saw a decline in the terms of trade, a decrease in private investment, and a more rapid decrease in economic activity. By the end of that year, export prices were about 20 percent lower than at their peak two years prior.

In 1999, Argentina faced another negative shock due to the depreciation of the Brazilian real. This caused greater downward pressure on Argentine exports. The appreciation of the US dollar also had a negative effect on Argentina's exports to Europe and the US. Even with these negative shocks, Argentina saw a short-lived increase in economic growth in the last quarter of 1999. The IMF issued a news brief commending Argentina's policies (Hausmann and Velasco 2002).

Causes of the Crisis

The glow of growth was short-lived. In January of 2000, new President Fernando de la Rua took office. The economy stagnated again and tax revenues began to fall. What is more, the government was increasingly deeper in debt. The external public debt was contracted, for the most part, in dollars (Lischinsky 2003). External public debt would rise to 30 percent of GDP by late 2000, while external public and private debt were even higher (Figure 7.4).

In response, Economic Minister Jose Luis Machinea implemented the *impuestazo*, a tax increase meant to decrease the financial deficit and in turn ease the private sector's concerns about debt sustainability. Unfortunately, the actual economic impact was negative, since citizens reduced their economic activity just after the announcement of the tax increase, even before taxes had actually increased. The decreases in economic activity led to a decrease in tax revenues which worsened the fiscal deficit. This had the result of increasing country risk as uncertainty of debt sustainability

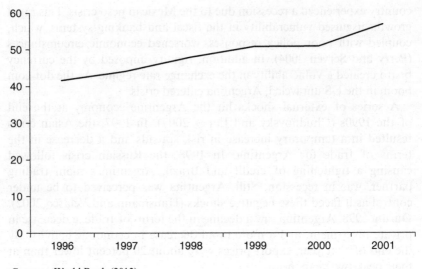

Source: World Bank (2012).

Figure 7.4   External debt stocks ($ of gross national income)

climbed. As a result, investment declined, causing economic activity to fall even further (Powell 2002).

Argentina was already vulnerable to external shocks, due to the rigidity of the exchange rate, the weak fiscal situation, and the fragility of the banking system. The rigidity inherent in the currency board arrangement prevented the free use of monetary policy in countering recession, and policy mechanisms became dependent on fiscal policy. Through the currency board, each peso in the economy was backed by a dollar and fully convertible. The currency board arrangement worked against the economy as exports became decreasingly competitive.

Macroeconomic stabilization was left to fiscal policy (IMF 2003). Argentina's fiscal spending was uncoordinated and over budget, and the increasing size of fiscal spending overshadowed the currency board arrangement which required the country to adjust fiscal policy according to money available after a fixed exchange rate was taken into account. This, however, could not be upheld. Money supply was dependent on foreign exchange earnings which, when they fell due to peso overvaluation, translated into low liquidity in the banking system. Hence saving and investment were dampened (Desai 2003). Nor could the exchange rate be painlessly devalued, since both the private and public sectors held a large amount of dollar-denominated debt (Hausmann and Velasco 2002).

The banking system was vulnerable since dollar-denominated bank loans were heavily extended to borrowers with peso-denominated incomes (De Krivoy 2003). Banks were also forced to invest in government bonds, which lost market value. As the economic climate worsened, bank runs occurred, especially in the two major publicly owned banks. Later "pesification" of bank assets and liabilities wiped out much capital in the banking system.

Fiscal policy was not overly effective, especially since Argentina had a fiscal system in which the central government set policies that were not necessarily in agreement with policies at the provincial level (IMF 2003). With a complex fiscal transfer system and little incentive for provinces to raise their own funds, Argentina's fiscal system faced challenges. Provinces had autonomy over spending and faced incentives to minimize tax transfers to the central government. In addition, government employment was much larger than average for middle-income countries and became a source of fiscal stress (Krueger 2002). Transfers to provinces comprised 30 percent of the budget, social security benefits comprised 30 percent, and interest payments comprised 10 percent, leaving little room to use fiscal policy where needed (IMF 2003). Sharply increasing public debt stemmed from the transition costs of the social security system, recession, and recognition of existing debts (Hausmann and Velasco 2002). With a problematic fiscal transfer system and yearly extra-budgetary spending due to tight fiscal constraints, Argentina's fiscal position declined.

Argentina's inability to reduce the fiscal deficit during the growth years led to the dilemma of choosing to maintain the exchange rate and suffer from deflation or float their currency which would cause immediate effects in its ability to pay their debts (Perry and Servén 2004). Alberola et al. (2003) find evidence that the peso became overvalued as the dollar peg appreciated relative to Argentina's main Latin American trading partner currencies. Appreciation was also caused by domestic wage and price rigidity (Desai 2003). All of these elements set the stage for potential debt default and a descent into crisis by late 2000.

Events of the Crisis

Argentina's crisis started in November 2000, as investors grew fearful of default on a mounting foreign debt (Desai 2003). The government became concerned that capital flight would occur en masse as default fears increased. In response, Economic Minister Machinea was able to negotiate a $30 billion support package, called the *blindaje*, $15 billion of which came from the IMF. The *blindaje* reverted deposit withdrawal until March 2001. Support from the IMF was conditional on Argentina meeting certain fiscal targets, greatly reducing fiscal spending. Although the announcement eased economic conditions, the economy did not show signs of recovery, and fiscal performance was unable to meet the targets set by the IMF.

On March 21, 2001, Machinea resigned, and was replaced by Ricardo Lopez Murphy as Economic Minister. Lopez Murphy focused on the need to reduce the deficit and proposed a program to reduce public expenditure. The decision was not well received by the political system or the public, since it was perceived as harmful to the public, and Lopez Murphy was forced to resign just two weeks after he had been appointed. He was replaced by Domingo Cavallo, the original architect of the convertibility plan of 1990. This political churning did not reassure foreign investors. Capital outflows put pressure on the dollar–peso peg.

Cavallo attempted to stimulate the economy through a number of policies such as: relaxing monetary policy, subsidizing certain economic sectors, implementing a financial tax (in order to reduce deficit) and increasing flexibility of the exchange rate regime. Efforts were made to reduce barriers to entering domestic industry for foreign investors. Associated taxes and import duties on capital goods were eliminated (Desai 2003). To increase flexibility in the convertibility law, the introduction of the euro into the currency basket was proposed, a measure that the central bank's President publicly opposed.

The resignation of Economic Minister Domingo Cavallo and President Fernando de la Rua added to the climate of uncertainty and worsened matters (BBC 2001). The resignation of Cavallo followed in quick succession the resignations of Jose Luis Machinea in March 2001 and Lopez Murphy that same month. The political climate led to reduced private sector spending (IMF 2003). IMF austerity measures forced Argentina to end budget deficits and cut state salaries and pensions, while private pensions were converted to government bonds (BBC 2001). Citizens protested such measures, and several members of the National Cabinet resigned (Cavallo 2002).

Country risk continued rising toward unsustainable levels, and therefore the *Megacanje* (megaswap) was introduced in June of 2001. The *Megacanje* exchanged government debt with shorter maturities for longer-maturity debt, and while it was able to improve liquidity risk, it also worsened solvency. On June 15, a de facto dual exchange rate on foreign versus domestic transactions was announced (IMF 2003). This new regime allowed the inclusion of the euro into the country basket for trade-related goods while keeping the exchange rate fixed for financial transactions. Banks' assets and liabilities were converted from dollars to pesos, which shifted devaluation to the banking system. At the same time, banks were required to pay out foreign exchange term deposits at the prevailing market exchange rate. The new regime caused concerns in the private sector since there was uncertainty about the IMF's reaction to the new plan. Argentina held that the new regime was not a dual exchange rate but a system that allowed for the subsidization of exports while it placed tariffs on imports.

On July 15, the government announced a reduction of 13 percent in government employees' salaries and individual pensions and a "zero-deficit" policy. Although the government employees had benefited from a policy committed to maintaining government employment, this announcement worsened the economic climate and financial markets reacted extremely unfavorably. Country risk continued to increase dramatically and this caused a continued decrease in bank deposits, owing to an increase in capital flight. On August 21, Argentina reached an agreement with the IMF, which included around $5 billion to increase bank reserves. By September, bank deposits had stabilized but the bank runs and the high-risk spreads caused a credit crunch, and once the poor fiscal revenue figures were announced for that month, risk spreads increased even further.

By November it was clear that Argentina would need to undergo another debt restructuring, but how it could achieve this was still unclear. Controls that limited deposit withdrawals and the outflow of capital were put in place, and were known as the *corralito*. The *corralito* attempted to "corral" capital flight and bank runs. Despite these controls, financial collapse could not be avoided. The currency collapsed in 2001 due to an overvalued exchange rate and the presence of foreign-denominated debt, along with an unfavorable trade imbalance in which the country could not earn enough foreign exchange to pay the interest on its debt (Feldstein 2002). The government was forced to default on its debt and devalue the peso. Since many businesses borrowed in dollars, they were unable to repay their loans. With banks exposed to government debt as well as foreign exchange shocks, bank runs ensued, and a day after bank runs began, on December 1, 2001, Cavallo restricted the amount of money the public could withdraw.

Public debt had greatly increased and at the end of 2001, the government defaulted on most of its public debt, representing the largest default on sovereign debt in history (Helleiner 2005). Banks were forced to "pesify" dollar-denominated loans, and dollar-denominated time deposits were coverted to pesos at a rate of 1.4 pesos to the dollar (Latin American Shadow Financial Regulatory Committee 2002). The government also suspended collection of private debt for six months.

With the onset of capital flow reversals from Russia in 1999 during the Russian crisis, the larger South American economies suffered, but unlike other Latin American countries, Argentina entered a prolonged

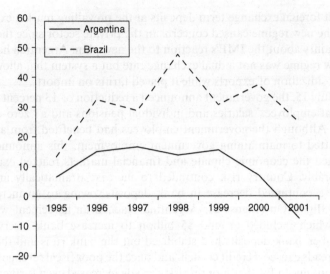

Source: World Bank data.

Figure 7.5   Net private capital inflows (billions of US current dollars)

recession. GDP was in a steady decline through 2002. IMF assistance was extended in 2003, to repay international financial institutions. The value of banks' assets deteriorated as a result of measures implemented to resolve the crisis. Argentina continued to restructure more than $100 billion of debt owed to foreign and domestic investors (Hornbeck 2004). By early 2005, bondholders had taken a 70 percent cut on their holdings (Helleiner 2005). In Figure 7.5, we show net private capital inflows in Argentina and Brazil.

Outcomes of the Crisis

The main culprits of the Argentine crisis have been identified as weak fiscal policy, with poor tax collection capability, and mounting overvaluation of the peso (Krueger 2002). Fiscal issues were presented due to lack of discipline at the provincial level, while the wage bill for public sector employees at the federal level increased and outpaced wage growth for private sector employees. In addition, Argentina's currency board arrangement was not as strong as had been projected, and became a liability as the economy deteriorated and monetary policy could not be used to combat recession.

Neither Argentina nor the IMF was aware of these growing weaknesses in the 1990s. Instead, Argentina was lauded for implementing measures to reduce inflation. As was stated in an IMF news brief (IMF 1995): "The IMF management welcomes the strong actions taken by Argentina. In the context of unsettled international financial markets, they demonstrate the firm commitment of the authorities to raise domestic savings, and to maintain fiscal and financial equilibrium and price stability." Even though attempts were made to stave off the crisis once it began (for example, imposing capital controls to prevent capital flight), crisis occurred and Argentina was forced to default on $132 billion of its debt and undergo debt restructuring for some time after the crisis ended.

Political Economy of the Argentine Crisis

Argentina, led by President Carlos Menem, had been a celebrated example of how Washington Consensus policies should be applied, but the status and the ideal were stripped away as the nation entered crisis. Fernando de la Rua succeeded Menem in December 1999 as President, but by 2001 the public was highly discontented with his leadership, which included austerity measures. His political party lost seats in the Argentine National Congress in October 2001. De la Rua was forced to step down in December 2001 due to domestic rioting and anger expressed by foreign bondholders after the *corralito* was implemented. Protests in the Plaza de Mayo had become deadly.

The short-lived administration of Interim President Adolfo Rodríguez Saá defaulted on much of the public debt, and lost political support in his attempt to implement a controlled currency devaluation. He was forced to resign after one week in office. Eduardo Duhalde was appointed President for the rest of de la Rua's term. He announced a plan to end the currency board and devalue the currency for major foreign commercial transactions, and adopt a floating rate for all other transactions. Debts were converted to pesos at a devalued rate. Larger dollar bank accounts were frozen for one year. Growth resumed in late 2002.

However, much damage was already done. Politicians were viewed as breaking the trust between the government and its citizens, and were seen as responsible for increasing poverty and unemployment. The economy had been stabilized but remained extremely fragile. The public was concerned about Argentina's repayment of debt to the IMF, which was later restructured by President Nestor Kirchner in 2003 and then canceled in 2005.

ECONOMIC THEORIES OF THE LATE 1990S AND EARLY 2000S

The breakdown of Washington Consensus policies, evidenced in the crises of the late 1990s and early 2000s, brought about a lacuna in theoretical consensus, and a strong challenge to neoliberal ideology. East Asia's growth indicated that the government could play an important role in bringing about economic reform, and Latin America's failure signified that full implementation of Washington Consensus policies was perhaps not entirely desirable, although there was a sense that market forces should continue to be emphasized. Growth, however, was not to be the only target of reform policies; equity and all-around well-being were increasingly emphasized (Stiglitz 2004).

Increasing emphasis was placed on improving institutions in the early 2000s. Institutions such as the rule of law, property rights, private incentives, and stable macroeconomic institutions were emphasized in place of outright liberalization. Rodrik (2004) classifies the types of reforms that fall under this category as governance reforms, and points out that such institutions are endogenous to income levels, rendering the practical study of the institution–growth nexus quite challenging. Still, a shift away from the neoliberal focus on government policy without sufficient attention to associated institutional infrastructure signified a movement toward inclusive growth rather than growth at any cost. Certainly, the fallout from the crises in Asia, Russia, Argentina, and Brazil comprised enormous economic and social costs.

CONCLUSION

In this chapter, we have examined the Russian, the Brazilian, and the Argentine crises in succession. All three crises were debt crises and currency crises, although the underlying causes and policy responses were different. In Russia, the immediate trigger for the crisis was a sudden outflow of capital while in Argentina the crisis built more slowly as policy makers attempted to stave it off by controlling capital flows, even though in both of these countries serious problems had been created long beforehand by serious fiscal shortcomings, particularly the inability to collect taxes. Brazil's crisis was created, in the short run, as a result of speculative attacks on the real. Attempts to fend off capital flight were overly simplistic and consisted of raising interest rates, which became decreasingly successful. Brazil's long-term problem was less serious than that of Russia or Argentina, and was due to overborrowing during the privatization process.

In all three cases, capital flight put pressure sooner or later on the exchange rates, and the IMF was forced to intervene to shore up capital and promote confidence. This did not always work, and grudging acceptance, at best, of IMF austerity conditions led to increased criticism of the IMF bailout and austerity policies. These criticisms would be echoed once again during the Great Recession of 2008, which was the largest crisis since the Great Depression, and which we turn to next.

NOTES

1. Government bonds, named GKOs (Государственное Краткосрочное Обязательство (pronounced "Gosudarstvennoye Kratkosrochnoye Obyazatyelstvo"), were issued in 1993 to finance the budget deficit.
2. Data are from the 1996 and 1998 Russian Longitudinal Monitoring Survey.

8. Late 2000s: the Great Recession of 2008

In the years just before the Great Recession, the global economy appeared to be running smoothly, with high levels of consumption in the West (due to cheap production in China) and a functioning eurozone. China and other emerging markets were growing rapidly, low-income Americans were able to purchase homes for the first time, and the world was becoming increasingly globalized or interconnected. Crises had occurred in emerging markets – Western economists viewed this as tragic but not shocking – and were never expected to happen in developed countries. Hence the Great Recession dumbfounded and dismayed economists and policy makers. It was never supposed to happen in developed, sophisticated nations; it could not happen.

Yet the unthinkable did occur. The Great Recession caused the most severe and globalized recession since the Great Depression.[1] Markets across the world, connected to the United States (US) financially or through trade, went into decline as US mortgage assets and their derivatives tumbled beginning in 2007.[2] We refer to this crisis as the "Great Recession of 2008" because it was in this year that global stock markets tumbled and global banks experienced failure on a large scale. This was the year that panic set in. Eventually the crisis laid bare and greatly exacerbated structural problems in the euro regions.

As is widely known at this point, the Great Recession began in the US with excessive overleveraging of subprime mortgage assets. Subprime mortgages were given out to individuals who lacked sufficient income or other financial resources to repay the loans. It was viewed at first as a problem among subprime mortgage owners; as these individuals lost their homes, the existence of new synthetic mortgage-backed assets based on these subprime loans came to light. These assets were widely owned across the financial system and worth billions of dollars. As US home prices fell, mortgage-based assets tumbled and threatened to bring down the most powerful financial institutions in the world. The crisis spread rapidly to Europe's financial system, bringing down some prominent financial institutions, and reversing carry trades. The crisis in Europe then gained virulence as it was brought to light that Greece's government had been covering up its true budget deficit, which was of course much higher than had been reported.

The causes of the crisis are numerous, and can be classified as both systemic and local, stemming from a lack of appropriate financial regulations, the enormous size of financial companies, problems inherent to the dollar-centered world financial order, and with the rules governing the European Monetary Union. Poor regulation and structural imbalances existed and wreaked havoc when the crisis hit. These were often worsened by political bickering.

As in other crises, such as the Nordic and the Japanese crises, the bursting of a real estate bubble in the US triggered the crisis. It was a very apparent symptom of underlying disease, excessive speculation in the real estate and financial sectors. The symptom forced economists and financial agents to question the stability of the financial system at its very core.

The crisis developed in the medium term as follows: a real estate bubble had developed after the dot-com crash of 2000, when the US Federal Reserve lowered interest rates. An increasing number of risky borrowers took out mortgages in this environment. Mortgage lenders pushed to customers excessively risky mortgages that were misleadingly highly rated by mortgage rating agencies. The Federal Reserve failed to take on the burgeoning real estate bubble and impose appropriate mechanisms to hinder runaway home prices and ensure transparency in banking and securitization practices, since the general consensus was to allow markets to resolve their own problems. When the real estate bubble burst, home prices fell, the risky mortgages failed, and the assets built upon those mortgages posed a threat to the entire US financial system. That a real estate bubble in a subsector of the US economy could have threatened to ruin the US financial system as a whole revealed that something fundamentally wrong was happening in the world of finance. And it was this: the financial system was not only underregulated, but it favored the pursuit of profit by any means while pushing risk to other subsectors, without attention to the impact of this activity. Incentives were wrong: bonuses were paid for this type of profit-seeking behavior rather than for building real economic value; the Federal Reserve was commended for maintaining monetary stability rather than for intervening in the creation of systemic risk.

The crisis spread directly to European banks that held these risky assets, and indirectly abroad through a sharp increase in unemployment and an accompanying decline in spending in the US. In the short run, countries for which the US and Europe are major export markets faced increasing unemployment and rising poverty. Carry trade reversals in Europe also forced several countries into near default. European problems became the focus of attention at the end of 2009, with the emergence of the Greek debt crisis and the eventual exposure of the eurozone's structural weaknesses that have yet to be resolved. In this chapter, we describe the causes, events, and outcomes of the Great Recession.

CAUSES OF THE CRISIS

The immediate causes of the crisis were far less conspicuous than the crisis itself. Therefore they went unnoticed as systemic risk increased. The crisis began at the bottom of the economic pyramid in the US, with new products that allowed subprime, or higher-risk, borrowers to take on risky loans. As housing prices declined and interest rates increased, the subprime borrowers were unable to repay the loans. Figure 8.1 shows the steep decline in home prices in the ten original Case–Shiller metro areas.

One can see from this graph that the home price index rose from 2003 through 2005, and then plunged from 2006 onward. The indices are calculated from data on repeat sales of single family homes. As home prices dropped, subprime borrowers were unable to refinance the new type of

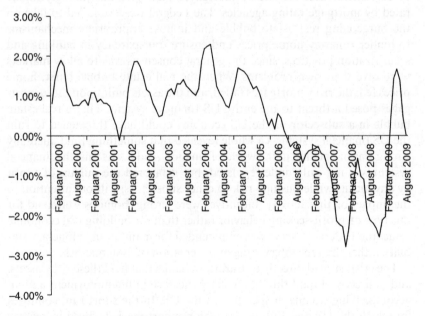

Source: Case–Shiller Home Price Index.

Figure 8.1   Percentage change in Case–Shiller Composite-10 Home Price Index

adjustable rate mortgage (ARM) loans to reasonable interest rates and began to default on their loans. These new ARMs that brokers had sold to risky borrowers offered low introductory interest rates that borrowers were able to pay initially. The ARMs then increased interest rates over time, which the risky borrowers could not pay and were not able to refinance. As a result, many subprime borrowers had their homes foreclosed upon by their banks.

Although the percentage of subprime loans was not high in comparison to the mortgage loan pool as a whole (about 20 percent at the peak of the subprime lending boom[3]), the failure of these loans to poorer individuals spread to mortgage brokers and banks who securitized the loans and sent them on to the large financial institutions, many of which leveraged the loans up to more than 10–12 times the original value (Laubsch 2009). The securitization of subprime loans involved reorganization of the loans themselves (slicing and bundling) and the tranching of risk in very complicated collateralized debt obligations (CDOs), collateralized loan obligations (CLOs), and structured investment vehicles (SIVs), all of which were instruments that did not trade on an exchange but rather traded over-the-counter (OTC). Because no public trading took place, market discipline which could have reduced the prices of these securities in tandem with the onset of falling home prices and increase in risk did not occur. The signal, then, that these were extraordinarily risky instruments was unavailable, and instead the assets were marked to model, not to market.

Marking to model implies that the financial model used to price assets is accurate. However, financial officials somehow did not realize that these bank models, especially the Gaussian Copula Function, did not include periods of prior crises or steep asset price declines (Salmon 2009). Therefore they mispriced the assets at a higher rate. Marking to model and the absence of a risk pricing signal resulted in massive "herd" behavior that failed to take into account the external financial climate.

The extensive use of over-the-counter trading for CDOs, municipal bonds, and credit derivatives created a climate of non-transparency. The volume of OTC derivative contracts expanded from $93 billion in 1997 to $595 trillion in 2007 (BIS 2009). As Dodd (2008) notes, often, in markets that do not electronically post trades, only the dealer and customer observe the price quotes and execution of OTC transactions. These transactions can take place between individuals and dealers, or between dealers themselves. In this climate, particularly when market disturbances occur, it is difficult to value securities or derivatives. After the crisis began, investors did not know who was or was not exposed to subprime risk (Dodd 2007).

It was not an easy task to monitor the bundling of subprime mortgages and their subsequent transfer to financial branches of banks or financial institutions. With the Gramm–Leach–Bliley Act of 1999, institutions could act as both banks and investment banks, and these were not subject to stricter banking regulations (that is, supervision by the Federal Reserve). Banks moved these subprime mortgage bundles off balance sheet and sold them to external investors (Crotty 2009). Therefore, the highly risky assets escaped the notice of auditors and regulators. In addition, banks were undercapitalized and had borrowed large amounts of money through repurchase agreements, leading to a tri-party repo market of possibly $2.75 trillion at its peak (Paulson 2010).

Many parties can be faulted for playing a role in building the excessive risk that caused the crisis. These include those who promoted the gross expansion of banking activities, financial analysts who used the mark-to-model pricing mechanism that could not account for market risk, mortgage lenders that offered excessively risky loans to high-risk borrowers, and credit rating agencies that marked up the rating of securities which did not merit this type of approval. Some also blame the US Federal Reserve for following a policy of low interest rates after the dot-com crash in 2000, but the Federal Reserve may be more to blame for failing to regulate a climate of improbable financial growth. Blame can be easily placed in retrospect; at the time, the lurking damage these assets could cause was entirely unforeseen. Indeed, the migration to usage of "shadow banking" (non-traditional banking) assets was part of a slow transition away from the traditional banking sector and toward the non-traditional banking sector, as the share of presumed-safe assets fell increasingly into non-bank categories. These include money market mutual fund shares, commercial paper, federal funds and repurchase agreements ("repo"), short-term inter-bank loans, Treasuries, agency debt, municipal bonds, securitized debt, and high-grade financial sector corporate debt (Gorton et al. 2012).

Fraud was also a factor. In a report put out in 2007 by Fitch Ratings, Fitch cited a study that was carried out by BasePoint Analytics LLC which examined more than 3 million mortgage loans originated between 1997 and 2006. This firm found that as many as 70 percent of early payment default loans contained fraudulent applications (Galbraith 2014). Sheila Bair and Neil Barofsky indicate in their memoirs that they became aware of pervasive financial fraud as a precursor to the 2008 crisis.

SPREAD OF THE CRISIS TO THE FINANCIAL SYSTEM

As subprime borrowers defaulted, hedge funds trading the bundled sub-prime securities stopped trading. Mortgage originators could not sell their loans, and therefore banks, mortgage brokers, and in turn, the six largest financial institutions that comprise 60 percent of gross domestic product (GDP) in the US (Johnson 2009a), began to face the specter of serious losses. The shocking losses announced by investment bank Bear Stearns in July 2007, the collapse of Germand Sachsen Landesbank in August 2007, and the run on Northern Rock in September 2007, revealed that the sub-prime trouble was beginning to spread. At year end 2007, the US Federal Reserve coordinated an action by five leading central banks around the world to offer billions of dollars in loans to banks (Guillén 2009).

Following that, 2008 was a year of excruciating financial drama. To start the year off, a group of US Treasury officials traveled to Europe to analyze the state of the European banking system, concluding that European banking was in a weak state (Paulson 2010). Global stock markets plunged in January, foreclosure rates increased, and US financial institutions suffered over the course of the year: Bear Stearns was bought out, Fannie Mae and Freddie Mac were taken over by the government, Lehman Brothers went bankrupt, and AIG received a government bailout. Indy Mac Bank became the largest thrift bank ever to fail in the US (Guillén 2009).

Fannie Mae and Freddie Mac were created in 1938 and 1970, respectively, and were both private institutions as of the 1970s that purchased and securitized mortgages (Dodd 2007). They were critical to providing financial backing for consumers to borrow home loans and obtain consumer finance. Due to fears over increasing losses from home foreclosures, these corporations were placed into government conservatorship in September 2008, bringing in new management and receiving injections of liquidity from the Treasury and Federal Reserve under close monitoring of these institutions.

Bear Stearns, exposed to the subprime securities crisis, was bought out by JP Morgan Chase in a Federal Reserve and Treasury-engineered purchase in March 2008. This angered some Congresspeople and frightened European leaders (Paulson 2010). In continuing government intervention, and just after the government takeover of Fannie Mae and Freddie Mac, the imperiled investment bank Lehman Brothers sought a buyer. However, when Lehman Brothers could not find a buyer, the Federal Reserve and Treasury were unable to bail out the firm, and on September 15, 2008, Lehman Brothers declared bankruptcy. Lehman Brothers' bankruptcy represented the largest bankruptcy in US history, at more than $600 billion dollars in debt (Mamudi 2008).

Ferguson and Johnson (2009) and others question the government's actions to bail out Bear Stearns and then refuse to bail out Lehman Brothers, which opened a floodgate of panic in the market. In light of US Treasury Secretary Henry Paulson's (2010) book on the subject, it is

clear that the Federal Reserve and Treasury were unable to legally bail out
Lehman Brothers due to its real capitalization, as opposed to liquidity,
problems. Paulson and other talented industry and government workers
worked strenuously to find a buyer for Lehman Brothers in a matter of
days, to no avail.

Due to large Lehman Brothers' losses in the Reserve Primary Fund,
the oldest US money market fund, the Fund reduced its share value. In
response, US Treasury Secretary Henry Paulson announced that the
Treasury would support all money market mutual funds for a fee (Weiner
2009). AIG, which had insured or purchased mortgage-backed securities to
cover large losses in its securities lending program, then facing potentially
further losses, was bailed out by the government one day after the Lehman
Brothers failure. Equity prices fell dramatically across the world, particularly after the Lehman Brothers bankruptcy, which caused banks to hoard
liquidity (Fender and Gyntelberg 2008). Figure 8.2 shows the fall in equity
indexes during this period.

The sharp decline in stock indexes reflects real losses of value and
a worldwide crisis of confidence in financial markets across the globe.
Grammatikos and Vermeulen (2012) show that financials in Europe

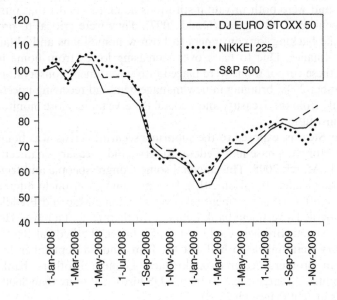

Note: Closing price on January 31, 2008 = 100.

Source: Tel Aviv Stock Exchange (2011).

Figure 8.2   Adjusted closing index prices

became much more dependent on Greek–German credit default swap (CDS) spreads after the collapse of Lehman Brothers.

It is difficult to convey the extent to which the suddenness of the downturn took individuals and policy makers alike by surprise. Former US Federal Reserve Chairman Alan Greenspan himself was startled by the crisis. As he testified in October 2008[4]: "In recent decades, a vast risk management and pricing system has evolved, combining the best insights of mathematicians and finance experts supported by major advances in computer and communications technology . . . This modern risk management paradigm held sway for decades. The whole intellectual edifice, however, collapsed."

In the US, it seemed as if the trouble would never end. Bank of America agreed to a $50 billion rescue package for Merrill Lynch. Morgan Stanley and Goldman Sachs converted from investment banks to traditional commercial banks. Washington Mutual, the largest savings and loan company in the US, was seized by federal regulators and sold to JP Morgan for $1.9 million (Guillén 2009). Wells Fargo acquired Wachovia Bank. Citigroup was bailed out in an asset relief package of $306 billion and eventually split into two entities. Larger financial institutions had engaged in much riskier behavior, mainly through increasing leverage (Bhagat et al. 2015). Tail risks of bank stocks surged in the US as the crisis hit (Straetmans and Chaudhry 2015).

The prospect of mounting failure created circular deterioration in balance sheets even among banks that did not hold claims against their cohorts. This is because, as overall asset prices declined due to the activities of some financial institutions, balance sheets of organizations that held such assets weakened, forcing the institutions to become overleveraged and reducing the size of their balance sheets (Brunnermeier et al. 2009).

In response to the crisis, and to prevent a downward spiral in asset prices, the US Federal Reserve's reaction was to again lower interest rates and work closely with the Treasury to "stop the bleeding." The first proposed solution was embodied in the Troubled Assets Relief Program (TARP), which initially set out to buy bad debts from failing institutions, but then was used to inject liquidity directly into failing institutions in return for government ownership of preferred stock. On behalf of the TARP, it was argued that the failure of large financial institutions would indeed cause a Great Depression rather than a large-scale recession. Large financial institutions were determined to be "too big to fail," even as issues of insolvency at the bottom of the pyramid, among the subprime mortgage holders, increased.

The TARP incited concern and even rage from a number of parties, including the United Steelworkers Union. In a letter to Treasury Secretary Paulson, the Steelworkers wrote on the overvalued purchase of assets:

Your investments do nothing to deal with the causes of the current crisis. Now that even Chairman Greenspan has discovered a "flaw" in his theories, wouldn't it make sense to have some reason to believe that the recipients of this government largesse won't just take the money and do it all again? Perhaps there is some reason I do not understand that you have seemingly handed this chicken coop back to the very same foxes who have been pillaging it for the last two decades? (United Steelworkers Union 2008)

In retrospect, economists such as Simon Johnson,[5] Joseph Stiglitz, and Paul Davidson have pointed out that policy measures such as the TARP contained critical flaws. Firstly, there was the failure to address the problem of risk after the crisis began. The main problem preventing resumption of normal financial activity was not of liquidity, which was provided in spades, but of risk, not knowing how much banks held in bad assets, since these could not even be quantified. Mortgages were allowed to remain on the books of financial institutions at face value, whereas the market value of these assets was obviously much, much lower.

Secondly, the TARP did not require financial institutions to refrain from paying out large bonuses to executives, which essentially transferred taxpayer funds to the wealthiest tier of American workers. There was much outcry over the payment of bonuses to top-level executives who were responsible for creating the crisis to begin with.

And finally, the underlying yet unstated contract behind the program itself was not really fulfilled. The idea was that the additional liquidity would be used to generate loans and alleviate the credit crunch. However, most of these funds were not lent despite prodigious growth in excess reserves, possibly because regulators or banks viewed themselves as under-capitalized due to higher expected losses (Edlin and Jaffee 2009).[6]

This series of events, particularly including the Lehman Brothers bankruptcy, as well as the AIG collapse, the run on the Reserve Primary Fund, and the political opposition faced by the TARP, had a significant negative impact on markets, and were reflected in the rising spread between the interest rate on interbank lending, measured by the London Interbank Offered Rate (LIBOR) on three-month eurodollar deposits, and the interest rate on three-month US Treasury bills, referred to as the "TED spread" (Mishkin 2011). Before this period, it appeared possible to contain the crisis. Afterward, however, it became apparent that the financial system was part of a huge "carry trade," borrowing at low interest rates and purchasing assets that promised higher interest rates along with higher risk. The series of events also strongly challenged government response, and the rejection of the TARP plan significantly weakened the credibility of the government in handling the growing crisis.

The Federal Reserve's creation of a temporary Term Auction Facility

(TAF) that enabled banks to borrow anonymously contributed positively to the view of government (Mishkin 2011). The Federal Reserve's purchase of mortgage-backed securities beginning in November 2008 was also a significant step toward lowering residential mortgage rates and improving housing demand.

Much damage, however, was already done. The American automobile manufacturing industry was the biggest non-financial industry victim of the crisis. The industry, which suffered from ongoing reduced competitiveness and a sudden decline in demand due to the crisis, was forced to turn to the federal government for assistance. General Motors, Ford, and Chrysler faced difficult times, and General Motors and Chrysler filed for bankruptcy.

The climate of uncertainty seeped into every pore of the economy, and was transmitted to Europe and beyond. Global losses due to the credit crisis jumped to $510 billion by the end of August 2008 (Fender and Gyntelberg 2008). In the United Kingdom (UK), the mortgage lender Bradford & Bingley was taken over by the government. The Belgian banking and insurance company Fortis, and Germany's Hypo Real Estate, received capital injections. Worse, as the carry trade, in which investors borrow in low-yield currencies and lend in high-yield currencies, reversed, currency crises loomed large in Eastern Europe. We next turn to the crisis abroad.

THE CRISIS ABROAD

The crisis was particularly virulent in Europe, but affected virtually all areas of the globe, as can be seen in Figure 8.3, which shows the annual GDP growth rate. Since the US was the center of the global economy, the crisis spread rapidly through a number of channels.

The crisis spread abroad directly, through falling values of subprime mortgages and falling demand for global goods; and more widely, indirectly, through a run on global financial institutions ("herd behavior"), the interconnection and dependence of financial systems on short-term funding, and increasing mark-to-market losses that resulted in large sell-offs of asset-backed securities (Kamin and DeMarco 2010). Financial institutions with heavy reliance on short-term funding experienced runs. The crisis in the asset-backed commercial paper market sharply reduced asset-backed commercial paper (ABCP) conduits' ability to fund assets. Foreign exposure to asset-backed securities backed at least in part by US loans was substantial, and declines in asset prices resulted in mark-to-market losses in foreign banks, amounting to $300 billion[7] by the end of 2008.

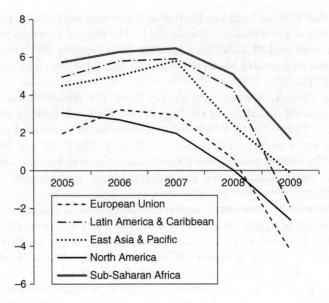

Source: World Bank.

Figure 8.3   Annual GDP growth (%)

Europe's trouble started with Northern Rock in 2007. Northern Rock, a UK retail bank, received emergency support from the Bank of England after losing money from flagging wholesale mortgage markets. The consequence was a run on some of the bank's branches, resulting in the UK government's full guarantee of all bank deposits. Fear in the mortgage market affected other UK banks, and in response, the Bank of England temporarily allowed banks to swap high-quality securities for Treasury bills (Goddard et al. 2009). Bradford & Bingley suffered from mortgage arrears and was split into two entities: half was nationalized, half was purchased by Spanish bank Santander. London Scottish Bank entered administration. Royal Bank of Scotland was affected by fear (not fundamentals) at the end of 2008, resulting in a low stock share price (Aldrick 2008); while HBOS was acquired by Lloyds TSB in order to prevent its collapse. To restore confidence, the UK government created in October 2008 a £50 billion recapitalization fund for troubled banks.

Like Northern Rock, Germany's IKB Deutsche Industriebank was affected in 2007, as its structured investment vehicle Rhineland Funding attempted to call on a line of credit underwritten by IKB and other banks. The line of credit was not universally delivered, and IKB had to be bailed out by Kreditanstalt fur Wiederaufbau (Goddard et al. 2009). Sachsen LB was acquired by Landesbank Baden Wurttenberg. Hypo Real Estate, a holding company for property finance banks, faced severe liquidity problems and was bailed out by the Bundesbank and a group of German banks in an initial €50 billion rescue package. The Bundestag issued an informal guarantee of all non-banks' bank deposits in October 2008. In December 2008, the German parliament passed a €31 billion stimulus package. Commerzbank, Germany's second-largest bank, was partly nationalized in January 2009. Germany then announced its second stimulus package of €50 billion.

Ireland entered crisis as the subprime bubble burst. Anglo Irish Bank, Bank of Ireland, and Allied Irish Banks encountered large losses as the Irish real estate bubble exploded, starting in 2008 (Lewis 2011). Ireland's large construction sector encountered rising unemployment. Irish banks had borrowed from abroad, mainly Germany, to finance the lending boom. The banks were bailed out by taxpayers, since the government issued a guarantee of bank bonds in September of 2008. Anglo Irish Bank was nationalized in January of 2009. Ireland received International Monetary Fund (IMF) and European Union (EU) bailout funds at the end of 2010.

UBS in Switzerland (and to a lesser degree Credit Suisse) also experienced heavy losses in mortgage investments (Goddard et al. 2009). UBS's troubled assets were transferred to a new fund, and the bank received a capital injection from the Swiss government through a convertible bond issue.

Although France did not experience extensive damage to its financial system, French savings bank Caisse d'Epargne announced large losses due to market volatility, and was later merged with Banque Populaire (Guillén 2009). French bank Societe Generale also showed a sharp fall in net profits in November 2008. French President Nicolas Sarkozy announced a €26 billion stimulus plan to invest in the public sector and to extend loans to troubled French carmakers.

Fortis Holdings, a large financial services corporation based in Belgium, the Netherlands, and Luxembourg, faced severe liquidity problems and was saved by the three governments. BNP Paribus acquired Fortis Bank while the governments became minority shareholders (Goddard et al. 2009). The same governments also recapitalized Dexia Group. The Dutch government also recapitalized ING Group and injected 3 billion Euros into the insurance company Aegon. The Belgian government injected €3.5 billion into KBC bank.

Non-European developed countries also suffered. Japan's Nikkei index fell by almost 10 percent, and the country entered recession in November 2008. The Japanese government injected funds into ailing companies in return for equity stakes (Guillén 2009). Japan also passed several stimulus packages to improve employment, help small businesses, and boost consumer spending (BBC 2010). Australia's second-largest investment bank, Babcock & Brown, went into administration in March 2009 (Guillén 2009).

Stress from the US and Europe resulted in increased volatility in exchange rates in emerging markets (Coudert et al. 2011). As contagion quickly spread to developed and then developing countries, many countries implemented fiscal stimulus packages and altered monetary policies in order to reduce unemployment and falling GDP. The central banks of the United States, European Union, United Kingdom, China, Canada, Sweden, and Switzerland made coordinated interest rate cuts for the first time in history. China, India, and the EU announced large stimulus packages to stir domestic demand and production. As Shirakawa (2009) points out, most of these stabilization programs were often implemented without global coordination, creating gaps in government guarantees for depositors and creditors between countries. Shirakawa and others viewed coordination as an important aspect of crisis containment because it directly affects the smooth liquidity transfer across currencies and regions. But policy makers were executing emergency measures.

The crisis continued and international and domestic authorities sought to stop the financial freefall, as international banks failed, the carry trade from Japan and Switzerland unraveled, and demand for exports in developed countries plunged. The IMF provided emergency loans to Hungary, Ukraine, Iceland, and Latvia, which had suffered severe reversals in the carry trade. Governmental collapse in Iceland was followed by that in Belgium and Latvia. The IMF also signed standby agreements with Byelorussia, El Salvador, Georgia, Greece, Ireland, Pakistan, Serbia, the Seychelles, and Romania.

Iceland's collapse occurred after the three largest commercial banks found they could not refinance their short-term debt. Iceland's crisis began before the global financial crisis (Landler 2008), as the country's commercial banks had expanded its assets to several times Iceland's GDP. The real exchange rate had fallen greatly in the lead-up to the debt default as foreign investors questioned whether Iceland's banks might default on their foreign loans. A number of Icelandic banks experienced sharp liquidity problems. Glitnir was the first, and was taken over by the government (BBC 2009). The nation's largest bank, Kaupthing, was also taken over by the government. The Icelandic Internet bank Icesave froze deposits in October 2008 (Guillén 2009). Landsbanki, first seized by the Icelandic Financial Supervisory Authority, entered bankruptcy in December 2008. A long boom period was threatened with imminent reversal and necessitated an emergency loan from the IMF.

Hungary's crisis occurred as foreign investors in the country's government securities withdrew their funds as the global crisis hit, causing enormous downward pressure on the currency. Many housing loans had been denominated in foreign currencies. Latvia requested IMF assistance after it found itself unable to pull out of a sharp recession, due to falling demand caused by high inflation and contagion from the global crisis. Hungary and Latvia both had net foreign currency liabilities of close to 50 percent of GDP in 2008 (Mihaljek 2009). These two countries were among a group of EU transition countries – including the Czech Republic, Hungary, Poland, Romania, Bulgaria, Estonia, Latvia, and Lithuania – that had formerly been Communist countries and were financially liberalized with accession to the EU (Gardó and Martin 2010). The EU transition countries experienced rapid growth and stronger integration with the EU leading up to the crisis, and strong, foreign-financed credit growth. It was reversals in foreign lending, as well as interruption of trade, which threatened the countries from the last quarter of 2008 through the first quarter of 2009. Hungary and Latvia were casualties of a severe credit crunch during this period.

Greece faced potential sovereign default due to excessive government deficits and cheap loans whose interest rates increased after the crisis hit. National debt was larger than the country's economy (CNN 2010). Greece's credit rating was downgraded to the lowest in the eurozone. The country was extended a loan by the IMF in May 2010, and leaders imposed austerity measures to sharply cut the deficit. Spain and Portugal were strongly affected by Greece's troubles due to their own indebtedness. Portugal negotiated loan terms with the IMF. Spain implemented a relatively large fiscal stimulus package of €1.1 billion to create 300 000 jobs in November 2008, but the stimulus package did not prevent continuing fears of a sovereign debt crisis.

Developing countries such as China, Thailand, and Vietnam experienced immediate shortfalls in their large export sectors (Johanssen 2010). The effect of a sudden decline in demand for exports abroad, as well as in external credit availability, strongly affected export-oriented economies. Export-oriented countries at a higher level of financial development weathered the crisis better than those which experienced a sudden tightening in credit. Sub-Saharan Africa, for example, was impacted by a sudden decline in demand for exports, as well as a decline in trade-related finance (Benedictus 2011). Sub-Saharan Africa lost access to global financial markets, although official development assistance continued to be honored (Bandara 2014). Countries and, in particular, industries that were financially vulnerable during the crisis were very sensitive to the cost of credit (Chor and Manova 2010).

China announced a $586 billion stimulus package to stimulate domestic demand by expanding infrastructure and improving social welfare programs. The stimulus package focused on spending, over two years, on health care, education, low-income housing, environmental protection, programs to promote technological innovation, transport and other infrastructure projects, and reconstruction after the Sichuan earthquake (*The Economist* 2008).

Singapore slid into recession in October 2008 (Guillén 2009). India's central bank cut short-term lending rates in response to the global crisis. South Korea announced a $130 billion financial rescue package for its faltering economy. Malaysia implemented two stimulus packages to boost the private sector. Pakistan, on the verge of default, was granted an emergency loan by the IMF.

Russia moved into crisis even before the global fallout hit. Threats by Prime Minister Putin against companies over back taxes and the Russian invasion of Georgia caused massive capital flight, resulting in a stock market plunge (Mankoff 2010). A fall in commodity prices due to reduced global demand greatly harmed Russia's export market and led the country into crisis (Gaddy and Ickes 2010). In response, the government implemented a large stimulus package, which helped to contain unemployment and poverty. The ruble underwent speculative attacks and was stabilized by a series of small devaluations.

SIGNS OF RECOVERY IN THE US, DOWNTURN IN EUROPE

As the crisis spread, US President Barack Obama was sworn into office in February 2009, and immediately instituted a large fiscal stimulus package to create jobs, increase welfare funding, and provide tax cuts. The package was a compromise between Democrats and Republicans, and its impact has been effective even though the components of the package itself have been criticized.[8] The US fiscal stimulus package provided $282 billion in tax cuts, and $505 billion on new projects in energy, science and technology, infrastructure, education, and health care (Teslik 2009). Quantitative easing, particularly under programs such as the Large Scale Asset Purchase (LSAP) program in which the Federal Reserve purchased long-term assets, provided a buffer against recession in the US and elsewhere (Chen et al. 2015).

In Europe, the European Commission put into place an economic recovery plan worth €200 billion to reduce unemployment and stimulate spending. The plan provided funds (outside of automatic stabilizers) to improve infrastructure, bolster key sectors, and provide social insurance for the unemployed (European Commission 2009). The goal was to promote regional competitiveness in the medium run.

At this point in time, despite the depth of the crisis, the international environment was hopeful and primed to instill a new financial architecture that could potentially address some fundamental problems with the existing world order that have created global imbalances and excessive financial interdependency. Much hope was pinned on the Group of Twenty (G-20) meeting in April 2009 to reduce the dominance of the dollar and reform the role of finance. Some economists hoped that a new, universal currency or basket of currencies might be created to reduce the hegemony of the dollar and shrink global trade and wealth imbalances, and that the role of finance in profit and politics, which has led to global instability, might be reduced.

However, this important meeting resulted instead in promises to improve financial regulation and commit some IMF funds for loans to developing countries in crisis. The moment for the creation of a new Bretton Woods-style financial restructuring passed, and this was underscored both by the quieting of voices for systemic reform, as well as by the US Treasury's proposal put forth in June 2009 (passed in 2010) for moderate reform of the financial regulatory system (US Treasury Department 2009).

Fortunately for the US, external funding through bond sales remained high as investors fled to safer assets (Caballero 2010). This was in sharp contrast to most other crises, in which investors fled the crisis countries, and it was continuing bond purchases that allowed the US to escape the same fate as crisis nations with less attractive assets. The flight to safety, however, harmed developed countries in Latin America, Africa, Eastern Europe, and Southeast Asia, resulting in a rise in interest rates (Soros 2012).

Although the impact of the crisis varied by country and social group, at the end of 2009, a few signs that the global economy was improving were present. In July 2009, China reported a 7.9 percent growth rate in the second quarter due to the effects of its stimulus package. In October 2009, the Dow Jones Industrial Average closed above 10000 for the first time since 2008, when it plunged under the benchmark number (Healy 2009).

Developing countries that had ample "buffer" space for absorbing shocks, that were able to implement countercyclical fiscal policy, and had strong banking and financial sectors before the crisis, appeared to recover quickly (Nabli 2010). Although global GDP growth was reported at 3.9 percent in 2010, and was at 3 percent in 2011, developing country growth rose to 7 percent in 2010, and to 6 percent in 2011 (World Bank 2011).

In Europe, however, trouble was brewing. In October 2009, Greece declared that its budget deficit was higher for 2009 than had been reported – much higher – and would be high relative to expectations for 2010 as well. This caused panic through the eurozone, as banks in many countries held Greek debt, which suddenly plummeted in value as its near risk-free status was lowered to "Very Risky." Greece's debt amounted to 113 percent of GDP, almost double the eurozone limit of 60 percent (BBC 2012a).

THE EUROZONE CRISIS

The eurozone crisis began with Greece and threatened other nations as well, as the fear of overindebtedness grew. Greece had engaged in over-spending before it joined the euro, and only increased spending afterward. Tax evasion prevented the government from obtaining much-needed funds to cover increases in spending. With the coming of the Great Recession, Greece experienced an external shock that exposed its high levels of indebtedness and made it impossible for the government to continue paying on its debts. The new Greek socialist government elected in October 2009 announced higher-than-reported debt levels.

The Greek crisis spread, as little to nothing was done to stop the decline in Greek debt. By May 2010, Greece was presented with a bailout package of €22 billion from the eurozone and IMF (BBC 2012a). The crisis spread to other countries that were in deficit, including Spain and Italy, and in response the European Financial Stabilization Fund of €750 billion was created. The fund did little to reassure markets, since conditions for fund distribution were dictated by Germany, which was unwilling to bail out deficit countries (Soros 2012). Germany fell back upon the Maastricht Treaty as a guideline for conducting emergency activity (stating that no bailouts shall be carried out) within the European Union, refusing to change the rules to meet the needs of debtor countries. Even so, due to the fear that Greece's descent into crisis would sharply damage the eurozone through interconnectedness of the financial sectors, a second bailout package of €109 billion was agreed upon to prevent contagion to other economies.

The peripheral eurozone economies had remained relatively uncompetitive before the crisis struck. Wages increased more quickly than productivity, while education and other institutions lagged behind. These countries were therefore quite susceptible to the crisis. Portugal fell into crisis and was bailed out at €78 billion by the European Union and the IMF. The country received funds for bank recapitalization – BCP and BPI received €3.5 billion and €1.5 billion in return for convertible bonds – and committed to austerity measures that would reduce wages and pensions and even cut some national holidays (Evans-Pritchard 2012). Portugal, like Greece, had engaged in overspending, and had an increasingly large current account deficit. The global crisis acted as an impetus for Portugal's debt crisis as investors withdrew funds from savings certificates and bonds, raising bond yields.

Spain was forced to bail out savings banks and municipalities. The country had also experienced a real estate boom, with housing prices rising 44 percent between 2004 and 2008, and a corresponding crash (BBC 2012b). By April 2012, the government had injected more than €34 billion into its banks. In addition, Bankia, the country's fourth-largest bank, received €19 billion before it was nationalized. Spain was to borrow up to €100 billion from the European Financial Stability Facility and the European Stability Mechanism to continue to shore up its banking sector.

Smimou and Khallouli (2015) find that contagion of the global crisis was transmitted to eurozone countries through liquidity channels, as wealthy investors in one nation reduced investment in another nation in an atmosphere of increased risk, and overall liquidity declined. Negative shocks stemmed from financial linkages within European stock markets and from US financial channels.

Changes in financial flows occurred as the crisis played out. Acharya and Steffen (2015) characterize changes in financial flows within the eurozone as carry trade behavior. The carry trade is generated by positive loading on peripheral bonds and negative loading on German bonds. The authors explain this behavior through regulatory capital arbitrage and risk shifting by undercapitalized banks, home bias of banks in peripheral countries, and inducement by sovereign bodies and home countries to maintain bond holdings. Large banks and banks with high levels of short-term leverage, high-risk weighted assets, and low Tier 1 capital ratios held larger quantities of peripheral sovereign debt. In addition, peripheral banks that were bailed out held higher levels of peripheral bonds.

Fiscal tightening at both the center and the periphery of the European Union did not help matters. France, Spain, Ireland, and Greece were ordered to reduce their budget deficits starting in April 2009 (BBC 2012a). Greece's austerity plan became a source of major unrest, as successive budget cuts were made to appease international lenders. Portuguese workers protested austerity measures as the government followed the measures closely. Spain passed a constitutional amendment that required limiting future budget deficits; while Italy passed a large austerity budget with an eye to balancing the budget by 2013.

In Europe, austerity measures bred anti-government protests, as social protection was in some cases decreased rather than increased even as workers lost their jobs. The decline in social protection was particularly worrisome in a region that already had a relatively high rate of unemployment, at 7 percent in 2007 and at 15.5 percent for younger workers, before the crisis took hold (Euzéby 2010).

Monetary policy measures carried out by the European Central Bank (ECB) were relatively cautious. Non-standard monetary policies included fixed-rate full-allotment for longer term refinancing operations (LTRO), the Covered Bond Purchase Program, Securities Markets Program, and Outright Monetary Transactions. The three-year LTRO carried out in December 2011 and February 2012 represented the biggest attempt to inject liquidity into the European banking system (Pronobis 2014). The ECB also purchased sovereign bonds in order to lower the borrowing costs of Greece, Italy, Portugal, and Spain.

As the crisis wore on, country debt was downgraded in the US and the eurozone. At the end of summer 2011, Standard & Poor's downgraded US debt for the first time, from AAA to AA+, due to the country's inability to curb deficits. In January 2012, Standard & Poor's downgraded sovereign debt ratings of nine eurozone countries: France, Austria, Spain, Italy, Portugal, Malta, Cyprus, Slovenia, and Slovakia (Gauthier-Villars 2012). Greece's sovereign debt rating slid far further down the ratings scale to "selective default" in February 2012. Sovereign downgrades, coupled with political uncertainty, played a key role in increasing Greek sovereign spreads (Gibson et al. 2014). To underscore this, Kazanas and Tzavalis (2014) find that credit ratings impacted Greece separately from economic fundamentals; these affected credit spreads independently from real indicators.

The EU approved a macroeconomic surveillance structure that consisted of a European Banking Authority, a European Securities and Markets Authority, a European Insurance and Occupational Pensions Authority, and a European Systemic Risk Board (ESRB) (European Commission 2010). These entities were set up to reduce systemic risk, ensure regional rule compliance, and regulate cross-border firms. However, it has become clear that there are structural flaws in the eurozone that must also be overcome if the eurozone is to survive long term. Eichengreen (2012) makes the case that these flaws in the eurozone are parallel to those in the global financial system. Specifically, the absence of a sufficient adjustment mechanism to account for imbalances, where devaluation of currency for one country is impossible given the zone-wide use of the currency, and the lack of bank regulation at the union level, which encourages neglect of cross-border impacts of policies, remain a problem. The European Banking Authority may ameliorate the latter problem, but implementation of policies is local. Similarly, currency and financial regulation policy imbalances remain problems at the global level.

Germany was strongly and negatively impacted by the global crisis through export channels, but rebounded rapidly. The cause of its resilience has been attributed to wage competitiveness as well as to technological prowess. Stockhammer (2015) states that German growth has been based on wage suppression. Storm and Naastepad (2015) make the case that Germany's technological, or non-price competitiveness and high-tech productive capabilities, trump other reasons for its rapid post-crisis restoration of growth, based on Kaldor's theory which states that the effects of relative costs on exports are relatively weak.

GREECE'S TRAGEDY

Greece had been considered a post-war growth miracle: economic growth was much higher than the Organisation for Economic Co-operation and Development (OECD) average in the 1960s and 1970s as Greece industrialized, according to Tsafos (2013). During the 1980s the state expanded sharply and state spending increased radically, as subsidies for state-owned enterprises and social transfers grew. Incentives to increase productivity declined, as did the process of industrialization. Growth prospects therefore declined.

Greece joined the eurozone on January 1, 2001. Greece's living standards were low in comparison to the rest of Europe in the early 2000s. State expenditures were only rising and increased greatly in 2009. Greece was also on a path of expanding neoliberalism before the crisis hit. Morales et al. (2014) argue that the crisis presented a critical juncture, at which Greece might have abandoned its neoliberal track, but that rather than doing so, Greece chose to consolidate the neoliberal agenda. In addition to short-term austerity measures, long-term neoliberal structural changes were recommended. An increase in labor market flexibility and emphasis on the tradeable rather than the non-tradeable sector was stressed. However, wages in the tradeable sector rose by 5.5 percent between 2000 and 2009, and 16.5 percent in the non-tradeable sector, indicating that adjustment should come from internal devaluation in the non-tradeable sector (Kouretas 2010). Much of the wage growth occurred in the public sector, and was coupled with an increase in the number of public sector employees. As such, Tsafos (2013) classifies Greek debt as a symptom of its structural economic problems, which arose from its inefficient civil service, excessive spending on pensions, corruption, tax evasion, a poor business environment, and an overregulated private sector. Greece also faced a current account deficit before the crisis began (Figure 8.4), revealing problems with its fixed exchange rate regime as well as a decline in competitiveness.

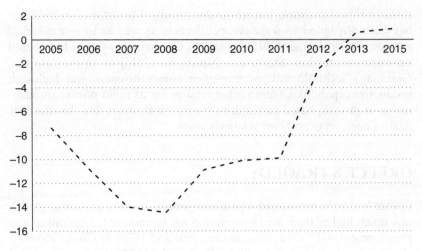

Figure 8.4   Greece's current account balance (% of GDP)

Greece's government sector was tied to the private sector, since most business contracts came from the government. This system failed to promote competition and innovation in the private sector. Tax evasion was rampant, limiting government revenues. Furthermore, the government preceding the crisis, from 2004 to 2009, even decreased capital taxation by 10 percent.

When the new Greek government announced a higher-than-realized government budget deficit in 2009, it became clear that Greece's case was serious. The country was at first not allowed to receive a bailout, to attain interest rate relief, or to default. The no-bailout clause was a component of the Maastricht Treaty. This posed an insurmountable barrier to debt reduction, as Greece was forced to borrow at very high interest rates to fund its deficit. Greece aimed to correct its own deficit by cutting bonuses and raising taxes. The aim was to reduce the deficit to 2.8 percent of GDP by 2012, from 12.7 percent of GDP in 2009. However, the results of these actions were relatively disappointing, and it had become clear that Greece would need a bailout to improve its debt position. After a liquidity crunch in global bond markets, finally, in May 2010, Greece received bilateral loans of €80 billion pooled by the European Commission to be disbursed between May 2010 and June 2013. The IMF financed a standby arrangement of €30 billion. Loans were to be aimed at covering the government's fiscal and medium to long-term liabilities until the end of 2011, and less thereafter. Greece attempted to eliminate some of its debts by reducing social security spending and pensions and privatizing public assets. The alternative to accepting a bailout and embarking on austerity measures was to default, which would most likely result in the collapse of the financial system and a severe depression. However, the market response to the bailout remained pessimistic, and the public response to austerity measures turned violent at times.

One of the major issues after the crisis began was that Greek labor markets increased in flexibility. Dismissal notice periods were shortened, permanent employees were replaced with part-time workers, collective dismissals (firing a large number of workers) were freed of restrictions, and employment protection declined. Gialis and Tsampra (2015) find that the negative impact of the crisis on national employment was severe and homogeneous across almost all regions. Closing businesses did not help matters either. Many skilled workers lost their jobs with little job growth to compensate for the losses. The Greek people voiced their dissent through protests, as well as through the promotion of the leftist, anti-austerity political party Syriza.

George Papandreou was not up to the task of saving Greece. Papandreou created political crises in November 2010, in June 2011, and in October 2011. In 2010 he made the elections about his premiership and the bailout agreements, declaring success after the ambiguous first-round results (Tsafos 2013). In 2011 Papandreou offered to the leader of the opposition to step down from his premiership but later announced a cabinet reshuffle. In October 2011, after a debt restructuring with the private sector, Papandreou requested a vote on the debt restructuring plan. All of these moves undermined confidence in the Prime Minister's ability to lead the country out of crisis. In November 2011 Papandreou resigned and Lucas Papademos became the new Prime Minister.

Events in 2011 cast a negative light on Greece's economic situation. Greece's 2009 deficit was revised upward to 16 percent of GDP, while the eurozone announced that crises after 2013 would require bailout participation of private creditors. Greece's implementation of austerity measures, strong through 2010, slackened in 2011 (Ardagna and Caselli 2014).

On March 14, 2012, the Second Economic Adjustment Programme for Greece was approved, with an additional €130 billion to be used for 2012–14, financed by the European Financial Stability Facility. Greece carried out a bond swap, swapping privately held bonds for longer maturity bonds at lower nominal values. Internal devaluation required the productive sector to devalue incomes, in an attempt to improve export performance. Elections held in May 2012 resulted in no overwhelming majority. A second round of elections was held in June 2012. Unemployment rose from 9.5 percent in 2009 to 24.2 percent in 2012, and surged to 27.5 percent in 2013.

A far-left, anti-austerity government headed by Syriza's Alexis Tsipras was elected in January of 2015, widening the gulf between Greek officials and European creditors. In June 2015, Greece defaulted on a loan payment to the IMF. In a referendum held on July 5, 2015, Greek voters rallied to reject austerity measures. One week later, Greece was given a third bailout package and Greece agreed to continue on the road to reform (Nelson et al. 2015). Reforms were to continue in the same vein of austerity as before, aiming to improve tax collection, expand market liberalization, and reduce spending on pensions.

Observers have searched for an explanation of why Greece and the eurozone failed to function in a healthy manner during the crisis. A dominant explanation is that within Europe, there were necessarily deficit and surplus nations with Germany being the most powerful surplus nation of all. Deficit nations had joined the eurozone in order to avoid constant devaluations. However necessarily low levels of inflation, required by the Maastricht treaty in exchange for joining the eurozone, led to a stagnation of wages in peripheral countries. Varoufakis (2013) makes the case that because Europe lacks an effective currency recycling mechanism in contrast to the United States its currency union has faced major issues. This is because Germany has relied upon peripheral countries as last resort sources of demand. In a deficit country the crisis would have an impact of requiring countries to reduce debt, cut spending; as a result, overall demand would decline, increasing unemployment and depressing prices; thus creating a cycle of debt and deflation.

To some degree, the problems with Greece were inherent to the eurozone. Because eurozone politicians guaranteed that no eurozone countries would default, Greece's debt was initially overvalued to begin with, as Greece was allowed to borrow at German-type low-level interest rates (Soros 2012). This allowed Greece to run up its debt to begin with. What is more, the eurozone lacked a common Treasury, so that individual countries were forced to take care of their own banks. Greece was unable to do so, even though Prime Minister George Papandreou insisted external assistance was unnecessary, and other countries were unenthusiastic about bailing Greece out.

Parallels have been drawn between the pre-1914 gold standard and other currency union crises, and the European monetary crisis occurring after 2008. Bordo and James (2014) identify similarities between the pre-1914 gold standard and European monetary union today. The authors note that both currency structures are based on fixed exchange rates, monetary and fiscal orthodoxy, and a relationship between peripheral and core countries. In the case of the gold standard, countries were able to temporarily devalue their currencies, but the European monetary union lacked such a recourse. Bordo and James also make the distinction between pre-1914 countries that were able to borrow in their own currencies versus countries that were unable to borrow in their own currencies, the latter which was dubbed "original sin." Financial centers without "original sin" and strong fundamentals were able to avoid financial crises. Similarly, core European countries remained stable during the current crisis while peripheral countries, particularly Greece, found it extremely difficult to absorb debt.

Another imbalance generated by the eurozone union was the inability of countries to alter exchange rates. Papanikos (2015) argues that the euro was overvalued, resulting in low levels of growth in Greece since Greece could not devalue the currency to promote exports and tourism.

When the eurozone crisis hit, European banks found they had a great deal of eurozone debt without a common European banking union. In response, the European Commission and the European Central Bank socialized bank losses and turned them into public debt. The makings of a public debt crisis were brought about by the surge in demand for credit default swaps taken out against peripheral countries like Greece.

SOVEREIGN RISK

Greece's floundering financial status has led some financial experts to closely examine sovereign risk. Sovereign risk can rise when sovereign debt increases as a result of regular government spending and when sovereign debt increases in response to an external shock, such as a banking crisis. Both of these occurred recently, in some places together. As the Bank for International Settlements has noted, sovereign credit quality in developed economies has declined in recent years, although at the same time, the global crisis has necessarily increased the level of protection implemented against sovereign risk.

The global financial crisis that originated in the US and spread to Europe was the first to increase sovereign risk, as countries sought to bail out banks and implement fiscal stimulus packages to prevent contagion. Ludwig (2014) refers to the repricing of sovereign risk after the common shock of the financial crisis "wake-up call contagion." Pricing of sovereign risk behaved differently before and after the crisis, as market participants became more sensitive to risk and were impacted by regional, rather than strictly local, macroeconomic fundamentals (Gomez-Puig et al. 2014). Fiscal stimulus, however, resulted in larger fiscal deficits and reduced the ability of governments to repay debt, pushing up sovereign risk. Banks and sovereigns became intertwined as the crisis spread. Heightened sovereign risk then impacted bank lending as funding costs increased, creating a liquidity squeeze (Cantero-Saiz et al. 2014). Funding costs may rise as lenders' perceived economic risk increases, and/or as strained public finances raise the cost of financial intermediation (Corsetti et al. 2012).

Banks' positions deteriorated as sovereign risk rose. Sovereign exposure by banks to potential contagion was impacted through several channels: a guarantee channel, an asset holdings channel, and a collateral channel (De Bruyckere et al. 2013). Assets or collateral held in the form of sovereign debt all faced potential losses, and explicit or implicit government guarantees lost credibility. Further, banks and sovereigns became further connected as the crisis wore on, as public sector balance sheets were used to shore up financial sectors.

Assessing the true level of sovereign risk became critical at this time, as credit default swap (CDS) spreads failed to fully reflect the reality of sovereign risk (procyclically overstating or understating risk). Pricing of sovereign risk pre-crisis reflected country fundamentals far less than pricing of sovereign debt during the crisis, especially in the peripheral European countries that underwent a deterioration in sovereign debt (Beirne and Fratzscher 2013). CDS spreads followed a weak form of price efficiency during the crisis but remained volatile (Gündüz and Kaya 2014). Greece and Portugal experienced increasing spreads that reflected not only their own default risk, but also spillover effects of default risk from other peripheral countries (Kohonen 2014).

A number of new models were proposed to better assess sovereign risk. Analysis based on macroeconomic fundamentals, most importantly the net international investment position to GDP ratio and the public debt to GDP ratio, has been proposed by Agliardi et al. (2014). Modeling of sovereign risk contagion ("default risk connectedness") based on CDS and bond yield data has been carried out by Gätjen and Schienle (2015). Commercial sovereign risk models have been created by Thomson Reuters (the Starmine Sovereign Risk Model), BlackRock (BlackRock Sovereign Risk Index), and others to prevent investment in countries with a Greece-like surge in sovereign risk. Even another aspect of sovereign risk was proposed, currency redenomination risk, referring to the risk that a euro asset would be redenominated into a devalued legacy currency (De Santis 2015).

At this point, it is well recognized that assuming zero risk for sovereign exposure is a mistake. European banks in particular held insufficient capital to guard against sovereign risk stemming from both domestic and non-domestic sovereign bond holdings. Korte and Steffen (2014) refer to this as the "sovereign subsidy," or amount of sovereign risk that is unaccounted for. The way in which the sovereign subsidy is applied is through classification of highly rated government bonds as highly liquid assets, exclusion of zero-risk weighted sovereign bonds from limits to large exposures, use of low capital requirements for government bond-collateralized exposures, and low capital requirements on select sovereign exposures. The European Systemic Risk Board (2015) produced recommendations to improve Basel III treatment of sovereign exposure. For banks, these include tightening Pillar 1 capital requirements to account for sovereign exposure, improving Pillar 2 requirements through implementation of stress tests or qualitative guidance on diversification, and enhancing Pillar 3 disclosure requirements on sovereign exposure. Still, reform is slow in the making because selling zero- or low-risk bonds is extremely attractive to governments. Governments are loath to reclassify sovereign bonds as risky.

Another issue is that resources for dealing with this type of financial destabilization within the eurozone must be strengthened. Macroeconomic stabilization tools available to countries within the eurozone are limited, as there is no regional fiscal policy, but interest and exchange rates are shared (Ballabriga 2014). Eurozone countries cannot issue debt in their own currencies, a fact that has helped to transform heightened sovereign risk into sovereign crisis. Therefore, while monitoring for sovereign risk is certainly important, it has limited effect if stabilization tools do not function well. Eurozone countries are not equal in terms of risk, yet they are forced to operate within the same monetary and currency specifications without sufficient fiscal coordination.

While the European Central Bank was forced to operate outside its mandate by purchasing sovereign debt as a lender of last resort, it was necessary to do so since member countries do not control the currency and therefore cannot guarantee that they will repay sovereign bonds. Going forward, however, a mechanism to promote the ECB as lender of last resort in the bond market would help to backstop sovereign bond markets in the face of increasing financial fragility. It has been noted that the lack of safe bonds presents a problem, as sovereign bonds reflect fiscal conditions outside the control of the central authority. To combat this problem, Illing and König (2014) suggest the construction of synthetic euro bonds, a portfolio of all euro bonds weighted by members' contribution to GDP.

Steps toward the creation of a European banking union have been made; this is one positive outcome of the eurozone crisis. The banking union requires an integrated supervision system. However, the process of setting up a banking union has slowed as countries with strong banks balked at turning over supervision to a central authority. Therefore, centralized banking control has been limited, and countries agreed to the supervision of the 130 largest banks (Eichengreen 2014).

Conditions in the eurozone's periphery gradually improved. Spain's level of sovereign risk has improved as fiscal austerity has been implemented to reduce the fiscal deficit. As Yuan and Pongsiri (2015) note, fiscal austerity practices generally led to reduction in CDS spreads. Ireland's sovereign risk has also declined due to the presence of economic growth and declining debt ratios. However, overall sovereign risk in the eurozone's peripheral countries remains somewhat high as fundamentals lag behind. France, for example, has insufficiently adjusted its fiscal deficit in the face of high structural unemployment and low growth. Italy has rebounded even slower than France and other eurozone peers as competitiveness has declined and unemployment has remained high. Cyprus continues to face high levels of debt and a weak banking sector. In the eurozone overall, signs of weakness in the core financial systems are still apparent. In EU-wide bank stress tests conducted in October 2014, 25 out of 130 banks failed. Credit risk exposure was responsible for the majority of these failures.

Greece in particular has faced a plunging sovereign rating, having been downgraded to CCC– by Standard & Poor's after defaulting on a €1.6 billion loan installment in June. Greece's fundamentals are quite poor, with extremely high unemployment and poor growth due to stifling austerity measures, an inefficient public sector, and burdensome pension system. It has been projected that Greek debt may peak at 200 percent of GDP and fall to 150 percent of GDP by 2024; however, Cline (2015) asserts that the debt burden is lower than it actually appears due to concessional interest rates on debt owed to the euro area's official sector.

Sovereign risk is in a state of flux at present as recovery from the eurozone crisis will take time to become fully established. Still, Calice et al. (2013) show that coordinated action from the eurozone dampened the sharply negative impact of the crisis on trade and sovereign debt instruments for several troubled eurozone countries. The authors use time-varying vector autoregression in order to illustrate the impact of cross-liquidity effects on eurozone sovereign debt and CDS spreads during the crisis.

The eurozone's quantitative easing policy has reduced returns on eurozone bonds, with some returns even being sold at a negative yield. This policy has reduced yield spreads relative to the German Bund, compressing risk and reducing the overall size of the sovereign bond market. The risk of sovereign debt default is being shared between the European Central Bank and the national central banks, which hold 92 percent of purchased bonds on their balance sheets. The extent to which quantitative easing will get the eurozone back on the path to growth and stability has yet to be seen; so far, the outcome is mixed. Going forward, it is hoped that Europe can overcome its exhausting state of sovereign fragility and move toward a unified recovery.

OUTCOMES

In September 2008, as bank failures spread and the depth of the crisis became clear, there was fear that the crisis would instigate a financial and economic disaster as profound as that of the Great Depression. Certainly, Eichengreen and O'Rourke (2009) show that the beginning of the US financial crisis was worse than the Great Depression in terms of declines in global stock markets and the volume of world trade. A Great Depression was avoided only through countercyclical fiscal and monetary policy. Indeed, the idea that fiscal and monetary policy used worldwide in the Great Recession, as compared to the Great Depression, effectively combated the crisis, has been successfully empirically tested by Almunia et al. (2010) and others. Without countercyclical policy approaches, the crisis would have a much worse impact around the world.

The extreme fallout from the US portion of the crisis had mainly dissipated by the end of 2009, but the real effects of the crisis continued to be strongly felt. Jobs continued to lag and many citizens in the US remained disgruntled, fueling union protests. The Occupy Wall Street movement included a series of continuing, national protests against corporate greed and unemployment. Sixty percent of American households experienced a decline in wealth between 2007 and 2009 (Deaton 2011). Corresponding worry and stress followed, particularly as unemployment climbed.

In the US, the Dodd–Frank Wall Street Reform and Consumer Protection Act of 2010 was passed to create a consumer protection bureau, discourage "too big to fail" bailouts, create an advance warning system of potential financial instability, and eliminate loopholes used to create destabilizing financial instruments (US Senate Banking Committee 2010). The law addressed both microeconomic- and macroeconomic-level regulation. In order to accomplish these goals, the bill created a Consumer Financial Protection Bureau, to regulate consumer protection, and a Financial Stability Oversight Council which would have the important responsibility of making recommendations to the Federal Reserve for stricter rules on capital and liquidity, increased regulation of non-bank financial institutions, and the break-up of large companies as a last resort. The Financial Stability Oversight Council would move toward designating particular shadow banking institutions as systemically important, and put them under further supervision and further regulation (Lowrey 2012). Creation of the council was an attempt to prevent future crisis caused by systemic financial failure; whether it will be successful has yet to be seen.

Emerging market economies were more strongly affected by the 2007–08 portion of the financial crisis (US and European financial crisis) than by the 2010–11 portion of the crisis (sovereign debt crisis) (Chudik and

Fratzscher 2012). The liquidity squeeze caused by a flight-to-safety reaction to the financial crisis in 2008 removed much-needed funds from emerging markets; but after the shock was overcome, funds to emerging markets resumed, and the eurozone crisis did not cause another reversal of capital inflows. Capital flows from emerging markets increased as a result of "push" factors (flight to safety) and flowed back into emerging markets because of "pull" factors (divergences in profitability between developed and emerging markets) (Fratzscher 2011).

There was little movement, at the national or regional levels, toward improving the impact of the current world financial order on the poor in both developed and developing nations. The United Nations (UN) and the World Trade Organization (WTO) made suggestions for revising the global financial structure to improve the lot of the poor (UN 2009a). Some suggestions were to reduce procyclicality and volatility, to protect food and energy (commodities) from speculation, to implement global stimulus measures, and to ensure that commercial practices do not destroy the environment. During the US financial meltdown, attention was certainly not trained on the world's poor, and eurozone austerity measures further impoverished families in the developed nations themselves. Although the IMF suggested that eurozone authorities refrain from cutting programs that provide assistance to the poor, there was little the countries could do to avoid it in meeting eurozone–IMF conditionality measures. What is more, the ongoing eurozone crisis is affecting developing countries through trade channels, as well as through declines in remittances, foreign direct investment, cross-border bank lending and aid flows (Massa et al. 2012).

The crisis disproved the idea that financial markets tend toward efficiency. It was largely assumed, before the crisis, that financial crisis was a developing-world phenomenon and that most developed countries did not experience such events because markets were efficient. However, the crisis showed that all financial markets are unstable and require constant supervision and regulation. In response to this the IMF, in 2009, included a successor to the Financial Stability Forum called the Financial Stability Board, which has a strengthened mandate to watch for systemic risks. In addition, the G-20 summit in April 2009 resolved to reduce procyclicality by year end, by working with accounting standard setters, including a requirement for banks to build buffers of resources in good times that they can draw down when conditions deteriorate (G-20 2009).[9]

A number of models examined the impact of the Great Recession, seeking to draw conclusions about crisis effects and policy impacts. As Sarafrazi et al. (2014) point out, the crisis experience throughout the eurozone countries was dissimilar. In some countries, the main trouble originated in the real estate market, while in others it stemmed from problems in the banking sector or from budget deficits. The extent and direction of the impact on eurozone countries varied; Matousek et al. (2015) find that bank efficiency in eurozone countries declined as a result of the direct and policy impacts of the Great Recession, with the exception of Belgium, Sweden, and Portugal in 2008, and Germany and Portugal in 2009. The UK was hit more strongly than other countries in terms of bank efficiency, while the highest efficiency level in 2012 was in Greece, whose crisis was not triggered by the banking sector. Bank efficiency levels were generally slow to rebound across what the authors classify as original EU-15 countries, as liquidity declined and non-performing loans rose. Relatedly, MacDonald et al. (2015) use a financial stress index within a multivariate analysis to find that eurozone countries are mainly responsive to their own financial stress, and to a lesser extent to regional financial stress. The financial stress index used is comprised of data from the banking sector, money market, equity market, and bond market. Financial conditions in Greece and Portugal were not found to strongly affect the eurozone area.

The study of regional and country-level impacts of the crisis has resulted in assertions of a decoupling–recoupling among international financial markets (Dooley and Hutchison 2009), with contradictory evidence in the case of Greece (Floros et al. 2013). Before the crisis hit in earnest – that is, up to 2007 – some economists asserted that emerging markets in Asia and Latin America had "decoupled" from advanced economies and in particular the US, in that they were able to generate growth without being affected by changes in the business cycles of developed nations. This can be explained, to some extent, by the emergence of China and its strength in the global economy, as some emerging markets "coupled" to the Chinese economy (Yeyati and Williams 2012). As the crisis spread abroad and heavily impacted emerging markets in late 2008, this theory was exchanged for the "recoupling" theory that emerging markets were closely connected to that of the advanced economies. Going even further, Felices and Wieladek (2012) provide some evidence that decoupling occurred in only a few cases and that "coupling" around global factors has remained the norm.

Galbraith (2014) puts forward the idea that traditional economics played a role in bringing about the 2008 crisis, at least in its ignorance of the necessary importance of government or money. Therefore, when the 2008 crisis hit, the crisis could only be conceived of as an external shock, rather than as a breakdown of the existing system.

What is more, the critical assumption in modern economics, which allowed the economics profession to become more like science, was that the economic future could be estimated based on past behavior. But, as we have seen, complex financial models cannot predict the future. Factors such as human psychology and people's expectations of the futures are not usually incorporated into such models. Pricing principles stem from a set of assumptions about the underlying asset as well as equilibrium criteria. Risk is hedged by balancing the asset with other assets that neutralize risk. Structured products are evaluated based on historical data, which in many cases is missing, requiring the input of results from simulations incorporating arbitrary assumptions on correlations between risk and default probabilities. These models incorporated many assumptions that are potentially pernicious, particularly when assumptions do not incorporate major changes in the economic reality (Colander et al. 2009).

In recognition of the riskiness of model-priced assets, banks in the United States became increasingly aware of the need to hold low-risk assets like cash and treasuries within liquidity pools, and of the need to stress test liquidity buffers. Stress tests were altered to reflect contingency risks: risks of off-balance sheet assets given a potential liquidity shortage (Sooklal 2012). This is a step in the right direction toward reducing financial sector risk. At present, however, the larger question of regulating off-balance sheet or shadow banking sector assets is still under consideration. Many assets are traded within the shadow banking sector and there is no guarantee that the pricing and risk of these assets will not present a future threat to financial stability.

The eurozone crisis demonstrated that the structure of the eurozone does not work for all countries. The eurozone does not allow for countries to engage in higher domestic spending, wage increases, and inflation (Moravcsik 2012). Deficit countries needed to be committed to adopting German spending behavior, at no small cost to the local populace. However, they were not, and external shocks from the US and European financial crisis induced a severe debt crisis in a number of nations. It is unlikely that the eurozone will be restructured after the crisis, but this remains to be seen.

The eurozone crisis was much more than a financial crisis. It also represented a challenge to European integration. Glencross (2014) discusses the importance of national leaders in determining the outcome of the eurozone crisis. This is because bailout funds for imperiled debtor countries had to be guaranteed by national leaders. What is more, in response to implementation of the European Stability Mechanism, creditor countries created the Treaty on Stability, Coordination, and Governance in the Economic and Monetary Union, which made it constitutionally impossible to run up long-term government debt. Eurozone countries were thus required to commit to balanced budgets. This exacerbated internal tensions within debtor countries, in particular regarding integration in the eurozone.

This type of crisis, preceded by the Exchange Rate Mechanism (ERM) crisis of the early 1990s and the Great Depression, in which nations faced adverse economic conditions transmitted in part by adherence to the gold standard, is more than "just" a currency crisis. It is a crisis caused by monetary union, in which a group of countries agrees upon a relatively rigid exchange rate or adopts a single currency through a region, and is as much of a currency crisis as it is a policy and political crisis. The policy crisis begins when necessary adoption of center country monetary policies results in a conflict of interest in peripheral countries, and the political crisis stems from rising political dissent as a result of economic hardship in non-core countries. Under the gold standard and the ERM crisis, the way out of the crisis was to end or alter the currency union. In the eurozone crisis, little was done to improve the economic structure of the European Monetary Union, which might attempt to improve the flexibility of the system and allow member governments to implement monetary and fiscal policies when needed. It does appear that austerity measures and conservative monetary policy from the center have created abysmal social and economic conditions in peripheral countries, namely Greece. To this author, based on the lessons from history, it does not appear that the European Monetary Union can continue without experiencing similar crises going forward.

POLITICAL ECONOMY OF THE GREAT RECESSION

Some analysts expected progressive politicians and policies to arise in response to the crisis which was caused by free markets, but this failed to come about. President Barack Obama, who was viewed as a potentially liberal politician, was a more center or center-right President than expected. Congressional liberals in the US were voted out of office in the 2010 mid-term election, while left-oriented governments in Portugal, New Zealand, and the UK lost their political base (Bartels 2013). Still, no consistent preference was shown for right- or left-wing governments in the five years following the crisis. Voters mainly sought to punish incumbents for slowing growth and other economic ills; voters acted much as they would under normal circumstances.

What was unique about this period is possibly the scale of political instability and public expressions of outrage, witnessed in protests and even riots. Discontent with the bailout packages, austerity measures, unemployment, and perceived favoritism toward particular groups or classes led to protests in the US, Iceland, Greece, Spain, Portugal, Italy, Ireland, Hungary, France, Belgium, and other nations around the world. Political instability in Europe arose as countries moved into crisis mode themselves, and as the eurozone debated whether, and how, to rescue Greece. Hostility toward austerity measures in particular, and the governments that accepted them, resulted in the rise of anti-austerity politicians.

The politics of the eurozone crisis were especially complex and has been the subject of entire books. Political leaders held different perspectives of how the eurozone should function, particularly between the core and periphery. The German core, led by Chancellor Angela Merkel, was devoted to fiscal discipline; while the debtor nation periphery tended to permit deficit spending. Germany was backed by the Troika of the European Commission, European Central Bank, and the IMF. Peripheral nations Italy, Greece, Spain, and Portugal protested against austerity measures that they felt punished taxpayers rather than those responsible for mounting debt.

Woodruff (2014) utilizes Polanyi's theory that market panic can be used as a political weapon to describe the reaction of European Central Bank and German leaders toward providing a palliative to peripheral countries. The "Brussels–Frankfurt consensus" required debtor nations to institute ordoliberal policies, which included commitment to stable money, sound finances, and efficient labor-factor markets under state guidance. The European Central Bank threatened to withhold financial assistance until these policy changes were adopted.

The political economy of the Great Recession is too extensive to discuss in this volume, since it encompassed many countries over a relatively long time period. Suffice it to say that some politicians benefited from the crisis while others lost ground. The latter was especially visible in the widespread rejection of incumbent politicians in favor of those who promised better economic conditions, which is a normal outcome when voters suffer from real or perceived government policy ills.

ECONOMIC THEORIES OF THE LATE 2000S

The post-Washington Consensus that developed in the early 2000s included requirements that differed somewhat from those of the Washington Consensus while continuing to maintain a market orientation. Post-Washington Consensus policies included anti-corruption, corporate governance, independence of the central bank, financial standards, flexible labor markets, WTO agreements, prudent capital account opening, non-intermediate exchange rate regimes, social safety nets, and targeted poverty reduction (Rodrik 2006).

The shift away from neoliberal policies in the early 2000s to a "post-

Washington Consensus Consensus" proved insufficient in checking the global crisis, either because of or despite the fact that neither the Washington Consensus nor the post-Washington Consensus could be applied wholesale to US policies. Still, in ideological orientation (if not in policy application, especially in the realm of fiscal discipline), the US leaned toward neoliberalism and augmented this with complex financialization. Germany, at the center of the eurozone, also favored neoliberal-type policies. Therefore, despite a general consensus during this period among economists that growth through market orientation should imply neither unchecked expansion of free markets nor punishment of the citizenry in order to achieve policy targets, both extremes were applied at this time, bringing about or exacerbating crisis conditions.

CONCLUSION

The Great Depression and many intervening crises taught us much about how policy should respond in the Great Recession, but again we face new challenges. The US component of the financial crisis clearly warranted more attention than was given to the Great Depression in the short run.[10] Governments around the world should be lauded for implementing fiscal stimulus packages and loose monetary policy to halt the crisis in its tracks. The eurozone component of the crisis is less clear, especially since the downturn worsens countries' debt positions, which in turn worsen the downturn, and the structural problem within the eurozone has yet to be addressed. The crisis has been so severe around the globe that it will take some time for economic conditions to improve.

NOTES

1. Bordo and Landon-Lane (2010) make the case that the Great Contraction is only fourth in ranking of severity compared to crises occurring in 1880, 1890–91, 1907–08, 1913–14, 1931–32, 2007–08. We find this result questionable, particularly because the authors include only countries that have consistent data in all of these periods (that is, other countries that were affected, in particular Eastern European and Asian countries, are not included in the analysis).
2. House prices began their decline in 2006.
3. See Katz (2007).
4. Concisely cited by Davidson (2009).
5. See, for example, Johnson (2009c), Stiglitz (2009), and Davidson (2009).
6. The Public–Private Investment Program (dubbed the "Legacy Loans program"), proposed in March 2009, which revived the original TARP plan in the sense of providing government backing for purchase of troubled assets, was, like its predecessor, so unpopular that it was canceled. This program proposed to guarantee private investment

in troubled assets through the Federal Deposit Insurance Corporation (FDIC), and to co-invest funds through the Treasury. Banks found the program so appealing that they requested to purchase these toxic loans from their own books (Enrich et al. 2009). This would have expanded the role of the government to become the "market maker of last resort" (Buiter 2007).

7. About $160 billion were linked directly to asset-backed securities.
8. See Zacharias et al. (2009).
9. Brunnermeier et al. (2009) recommend setting up countercyclical measures on a country-by-country basis, since business cycles vary by nation. Rodrik (2009) also makes the case that national regulation should be emphasized, with a thin layer of supranational regulation, since rules of sovereignty are not easily superceded, and when they are, a supranational regulator may create inadequate policies.
10. Some economists continued to vilify government intervention even after the crisis (Galbraith 2014). Even former Federal Reserve Chairman Alan Greenspan stated that post-crisis government intervention hobbled markets.

9. Global imbalances

Global imbalances have generated the conditions for crisis, from the Great Depression through the Great Recession. Imbalances in currency stability and power, government debt, trade deficits, financial stocks and flows have repeatedly laid the foundation for crisis. The success of the intentional, imposed stability and balance of the Bretton Woods period provides the exception that proves the rule: global imbalances allow crisis conditions to arise and ripen.

Global imbalances have referred mainly to current account deficits in the United States (US) and the European periphery, as separate but destabilizing issues. The former issue came to light in the early 2000s. In this case, Bernanke (2005) dubbed the imbalance of the US trade deficit with other nations, notably China, the "global saving glut." Surpluses of developing and emerging market economies drove purchases of dollar-denominated assets, especially US government bonds, pushing down US interest rates which expanded the supply of available credit. This allowed credit to be extended for the purchase of risky assets in the lead-up to the recent financial crisis.

After the crisis hit, much was written about global imbalances and the Great Recession. Obstfeld and Rogoff (2009) assert that financial innovation, coupled with loose monetary policy and credit market distortions, created conditions for financial crisis starting in the United States. Large current account deficits, rising real estate values, and high leverage across many countries posed risks to global economic stability. The United States possessed all of these risks. The US borrowed in dollars at low interest rates to purchase consumer goods, homes, and other assets. The United States' main trading partner, China, did not allow its currency to appreciate to reduce these imbalances. The global imbalance caused by China's sterilization of foreign currency inflows allowed exporters to continue to manufacture goods for sale abroad at no extra cost (that is, at appreciated value), thereby perpetuating the current account imbalances (Obstfeld and Rogoff 2009).

The global imbalances prevented the dollar from weakening and therefore prevented an increase in world real interest rates, and blocked the reduction of the US current account deficit. Deficits of the advanced countries rose on average after 2004 (Obstfeld and Rogoff 2009). What is more, loose monetary policy in the US impacted not only borrowing in the US but also eased global credit demand. The undervalued renminbi (RMB), combined with easy credit in developed countries, led to extensive capital inflows from abroad, legally and in the form of "hot money." This made conditions ripe for asset price bubbles to appear.

Other authors focus on the concept that excessive holding of reserves generated conditions for crisis. Even though countries with large reserve accumulations are protected to some extent against destabilizing international currency flows, reserve currency countries find themselves with a much lower financing constraint, which may create the conditions for global crisis by allowing reserve currency countries to borrow more (Steiner 2014). Although in the wake of the Asian financial crisis the International Monetary Fund (IMF) had urged countries to maintain large reserves in order to prevent worsening of financial crises, this new wisdom realized after the global financial crisis has shown that excess liquidity can increase the risky asset holdings of large financial institutions.

Conversely, the idea that a "global savings glut" caused the recent crisis has been questioned by scholars such as Borio and Disyatat (2011), who write that it was not excess saving, but instead "excess elasticity" of the global monetary and fiscal system (that is, excess credit creation), that caused the crisis. That is, existing monetary and fiscal regimes did not prevent the creation of excessive credit and asset price bubbles. A key component of this thesis is the fact that current accounts and net capital flows provide insufficient information about financing, failing to reveal information about changes in existing stocks, especially stocks of financial assets. The same level of saving may be associated with various levels of financial assets and liabilities. Borio and Disyatat separate the concepts of saving and financing; the latter is required for investment, and can reveal borrowing and lending patterns. Furthermore, they discuss how monetary and fiscal regimes allowed market interest rates to diverge from a "natural" interest rate, reflected in savings and investment, and other real (non-monetary) factors. Divergence between the rates may reflect unsustainable asset price bubbles.

Borio and Disyatat (2011) also present evidence to flout the excess savings hypothesis. The authors note that there is an insufficient link between current account balances and long-term interest rates, that the depreciation of the US dollar should have rendered US assets less, rather than more, attractive, that the link between the US current account deficit and global savings is tenuous, and that there is no clear link between the global savings rate and real interest rates. They write further that credit booms were not restricted to deficit countries, that the countries from which net credit flows stemmed were least affected by the crisis, and that global growth should not have continued, given *ex ante* global saving, which would depress aggregate demand.

Obstfeld (2012) answers the arguments against the excess savings hypothesis by reaffirming the importance of current account imbalances, and coupling this indicator with global gross assets and liabilities. Global gross assets and liabilities generate higher systemic financial instability, since in many financial transactions there is no net financial flow, and also no rise in capital buffers against potential default. Obstfeld asserts that low interest rates and accommodating monetary and regulatory policies created an environment ripe for overleveraging. The US current account deficit was a symptom of this disease, as current account deficits are often accompanied by unsustainable financial trends.

In any case, imbalances persisted not only with the dollar and the rest of the world, but with the euro, with Germany at its center, and the eurozone periphery. The eurozone lacked sufficient surplus recycling mechanisms. The surplus recycling mechanism, as explained by Varoufakis (2013), includes the transfer of surplus from the present to the future and from surplus regions to deficit regions. Eurozone countries' public debts remained separate, so that flagging nations such as Greece remained wholly responsible for their own debt positions and there was no mechanism to address fiscal imbalances. Greece and other deficit nations therefore bore the main brunt of the crisis.

Core eurozone countries also pursued export-led growth policies, resulting in mounting deficits in the periphery prior to and during the crisis. It is notable that even before the crisis, the core countries, Germany and France, missed the mark on Stability and Growth Pact fiscal conditions, even though most eurozone fiscal policies remained relatively conservative (Holinski et al. 2012). Countries were generally fiscally conservative, though without a common treasury to enforce this obligation (Anand et al. 2012). Wage divergence between core and periphery countries exacerbated deficits and increased the competitiveness of core countries, as wages increased in periphery countries and declined in core countries. Core countries such as Germany increased exports to a rising China, while peripheral countries were edged out of export markets also due, perhaps ironically, to a rising China.

Furthermore, in the lead-up to the crisis, Greece and Portugal experienced a consumption boom, while Ireland and Spain underwent housing booms (Diaz Sanchez and Varoudakis 2013). Credit growth in the periphery grew much faster than that in the core, while savings in the periphery fell.

On the whole, underlying structural differences in inflation rates, specialization, and financial and real economic structures have increased the costs and risks associated with operating the eurozone. Countries did not have the ability to influence currency values or short-term interest rates. As fragility set in, low interest rates across the eurozone led to diverging long-term interest rates starting in 2006.

Before the crisis, uniting the currency had reduced financial transaction costs and united bond markets, leading most investors to believe that all European bonds were created equally, revealed in the convergence of bond yields between 1999 and 2002 (Anand et al. 2012). When the crisis broke out, sovereign debt ratings for Greece, Ireland, Portugal, Spain, and Italy were downgraded as investors feared default. It became clear that viewing all European bonds as similar in terms of risk was foolhardy.

Post-crisis eurozone policy exacerbated rather than alleviated imbalances. Instead of increasing government spending in peripheral countries to make up for a lack of demand, the IMF and creditor nations have forced into place austerity measures that have only worsened growth, employment, and in some cases debt positions. Furthermore, as Shambaugh (2012) points out, the Maastricht Treaty and Stability and Growth Pact focused on public budget deficits, but neglected banking issues, unemployment, and other important issues.

In both the case of US–China and eurozone imbalances, the current account plays an important role. However, it must be underscored that both of these cases are somewhat unusual circumstances. It is the current account deficit in the face of the center country (in the first case), which happens to issue assets issued in the most important global reserve currency, and in the face of a currency union with little to no fiscal firepower (in the second case). Furthermore, the current account balance indicator does not stand alone in determining crisis conditions. In the case of the US–China imbalance, it is essential to capture stocks of financial assets. In the case of eurozone imbalances, government debt, savings, and competitiveness indicators play a key role. For the eurozone, the inability to depreciate the currency has sentenced peripheral countries to poor trade outcomes, and this, coupled with austerity measures straitjacketing peripheral governments, has led to a lack of demand and painful internal adjustment.

These imbalances have historical and institutional roots, in the demise of the Bretton Woods system. The Bretton Woods system unraveled as trade imbalances could not be kept in check, and the US transformed from a surplus country to a deficit country as the Vietnam War siphoned away resources, even as the dollar remained at the center of the global financial architecture. Excessive amounts of dollars resulted in inflation abroad and created the possibility of a run on the dollar in the face of a constant gold stock (Varoufakis 2013). When President Nixon closed the gold window in 1971, the dollar remained the global reserve currency, and US current account deficits persisted. The days of balanced trade and stabilized currencies were gone.

What arose was a system of hegemonic economic power in the US, as the dollar became a replacement for gold. The dollar, however, was not a commodity like gold, but mere fiat money. Still, the US could "strike gold" at its own whim by printing more money, as the dollar took on in part the intrinsic value characteristic normally reserved only for commodity money. The US was able to run large trade deficits, tapping into seemingly endless global demand for its currency.

In the post-Bretton Woods period, finance innovated, corporations grew tremendously, and wages stagnated. Imbalances were therefore created not only between the US and the rest of the world, but also between corporations and workers, and between the financial sector and real sectors. The tenets of neoliberalism, free market economics, became most powerful. The most dangerous challenge to global stability was the idea that with free markets, fragile economic imbalances would stabilize themselves. While this may have been true for the US, which contained the automatically stabilizing mechanism of reserve currency status, this was not true for other countries. Financial deregulation that led to fast-moving financial inflows and outflows created crisis conditions in many nations, as examined in previous chapters. Financial imbalances were created by market liberalization without sufficient real economic and regulatory checks to stabilize or stop sudden flows.

This brings us to the next point, which is that imbalances require not only stabilization of unbalanced indicators, such as current account deficits or savings, but also stabilization of the greater institutional environment. We note that in the aftermath of the crisis, none of the institutional imbalances that gave way to excess liquidity in the US or to loss of competitiveness in the eurozone have been sufficiently corrected. Policies to implement financial stability in recent crisis-ridden countries have been subject to the same blinders that have often prevented policy makers in emerging markets from implementing deeper stabilizing mechanisms in the nineties and early 2000s.

Additional global and domestic destabilizers are also present, in particular the surge in income inequality. While we cannot state that inequality directly causes financial crises, just as we cannot say that a current account deficit will result in crisis, inequality may create conditions for economic and financial fragility. Rajan (2010) has made the case that rising inequality led to pressures to redistribute in the form of subsidized finance. The expansion of credit to risky households brought about the circumstances for the subprime crisis in the United States. Stockhammer (2015) asserts that another channel in which inequality led to increased risk is through risky investment on the part of wealthier classes, who invested in risky assets in the run-up to the global crisis. This activity was permitted by financial deregulation.

Post-Keynesians would also support this idea, as they believe aggregate demand drives the economy. As wages are eroded and inequality grows, aggregate consumption demand declines, as lower-income groups have higher marginal propensities to consume. Lower demand leads to lower investment by firms, and lower output, potentially creating the conditions for crisis in a wage-led economy. In addition, increasing wage share of the rentier can lead to increased borrowing on the part of households in order to maintain living standards, creating additional conditions for crisis. The latter was the case in the United States as well as in the Great Depression. Furthermore, the rise in profit share led to the creation of cash pools held by firms and invested in the riskier shadow banking sector (Pozsar 2011). Pozsar conceives of institutional cash pools' demand for highly rated short-term assets as the flip side of foreign central banks' demand for highly rated long-term assets within the context of the global savings glut hypothesis. Due to a shortage of treasuries and other safe, liquidity assets for placement of cash pools, cash pool managers have been forced to place funds in privately guaranteed assets issued by the shadow banking system.

Inequality generated crisis conditions in the center country, the United States, that emanated to the rest of the world in both the Great Depression and the Great Recession. In that sense, inequality has acted as a global destabilizer. Inter-country inequality may become a larger factor within regional economic blocs, such as the eurozone, as political and financial conditions become more integrated.

Addressing global imbalances is an important component of preventing future crises. In the next chapter, we delve into this topic, first examining financial crisis models and empirical studies that have arisen in particular after the most recent crisis, then making policy recommendations on the prevention of future crises.

10. Preventing future crises

FINANCIAL CRISES: A SUMMARY

The idea that a sophisticated, financially liberalized country could enter crisis was unthinkable until the Great Recession. It will take some time before the academic understanding of financial crises catches up to this event. European countries that believed themselves to be integrated into the European Union, and therefore immune from sudden crises of confidence, experienced a psychological shock as they entered crises of their own and had to be bailed out by the International Monetary Fund (IMF). For once, developing countries watched as developed countries experienced economic degeneration.

That being said, contrary to what some people expected, a new economic superpower, such as China, did not arise. Much of the status quo in the financial architecture has been preserved. This only underscores the need for preventing future financial crises, as the Pandora's Box of financial profit-seeking has been left open since the 1970s. Developing countries are still just as much at risk of experiencing the negative effects of short-term capital outflows.

As James Galbraith (2008) puts forth, political economy itself has been at fault for allowing the causes of financial crisis, in the name of free markets and free trade, to arise. The current policy arena prevents proper crisis prevention policies from being put into place. Within this policy arena, he writes, "we see the grip of 'free market economics' on the public stage; to be taken seriously, one must be able to profess a belief in magic with a straight face." The idea of constraining financial capital is not generally accepted. Galbraith shows that the Bretton Woods system of regulated exchange rates and capital controls allowed free trade to work. During this period, fixed exchange rates reduced uncertainty and low tariffs allowed more trade to occur. As discussed in Chapter 3, the Bretton Woods era certainly provided real and financial sector stability for some time. A similar, globally coordinated regime could improve economic stability. It is unlikely that a "New Bretton Woods" agreement will occur, however. Below, we discuss new financial crisis models and policies to prevent future crises.

FINANCIAL CRISIS MODELS

By now, it is well known that few economists were able to predict the 2008 global financial crisis. This is despite the fact that a large literature previously existed in an attempt to develop early warning signals. Many of the early warning signals contain information about indicators such as the level of reserves and exchange rate appreciations. Christofides et al. (2015) test a set of early warning signals to find out whether any of these signals could have single-handedly predicted the 2008 crisis. The authors find that no single early warning signal could alert to all dimensions of the 2008 crisis. Rather, separate sets of signals might predict different aspects of the crisis, including the banking, balance of payments, exchange rate, and growth crisis.

By contrast, other authors have found that certain indicators can indeed predict financial crises. Kauko (2014) summarizes existing literature on various indicators, noting that the credit-to-gross domestic product (GDP) ratio is not a strong crisis predictor, as evidenced in Hahn et al. (2011), Joyce (2011), and others. However, credit growth lagged does increase crisis probability (Bordo and Meissner 2012). Rising asset prices result in asset price bubbles that lead to financial instability and crises.

Jing et al. (2014) construct a money markets pressure index based on central bank reserves and short-term nominal interest rates to identify banking crises. The authors find that this index identifies more crises than the Laeven–Valencia database. Dabla-Norris and Gunduz (2014) develop an early warning system for crises in low-income countries. In the face of a large, negative shock, low-income countries have insufficient resources and policy buffers to absorb shocks. Dabla-Norris and Gunduz develop the crisis index based on multivariate regression and univariate signaling analysis to create a composite vulnerability index. Miao and Wang (2015) illustrate a macroeconomic model with a banking sector in which changes in household confidence trigger a financial crisis. Bicaba et al. (2015) show that investment growth, terms of trade, the real interest rate, and the M2-to-reserve ratio can predict policy or macroeconomic stability between currency crises, and that the real interest rate predicts stability between debt crises using data between 1960 and 2008.

Garcia-Palacios et al. (2014) construct a model in which policies to correct banking crises depend on the public's preferences; when individuals highly value public services, a sound resolution to banking crises is to tax early withdrawals; but if individuals do not value public services, the best resolution to banking crises is to recapitalize banks. Chang (2007) goes even further in describing the interaction between society and financial crises: Chang lays out a model in which political crises accompany debt default due to an information transmission conflict between the government and the public.

Some crisis models in the late 1990s and late 2000s theorized that a strong cause of crises is the run-up of debt in normal times, implying that pre-crisis macroprudential policies and debt control are essential to preventing financial crises or controlling the impact of crises. Benigno et al. (2013) model a crisis situation in which policies made both before and during the crisis are relevant. They find that policy makers should not subsidize borrowing to restore economic efficiency, but rather that they should allocate resources in both normal and crisis periods to maximize borrowing.

Boschi and Goenka (2012) examine how investor behavior influences transmission of crises, using a second-generation currency crisis model to show how contagion is spread through fundamentals. Risk averse behavior translates into negative wealth shocks, which raises the risk premia on risky assets. This increases the possibility of devaluation, for which the solution is to impose capital controls of a Tobin tax.

Models also attempted to find better methods for evaluating risk. Poledna et al. (2015) model the Mexican banking system between 2007 and 2013 to identify systemic risk. The authors divide the banking system into four layers, revealing that focusing on a single layer underestimates total systemic risk by up to 90 percent.

Empirical Examinations of Multiple Crises

Economists today have the benefit of being able to analyze multiple crises over a longer time period. These conclusions have helped to shaped some of the models discussed above, and to provide indications for economic and financial policy.

Babecký et al. (2014) examine crisis episodes over 40 countries between 1970 and 2010, finding that banking and debt crises often precede currency crises, but not vice versa. The authors also find that banking crises are more costly than other types of crises, and take on average six years to recover from. The long-lasting effects of banking crises have been confirmed by various studies, including Reinhart and Rogoff (2014) and da Rocha and Solomou (2015). Furthermore, countries that have experienced one banking crisis have a higher likelihood of having another banking crisis in the future (Aizenmann and Noy 2013). Qin and Luo (2014) examine data from G-20 countries between 1989 and 2010, showing that capital controls play an important role in predicting banking crises. Reducing capital account openness somewhat in high-income countries, they find, can reduce the incidence of banking crises; while increasing capital account openness in low-income countries can have the same effect.

Examining financial crises in Organisation for Economic Co-operation and Development (OECD) countries between 1960 and 2008, Furceri and Mourougane (2012) find that financial crises lower potential output by around 1.5–2.4 percent on average, due to a decline in capital. Cohen and Villemot (2015) use data from 97 countries over the period 1970 to 2004 to show that, while exogenous shocks account for most debt crises, self-fulfilling crises occur in 6 to 12 percent of cases, as financial markets panic, leading the debt-to-GDP ratio to stray from its pre-crisis path.

Despite the going wisdom from the most recent crisis, Bretschger et al. (2012) find that banking concentration ("too big to fail") may lead to financial stability or to financial fragility; there is no evidence that it is one or the other in all cases. Using data from 160 countries between 1970 and 2010, the authors show that market concentration, then, has no direct effect on systemic crises. Still, banking indicators matter. Lainà et al. (2015) find that indicators that best predict systemic banking crises in 11 European Union (EU) countries between 1980 and 2013 include growth rates of loans-to-deposits and house prices. Market power has also been shown to exacerbate a downturn in industries that are more dependent on external finance, based on data from 36 banking crises in 30 countries over the 1980 to 2000 time period (Fernandez et al. 2013). By contrast, inter-connectedness to global markets has been shown to reduce the incidence of banking crises (Caballero 2015). This may be because more globally interconnected banking institutions have access to liquidity in the face of negative shocks.

Currency crises became more internationally synchronized over the twentieth century, while banking crises became first more international in the early twentieth century, then less so with the rise of banking regulation after the Great Depression. After the rise of neoliberalism in the 1980s, banking regulation declined, resulting in a rise in banking crisis incidence through the Great Recession (Dungey et al. 2015). Twin crises, or concurrent banking and currency crises, arose. Twin crises have led customers in the crisis-affected country to bank abroad in unaffected countries (Kleimeier et al. 2013).

The impacts of financial crises on exchange rate regimes and vice versa have been studied for many years. Some have argued that the optimal exchange rate regime is a floating rate, while others argue that a pegged exchange rate provides the most credibility. Esaka (2014) and Domac and Martinez Peria (2003) find that consistent pegs, or de facto and de jure pegged regimes, are significantly less likely to experience a currency crisis than countries with other exchange rate policies. The reason for this may be that countries with consistent pegs increase the credibility of their currency regime by clearly committing to a pegged regime. Angkinand and

Willett (2011) show that countries with a soft exchange rate are the most vulnerable to currency crises.

Financial crises result in the deterioration of labor rights practices, due to increases in unemployment as firms cut costs. Blanton et al. (2015) use data from 46 countries between 1985 and 2002 to show that while crises do not impact labor rights laws, they adversely affect labor rights practices, lasting into the early years after the crisis.

The recent global crisis has brought the study of financial crises more into vogue, and new crisis models reflect the latest understanding of how crises arise and are transmitted. Pre-crisis monitoring, particularly of banking systems, to intercept building crises has become an important component of the global financial architecture. Monitoring systems may include some of the indicators found to be relevant in the academic literature. In what follows, we discuss policies to prevent future crises, based on our present knowledge of crisis prevention and containment.

POLICIES TO PREVENT FUTURE CRISES

Many economists agree that crises will return, and that global imbalances persist. However, economists agree little on solutions that can be used to prevent future crises. This is because crises are unique and to a large degree unpredictable, often a product of not only poor policy or an economic shock, but also a crisis of confidence. The idea that the world is increasingly globalized does not negate the fact that nations are sovereign, and therefore the extent of control and even supervision governments have over the economy is limited all around, especially for developing countries. Hence most crisis prevention policies have been implemented at the domestic level; while possibly better, more comprehensive global schemes remain an issue of academic interest alone.

To take a logical approach to crisis prevention, one must go back to the basics of the shock and crisis response themselves (Caballero and Kurlat 2009). In orthodox economic theory, three events create the crisis: a negative shock or surprise that is new and confusing; the concentration of risk (rather than leverage per se) in a single area, such as highly leveraged financial institutions; and a policy response that is too slow in addressing these issues. Confusion brings panic, and panics increase the demand for explicit and implicit insurance.[1] The characterization of a crisis as a surprise is universal and important, for in considering policy remedies to prevent fallout the chaotic nature of the shock has to be accounted for. Hence the response to a developing crisis should be one of containment even before the crisis has fully blossomed. Crisis resolution and then prevention should impose policies to wind down the crisis and minimize the possibility of crisis occurrence in the future, respectively.

Containment

Containment is the process of preventing the expansion of financial crisis, which seeks to make up for the lack of policy response before the crisis in preventing the build-up of risk. Bagehot's policy recommendation for containment is to ensure liquidity is present, lent freely by the central banks to solvent banks. There is difficulty, however, in recognizing solvent banks during a crisis; improvements in information availability before a crisis are necessary to fulfill this recommendation (Demirgüç-Kunt and Servén 2009). The government must also maintain a substantial capacity for absorbing losses prior to the crisis in order to maintain credibility of guarantees during the crisis; not a simple task. Free-flowing liquidity per Bagehot's advice is often essential but in actuality not easily achieved, since liquidity support may not have its intended effect, as in the Great Recession, in which banks held on to liquidity from the Central Bank in the form of reserves. An alternative may be a relatively short "banking holiday" to examine financial institutions for solvency and impose hair-cuts on uninsured depositors and creditors before they remove funds (Demirgüç-Kunt and Servén 2009).

Containment in a currency crisis requires alleviating pressure (that is, speculative attacks) on the currency by floating or devaluing the currency. In few currency crisis scenarios has a commitment to the existing exchange rate been credible. Devaluation has real effects, and in the absence of capital controls results in capital outflows and a higher cost of imports, and is a shock to the system. Foreign and domestic lending may be choked off under these circumstances and the government as well as international lenders must attempt to restore confidence in the economy by providing additional funds in the financial market.

Resolution

After the containment stage, the crisis should enter the resolution stage. In the resolution stage, the causes of the crisis are analyzed and addressed in order to improve the economic situation. The resolution stage can be applied to both banking and currency crises.

Calomiris et al. (2004) discuss seven potential resolution policies, including (capital) regulatory forbearance, across-the-board incentives for loan loss write-offs, conditional government subsidized workouts of assets, debt forgiveness, the establishment of a government-owned asset management company, government-assisted sales of financial institutions, and government-assisted recapitalization. Some of these are more effective than others; for example, regulatory forbearance caused more problems than it resolved during the United States (US) savings and loan crisis in the 1980s, as financial institutions took advantage of a delay in regulatory enforcement by accumulating loan losses. Other practices, such as loan loss write-offs, promote good behavior such as transparency in banks' balance sheets but must also be accompanied by other policies, such as in this case, those to prevent continuing poor lending practices. Some policies must be accompanied by appropriate institutions. The conditional sharing of loan losses between financial institutions and the government must make use of a credible supervisory authority to enforce loan loss recognition and an appropriate legal system to enforce lending laws.

The resolution stage in a banking crisis may make use of recapitalization of the banking system (designed to enhance incentives to limit taxpayers' losses), transfer of non-performing assets to government ownership, or government-assisted sales of financial institutions, as possible methods of resolving a banking crisis (Demirgüç-Kunt and Servén 2009). In the Nordic country crises, resolution involved temporary nationalization of struggling banks. These banks were nationalized and later recapitalized to minimize spread to the rest of the banking sector. Toxic assets were separated from healthy assets, and the latter retained (Dewatripont et al. 2010). Government-assisted sales of financial institutions were carried out in the Great Recession to prevent their failure.

Prudential regulations (which will also be discussed as crisis prevention tools; they are that important) can also simultaneously be improved to reinforce positive banking practices. Implementation of Basel III standards will likely help. Basel III banking regulation, discussed in Chapter 1, was put forward in June of 2011 to improve systemic banking oversight, as well as to improve banks' risk management and transparency (BIS 2011). Other regulations may prevent further loan losses, as in the Nordic crisis, or enhance consumer protection, as in the Great Recession.

The resolution stage in a currency crisis includes imposing controls on capital inflows if judged to be necessary. Capital controls can provide another regulatory backdrop against which currency stability is maintained. Controls can limit capital inflows or outflows through a country using restrictions on financial or foreign exchange transactions. Controls on capital outflows have been used to contain crises, as in the cases of Malaysia and Thailand. Malaysia's capital controls, which temporarily prevented outflows of short-term capital during the Asian crisis and made it compulsory for exporters to exchange foreign currency for the ringgit at the new exchange rate, allowed Malaysia to defend the new currency peg until the situation was stabilized (Blecker 1999). Thailand's controls on outflows during the Asian crisis provided only temporary relief of pressure on the exchange rate, which eventually had to be floated.

Crisis Prevention

Financial liberalization has increased in the past five decades, and appears to be increasing rather than decreasing. Policy makers have recognized that financial liberalization must be accompanied by transparency and regulation, but few have gone further to suggest more comprehensive changes to the global financial architecture in order to prevent future crises, since politically the task is wildly difficult to achieve. The likelihood of installing a new global financial structure like that created at Bretton Woods is unlikely, despite the fact that experts the world over have made strong recommendations to this end.[2] Bretton Woods was, after all, a major exception to efforts in creating international agreements to change the international financial architecture (Boughton 2009). This type of reform requires strong leadership and participation, clear and shared goals, and a realistic approach to achieving those goals. Today, goals are heterogenous and hence reform proposals must necessarily be less involved.

However, reform must be undertaken, since:

> viewed from an ex ante perspective, an ex post rescue seems completely unwarranted . . . [and] it becomes urgent to take measures to prevent authorities in the future from being held hostage by the risk of an unregulated institution defaulting, because it cannot be right that firms subject to no external controls should enjoy access to taxpayer funding. (Dewatripont et al. 2010)

Crisis prevention as a financial goal is imperative if financial harm to the population is to be minimized. Below, we discuss several prevention policies as potential steps toward improving domestic and global financial frameworks.

Frenkel and Rapetti (2009) suggest that financially "under"-liberalized or liberalizing countries should focus on stabilizing their economies through maintaining stable macroeconomic regimes, with exchange rate systems that prevent speculation, appropriate capital account management techniques, and policies that maintain stable external accounts; while financially liberalized countries should be prepared to implement expansive fiscal packages in the case of crisis, as the demand for money and public bonds increases. The idea is that liberalizing countries should prevent crisis, while liberalized countries should build up safeguards against crisis, should it occur. There is more that can be done, however.

Below, we discuss some of these suggestions and more, starting with regulating capital flows through domestic controls, discussed in part in the previous section; reforming the IMF; implementing countercyclical macroeconomic policy; coordinating macroeconomic policy; and creating a global managed currency regime.[3]

Regulating capital flows through domestic controls
Capital controls are as much a means of crisis prevention as they are of crisis resolution. Controls on capital inflows, as in Chile and China, have been designed to prevent the build-up of crises. However, capital account management techniques must fit the needs of the individual nation. The extent to which countries should control the capital account continues to be a subject of debate. Economists and policy makers favoring less control have argued that liberalization allows capital to flow to projects with higher returns that have better allocative efficiency (Blecker 1999). In transferring funds to more efficient projects, investors demand better financial services and sound macroeconomic fundamentals, which put pressure on local institutions and governments to improve these structures. Arguments in favor of capital controls have been supported by empirical evidence, which shows that reduction in capital controls cultivates instability (Bruner and Ventura 2010). Data also show that reduction of capital controls does not necessarily lead to investment or growth, while it does increase output volatility. Maintaining low levels of capital controls can also reduce monetary policy autonomy; offshore banking is a prime example, in which capital outflows escape the management of domestic financial authorities. A contractionary macroeconomic policy bias may be produced with liberalization since financial capital prefers somewhat deflationary policies to preserve the value of assets. To compound matters, international capital tends to act procyclically and exacerbate downturns, leading to potential repeat of financial crises.

Capital controls went out of fashion in the early and mid-1990s, came back into fashion after the Asian financial crisis, and currently remain a subject of debate. China's monumental economic growth while maintaining capital controls on a whole host of financial and foreign exchange transactions, including limiting residents' ownership of foreign assets and limited foreign access to Chinese stock and asset markets, has proved that capital controls do not prevent wholesale growth per se. Chile's experience of capital controls is also often invoked as a successful case, but its specific type of controls may not have worked altogether in its favor. The controls, which stipulated a reserve requirement on short-term financial inflows, are viewed as having worked in the short run, but not in the long run when expectations of currency appreciation grew.

In the case of capital controls on both inflows and outflows, enforcement is a major duty that must prevent the use of loopholes. Capital outflows from developed countries provide most of the inflows into developing countries, and control of these flows would stabilize less developed economies. To this end, Jane D'Arista (2002) proposes that investors use a closed-end fund for emerging markets run by an international institution like the World Bank. The fund would issue liabilities to private investors and purchase stocks and bonds of private enterprises and public agencies in developing countries in cooperation with the government. The fund could be capitalized by government securities of major industrial countries in amounts equal to the proportion of residents in those countries who hold shares of the fund. Underlying assets would not have to be sold as the value of fund shares fluctuated, protecting emerging markets from capital flow volatility.

In recent years, some Latin American countries have also used reserve requirements to control monetary policy while preventing capital from rushing into or out of the economies. Rather than implementing outright capital controls, Brazil, Columbia, and Peru have used reserve requirements as a tool in inflation targeting, which has allowed these countries to check capital flows as well (Montoro and Moreno 2011). This was useful during times of economic stress before and after the bankruptcy of Lehman Brothers. Bussiere et al. (2015) show that countries with high reserves relative to short-term debt and some capital controls suffered less from the 2008–09 global crisis. Using reserve requirements to adjust monetary policy while controlling capital flows can be effective in particular circumstances, although policy makers must weigh the use of this tool against potential side effects, including a larger spread between lending and deposit rates, which increases the cost of credit, and the necessity for banks to deposit a larger portion of their assets with the central bank, lowering bank profits.

Reforming the IMF

The IMF was created at the Bretton Woods conference to extend credit to countries that have short-term balance-of-payments problems. It currently describes itself as "an organization of 187 countries, working to foster global monetary cooperation, secure financial stability, facilitate international trade, promote high employment and sustainable economic growth, and reduce poverty around the world" (IMF 2011).

Since its inception, the IMF's role as lender of last resort has expanded. After the Asian financial crisis, the IMF was reviled for imposing poor policies on the weakened crisis countries in return for a loan. Blecker (1999) records criticisms post-Asian crisis against the IMF, as follows, for:

- Imposing excessively harsh austerity policies that unnecessarily depress a country's economy as a condition of obtaining bailouts;
- Inviting speculative attacks by encouraging countries to maintain indefensible exchange rate targets with unsustainably high interest rates;
- Worsening moral hazard problems by repeatedly bailing out foreign investors who take imprudent risks (and thus encouraging them to overinvest again);
- Exacerbating financial panics by announcing that countries with temporary illiquidity problems and fundamentally sound economies were suffering from deep structural flaws;
- Pushing capital market liberalization on countries that lack the requisite internal institutions and regulations to manage the resulting capital inflows;
- Unduly interfering with domestic institutions and practices that are unrelated to the IMF's core mission of solving balance-of-payments problems;
- Prescribing macroeconomic and financial policies that ignore structural features of national economies and that fail to take into account their likely social and political effects; and
- Worsening inequality by making ordinary workers and citizens bear the burden of adjustment through increased unemployment and reduced incomes, while bailing out wealthy creditors (both domestic and foreign).

Some of this was debatable at the time; Eichengreen (1999) noted that the IMF is a necessary institution since systemic risk continues to exist, and that the concern that the IMF presents moral hazard risk must be measured against the risk of systemic crisis. Evidence supporting creditor moral hazard associated with IMF bailouts has come to opposite conclusions, and further, some scholars believe that the risk of moral hazard may be constrained by conditionality (Bird 2007). The idea of conditionality itself is still a subject of debate.

Conditionality attached to IMF loan packages requires countries to implement policies that may or may not be in their favor. Certainly the intent of the IMF has been to improve the macroeconomic outlook of countries in crisis, but conditions imposed have often had a negative impact on the economies. Opponents of conditionality have argued that it may create uncertainty in policy ownership, and that it disempowers countries in making their own policies (Bird 2007). IMF policies have rarely been fully implemented (Ivanova et al. 2003), and there is no clear evidence that conditionality policies positively impact growth. In defense of the IMF, Kenneth Rogoff, former IMF Chief Economist, makes the case that countries must face budget constraints even in hard times since it is unrealistic to expect that running a budget deficit will eventually stimulate enough growth to make up for the increased debt levels (Rogoff 2003). While IMF intervention has been seen as exacerbating crises, it has also been seen as imposing a force of stability in crises. Rogoff (2003) also explains that the IMF has sided with neither private investors nor regular citizens.

The IMF, aware of these issues, set out to create new conditionality guidelines in 2000. These were approved in 2002, and set out to improve the implementation record and country ownership of conditionality guidelines. These guidelines also strove to ensure that the guidelines are appropriate to each case and to lay out specific performance criteria and benchmarks (IMF 2002).

Since the late 1990s and early 2000s, after the Great Recession, the IMF's image has improved. The IMF played a partly uncontroversial role in the Great Recession due to the clear need to bail out Latvia, the Ukraine, Hungary, and Iceland (Bordo and James 2010).[4] Austerity measures imposed as conditionalities on IMF–eurozone loans in Europe have, however, incited protests in several crisis-enveloped countries.

The US crisis of 2008 led G-20 countries to resolve to reform the IMF, in particular to ensure that the IMF better represented developing countries. The IMF agreed to governance reforms in November 2010 to better reflect the presence of developing countries. Brazil, Russia, India, and China (the BRIC countries) will become top ten shareholders, and 110 out of 187 countries will maintain or increase quota shares (IMF 2010b). The shift toward major emerging economies is slight but encouraging.[5]

The criticism that the IMF has failed to properly survey global imbalances was taken up in the replacement of the Financial Stability Forum with the Financial Stability Board (FSB), which has set out to improve surveillance of countries' economic status. The Financial Stability Forum was created in 1999 to promote international financial stability, improve market functioning, and reduce systemic risk. The Financial Stability Board was assigned the tasks required of the Financial Stability Forum, as well as to monitor and advise on market developments and on the meeting of regulatory standards, review policy development work of the international standard-setting bodies, put forth guidelines for the establishment of supervisory colleges, manage contingency plans for international crisis management, and collaborate with the IMF to carry out Early Warning Exercises (Financial Stability Forum 2009). The FSB is still considered "soft" law rather than "hard" law, less enforceable than regulations drawn out by the World Trade Organization (WTO), for example (Arner and Taylor 2009).

Implementing countercyclical macroeconomic policy
Macroeconomic policy is a necessary tool in crisis containment and resolution. Countercyclical macroeconomic policy can dampen an overly exuberant upswing and cushion a precipitous downturn. Countercyclical

macroeconomic policy consists of anticyclical monetary and fiscal policy, as well as macroprudential regulation.

Since the 1980s, rather than focusing on economic activity, monetary policy has generally focused on inflation (Blanchard et al. 2010). Monetary policy made use of the short-term interest rate that the central bank could directly control. Whereas it may be an important countercyclical measure, the focus has not been on dampening the business cycle per se. One issue of caution in using monetary policy is that using it to prick a bubble can be dangerous and difficult. Normally there is disagreement among policy makers as to whether a bubble indeed exists and is harmful to the economy. In addition, a sudden tightening of monetary policy can have larger effects on the economy than anticipated. An increase in interest rates may not only prick the bubble, but also lead the economy into a downturn. Monetary policy would be better used in conjunction with macroprudential regulation that would dampen, rather than amplify, the business cycle. This type of regulation places emphasis on controlling leverage ratios, loan-to-value ratios, and other capital buffers (Demirgüç-Kunt and Servén 2009).

Soros (2012) makes the case that monetary tools are insufficient to control asset bubbles. He writes that credit controls such as margin requirements and minimum capital requirements must be implemented to prevent loss of capital. This would provide the financial system with more control at the microeconomic level to ensure capital is present in the areas that most require it in the case of a financial downturn.

Countercyclical fiscal policy is also important but has become less of a focus than monetary policy. The effects of fiscal policy became a matter of debate given Ricardian equivalence arguments and lags in implementation (Blanchard et al. 2010). However, use of countercyclical fiscal policy, including changes in both taxation and spending according to the phase of the business cycle, can be helpful in the recognition that there are social effects of economic activity, and can be used to maintain income and employment. Countercyclical fiscal policy does not exclude decreasing government expenditures and increasing revenues as a percentage of GDP during a boom, and should be used to counter the formation of a bubble. As Alesina et al. (2008) point out, fiscal policy is procyclical in many developing countries (to prevent governments from appropriating rents during upswings) and generally countercyclical in OECD countries. Appropriate countercyclical fiscal policy should ideally focus on creating fiscal space during booms by reducing debt-to-GDP ratios, so that net government expenditures can be increased during downturns.

Macroprudential regulation, mentioned above, is a useful accompaniment to both monetary and fiscal policy. It also addresses problems that cannot be targeted by fiscal or monetary policy. Rather than focusing on regulation of individual institutions alone, macroeconomic financial regulation focuses on systemic risk and can enhance countercyclical monetary and fiscal policy by ensuring financial markets are properly cushioned with limited exposure to risk. Deviations of asset prices from fundamentals, excessive risk taking, and excessive leverage can be restricted by macroprudential regulation (Blanchard et al. 2010). Macroprudential regulation is supposed to be managed by the new US Financial Stability Oversight Council and the European Systemic Risk Board and European System of Financial Supervisors.

Coordinating macroeconomic policy

The concept of macroeconomic policy coordination has been around for decades, and was created with the recognition that policy in one country creates externalities in other countries. For example, macroeconomic policy coordination feeds into stabilization of exchange rates, since differences may lead speculators to pull money out of one country and place it in another. Monetary policy coordination that changes interest rates among countries in tandem can halt this type of speculation (Blecker 1999). Fiscal policy coordination can be used to ensure fiscal discipline of coordinating countries to control inflation (Eggertsson 2006) and reinforce monetary policy coordination.

There are small gains (between 0.5 and 1 percent of GDP) to macroeconomic policy coordination (Oudiz and Sachs 1984). This is the generally accepted quantification of gains from policy coordination for developed countries; developing countries may experience higher gains (Meyer et al. 2002).

Policy coordination in practice has been difficult to achieve. The first attempt at macroeconomic policy coordination occurred in 1973 in the face of the oil price shock. Countries experienced higher inflation and devaluation, and countries were poised to engage in monetary tightening. Coordination did not occur at this time, but a conversation among the Group of Five (G-5) resulted in creation of an oil facility as an alternative to fiscal tightening (Meyer et al. 2002). Serious attempts at policy coordination ended after the failure of a coordination in 1978 that was interrupted by the second oil shock in 1979, and by the election of Ronald Reagan in the US and Margaret Thatcher in the United Kingdom (UK) in the 1980s, who were generally opposed to coordinated policy maneuvers. Policy coordination was attempted in 1985 under the Plaza Accord, and in 1987 under the Louvre Accord, but neither implementation was particularly effective (Meyer et al. 2002).

Policy making at the national level once again became the norm. Fiscal policy was seen as a less effective tool for economic fine-tuning. Even more generally, officials particularly in the United States felt, after the failure of the Plaza and Louvre accords, that coordinated policy making was not worthwhile (Sobel and Stedman 2006).

After the Asian financial crisis, however, global coordination was again discussed. The Financial Stability Forum was created to bring finance officials, regulators, and central bank officials together to discuss financial stability, even if this was not a forum for coordinated policy making per se. After the Great Recession of 2008, the Financial Stability Forum was regrouped as the Financial Stability Board.

Academics and officials alike desired global macroeconomic policy coordination in the wake of the US crisis, but this was not accomplished as G-20 leaders met in April 2009. The most recent crisis reinforced the importance of using regular automatic stabilizers in the case of any recession, since once a crisis begins, discretionary fiscal spending comes too late (Claessens et al. 2010). Macroeconomic policy coordination among regions at least is desirable to provide countercyclical fiscal stimulus (Takagi 2009) while preventing cross-border shifts in deposits and other destabilizing effects, but it has not gotten any easier, as individual countries find it difficult to make concessions to others (Jones 2009).

Creating a global managed currency regime
Imbalances created by the current currency regime have led many economists to call for the creation of a single world currency. The dollar standard has created imbalances between core and periphery countries, exposing export-oriented periphery countries to deflationary pressures as they engage in dollar-denominated trade (McKinnon 2005). The periphery's often hard or soft dollar (or euro, or yen)-pegged exchange rates expose the countries to exchange rate risk, both through trade and, particularly, through short-term borrowing from abroad. This in itself increases the potential for developing countries to experience crisis. In addition, confidence in the dollar has not been consistently strong, leading to volatility in the dollar's effective exchange rate and increased uncertainty among countries pegged to the dollar (UN 2009b).

As a solution, neither of the two extreme exchange rate regimes of purely fixed or floating regimes appears to be entirely desirable (although McKinnon advocates a universal fixed exchange system): fixed regimes because of the necessity to therefore impose capital controls to maintain the peg; floating regimes because of developing countries' fear of exchange rate volatility. The third alternative global exchange rate regime aside from the current mixed regime, which may provide a new measure of stability, is a managed system based on international cooperation. There have been several proposals in this direction.

The simplest suggestion has been to simply create one global currency as a store of value and unit of exchange. Using one global currency not tied to any particular country could eliminate the "Triffin dilemma" (see Chapter 3) and reduce imbalances between center and periphery nations. One of the first suggestions for a world currency was proposed by Keynes at the Bretton Woods conference in 1944, and was more complex than the simple proposal. Keynes proposed a world clearing currency, called "bancor," that would be tied to the price of 30 commodities. Domestic currencies would be fixed but adjustable to bancor and cleared through an International Clearing Union (Hockett 2002). In fact, no world clearing currency was created until 1970, when the Special Drawing Right (SDR), was introduced by the IMF. The SDR, valued using a basket of currencies, has mainly been used as a tool of the IMF to allow countries to purchase their currencies using SDRs when they are in a weak external position (IMF 2010a). Yet, more extensive use of SDRs has not occurred. To this end, some have encouraged the use of SDRs in trade, financial transactions, and reserves (Saccomanni 2010).

Davidson (2009) presents what he dubs an "updated" version of Keynes's proposal, to create an International Monetary Clearing Union (IMCU) that would require all foreign exchange transactions, for any purpose, to go through the IMCU. The objectives of the IMCU would be to improve financial transaction monitoring, place the burden of resolving trade imbalances on surplus nations, and prevent holdings of excessive reserves.

The UN Commission of Experts (UN 2009b) also recommends a single global currency, managed by the IMF or a Global Reserve Bank. Countries could exchange their own currencies for the new currency, and the global currency would be therefore backed by the currency of all the members. It is not necessary that the global currency be backed by member currencies, however, as long as central banks commit to accept the new currency. Countries would hold some of the new currency as reserves and use the exchange rate regime of their choice. This new currency would be allocated to countries based on their weight in the world economy or on their needs (based on the demand for reserves). Excess reserve holdings would be discouraged.

Although creating a single world currency may eliminate exchange rate crises, it may not remove imbalances that create crises. Using Europe as an example, Eichengreen (1999) notes that, first, creating a single regional currency took years of political institution building to arrive at. Second, rather than preventing crises, the single currency may transmit the crisis to other nations more rapidly. And third, some countries may allow for lax regulation, creating a free rider problem.

Maintaining the dollar standard requires better exchange rate policy, but it is not clear what a better policy is. Developing countries that float their currency may benefit from an increase in export earnings after a devaluation, but several countries that float together will face fierce competition without the same growth outcome (Blecker 1999). Debts denominated in foreign currency held by domestic residents would create a sudden debt burden with devaluation. A devaluation can have the unintended effects of severe inflation and a free-falling currency, which undermines both domestic economic activity and international investment.

A fixed global exchange rate has been proposed as a partial solution to the dollar standard problem. McKinnon (1988) suggests that countries fix their currencies to the three dominant currencies (then the dollar, yen, and German Mark), at purchasing power parity. This would occur through adjustment of the money supplies; therefore inflation would converge to the same rate. Others criticize this solution since it would require a great deal of policy coordination and a loss of ability to conduct monetary policy, which is unlikely for countries to support (UN 2009b).

ARE CRISES INEVITABLE?

A question that arises from this survey is, are crises inevitable? Can they be prevented even with the solutions suggested above? Certainly we have much to learn from previous crises. Rapid capital account and banking liberalization often lead to crisis. Incurring a large amount of foreign-denominated debt as a developing country is unwise, particularly if there are pressures on the currency to depreciate. Large gains in asset prices likely represent a bubble, and the bubble will burst. Quick and "correct" policy action is essential.

Some economists have argued that crises are endemic to capitalism, and this may apply doubly to financial capitalism. These economists are all considered heterodox, not believing in the efficiency of markets and rationality of individuals. Karl Marx was the first economist to successfully argue that capitalism is by its nature unstable and will give way to crises due to the tendency of the profit rate to fall. Following in the Marxist tradition were John Maynard Keynes, Paul Baran, and Paul Sweezy, who viewed capitalism as tending toward crisis-causing stagnation (Keynes argued that overinvestment led to industrial overcapacity, while Baran and Sweezy argued that the culprit was underconsumption). Hyman Minsky, a macroeconomist unassociated with Marx and therefore more palatable to the public, also believed that capitalism was unstable. Minsky observed the rise of modern finance and saw irrational exuberance as particularly pernicious, creating crises out of excessive speculation.[6]

At the other extreme, some economists of the inevitability-of-crises school argue that crises should be viewed as market corrections, penalizing imprudent decisions. This view is related to the efficient-markets hypothesis, which states that financial markets reflect all available information.

In between the extreme views that markets can be entirely efficient (or self-correcting), and that markets cannot possibly be efficient (that is, capitalism is unstable), the question of whether crises are inevitable remains. Potential for crisis begins with differences between exchange rate regimes, monetary policies, productive potential, and strength of political and economic institutions, with capital flowing to the temporarily most attractive areas. Information and uncertainty, along with random shocks, only serve to exacerbate these differences, as squeamish investors flee from areas that lose appeal to those that gain appeal. Even where asset prices reflect historical information, and are weakly efficient, tail risks may present a financial threat.[7] These factors, which can be viewed as economic "fault lines," can agitate confidence and perceptions of profitability in various regions.

Constraints bear down on policy makers despite their best efforts to move in the direction of growth. If policy makers were willing to sacrifice growth for stability, perhaps crises could be prevented. Growth requires the attraction of capital. Creating a unique environment, within a country, for domestic and foreign investment and increased production is ideal for that country, but it can lead to global instability both in and of itself, and through competition and retaliation from other countries. The pre-eminence of country sovereignty and competitiveness over global financial stability ensures that fault lines will exist and expand, and that crises will continue to occur. Should country priorities shift en masse from economic growth to economic and financial stability, there is a much greater probability that future financial crises might be prevented.

Strong, stable institutions and stabilizing government policies are more likely to help a country resist crisis. Strong institutions include effectively governed and supervised banks, as well as an effective system of taxation, while stabilizing government policies include preventative macroprudential regulations noted above. As a bulwark against crisis, every institution counts: good homes, a network of utility and road infrastructures, a legal system that prevents widespread gross injustice, a functioning system of taxation, available formal sector jobs, and sound financial systems. None of these institutions is easy to implement, particularly for less developed countries, and the persistence of institutions across countries over time is strong. We can only hope that economic leadership will not sacrifice essential institution building as economic growth is carried out, throwing out the proverbial "baby" with the "bathwater."

CONCLUSION

Hyman Minsky was right in the sense that given free rein, capitalism has created instability and unanticipated crises. Deregulation of the financial sector and breakdown of the global monetary and economic cooperation of Bretton Woods has led to more pronounced and rapidly developing crises. At present, we need not only financial and economic regulation, but also some economic restructuring to reduce the role of finance in the global economy and increase the role of real economic activity. After all, real economic gains are based on real production, and we must reorient our focus to this aim.

NOTES

1. Caballero and Kurlat (2009) recommend that the government issue tradable insurance credits, which would entitle institutional holders to central bank guarantees during a systemic crisis.
2. For example, the UN Commission of Experts (UN 2009b) headed by Stiglitz.
3. Less seriously considered is the idea of creating a World Financial Authority (WFA), suggested by Eatwell and Taylor (2000), who propose an international institution that would control financial externalities, such as potential losses, that impact societies but are not paid for by markets. The WFA would regulate systemic risk and coordinate national action against market abuses and international financial crime.

   Although the main argument against such an institution is that nations would oppose such an authority as an infringement upon their sovereignty, Eatwell and Taylor make the case that similar international institutions have been created in the past. Rather than think of a WFA as a new type of entity, Eatwell and Taylor view the WFA as an extension of the Basle Committee on Banking Supervision (based at the Bank for International Settlements in Basle), which sets regulatory standards for financial institutions; the International Organization of Securities Commissions, which creates regulatory standards on cross-border securities transactions; and the International Association of Insurance Supervisors, which sets standards on insurance transactions. In addition, the Financial Stability Forum, now the Financial Stability Board, was organized to promote financial stability by addressing current issues.

   Eatwell and Taylor define the "social spread" as the difference between costs associated with social risk, and those associated with private risk. One task for global financial regulation is to build the social spread into the investors' calculations where possible, and where not possible, to limit excessively risky financial activities. Risk control would be accomplished at both the macro and the micro level. The IMF, not the WFA, would remain the lender of last resort. Generally, creating a WFA is seen as an unlikely event, and without change among national leaders, there is little evidence to support the notion that the WFA would not face the same ideological and practical problems facing the IMF today.
4. Bordo and James (2010) argue that three issues dominate the debate about the IMF: the design of the exchange rate regime, in which some Asian economies have been accused of maintaining an artificially low exchange rate; the question of reserve management, where there is concern over a build-up of large surplus reserves; and the management of financial globalization, particularly on financial instability.
5. Woods (2010) views this change as too small to include the developing world per se.

6.　Minsky viewed the process of expansion as creating increasingly greater potential for a debt–deflation process to occur. Although we do not necessarily agree with this assessment (financialization beyond lending money has created value in assets), his overall framework that pinpoints excessive speculation as dangerous still holds today.
7.　Righi and Ceretta (2013) find that European markets are weakly efficient but that tail risk is present.

References

Acharya, Viral V. and Sascha Steffen. 2015. The "Greatest" Carry Trade Ever? Understanding Eurozone Bank Risks. *Journal of Financial Economics* 115: 215–236.

Agliardi, Elettra, Mehmet Pinar, and Thanasis Stengos. 2014. A Sovereign Risk Index for the Eurozone based on Stochastic Dominance. *Finance Research Letters* 11: 375–384.

Aizenmann, Joshua and Ilan Noy. 2013. Macroeconomic Adjustment and the History of Crises in Open Economies. *Journal of International Money and Finance* 38: 41–58.

Akyuz, Yilmaz and Korkut Boratov. 2003. The Making of the Turkish Financial Crisis. *World Development* 31(9): 1549–1566.

Alba, Pedro, Amar Bhattacharya, Stijn Claessens, Swati Ghosh, and Leonardo Hernandez. 1999. The Role of Macroeconomic and Financial Sector Links in East Asia's Financial Crisis. In *The Asian Financial Crisis: Causes, Contagion and Consequences*, ed. P.-R. Agenor, M. Miller, D. Vines, and A. Weber. New York: Cambridge University Press.

Alberola, Enrique, Humberto Lopez, and Luis Serven. 2003. Tango with the Gringo: The Hard Peg and Real Misalignment in Argentina. Banco de Espana.

Aldrick, Philip. 2008. Royal Bank of Scotland: Why One of Britain's Biggest Banks is Trading like a Penny Stock. *Telegraph*. http://www.telegraph.co.uk/finance/newsbysector/banksandfinance/3151276/Royal-Bank-of-Scotland-Why-one-of-Britains-biggest-banks-is-trading-like-a-penny-stock.html.

Alesina, Alberto, Filipe R. Campante, and Guido Tabellini. 2008. Why is Fiscal Policy Often Procyclical? *Journal of the European Economic Association* 6(5): 1006–1036.

Almunia, Miguel, Agustin Benetrix, Barry Eichengreen, Kevin H. O'Rourke, and Gisela Rua. 2010. From Great Depression to Great Credit Crisis: Similarities, Differences and Lessons. *Economic Policy* 25(62): 219–265.

Amann, Edmund and Werner Baer. 2000. The Illusion of Stability: The Brazilian Economy Under Cardoso. *World Development* 28(10): 1805–1819.

Anand, M.R., G.L. Gupta, and Ranjan Dash. 2012. The Euro Zone Crisis:

Its Dimensions and Implications. India Ministry of Finance Working Paper.

Andrade, Joaquim P. and Vladimir Kuhl Teles. 2004. An Empirical Model of the Brazilian Country Risk – An Extension of the Beta Country Risk Model. Econometric Society 2004 Latin American Meetings 284, Econometric Society.

Angkinand, A.P. and T.D. Willett. 2011. Exchange Rate Regimes and Banking Crises: The Channels of Influence Investigated. *International Journal of Finance Economics* 16: 256–227.

Ardagna, Silvia and Francesco Caselli. 2014. The Political Economy of the Greek Debt Crisis: A Tale of Two Bailouts. *American Economic Journal: Macroeconomics* 6(4): 291–323.

Arner, Douglas W. and Michael W. Taylor. 2009. The Global Financial Crisis and the Financial Stability Board: Hardening the Soft Law of International Financial Regulation. *UNSW Law Journal* 32(2): 488–513.

Atinc, Manuelyan and Michael Walton. 1998. *Social Consequences of the East Asian Financial Crisis*. Washington, DC: World Bank.

Babecký, Jan, Tomáš Havránek, Jakub Matějů, Marek Rusnák, Kateřina Šmídková, and Bořek Vašíček. 2014. Banking, Debt, and Currency Crises in Developed Countries: Stylized Facts and Early Warning Indicators. *Journal of Financial Stability* 15(C): 1–17.

Baig, Taimur and Ilan Goldfajn. 1999. Financial Market Contagion in the Asian Crisis. *IMF Staff Papers* 46(2): 167–195.

Balin, Bryan J. 2008. Basel I, Basel II, and Emerging Markets: A Nontechnical Analysis. Johns Hopkins University School of Advanced International Studies, Washington, DC.

Ballabriga, Fernando. 2014. Euro Zone Crisis: Diagnosis and Likely Solutions. ESADEgeo Position Paper 35.

Bandara, Amarakoon. 2014. How Effective are Countercyclical Policy Tools in Mitigating the Impact of Financial and Economic Crises in Africa? *Journal of Policy Modeling* 36: 840–854.

Barro, Robert J. 2001. Economic Growth in East Asia Before and After the Financial Crisis. NBER Working Paper 8330.

Bartels, Larry M. 2013. Political Effects of the Great Recession. *Annals of the American Academy of Political and Social Science* 650(1): 47–76.

BBC. 2001. The Events that Triggered Argentina's Crisis. December 21. http://news.bbc.co.uk/2/hi/business/1721103.stm.

BBC. 2003. History of the Euro. http://news.bbc.co.uk/2/hi/uk_news/politics/2450825.stm.

BBC. 2009. Timeline: Iceland Economic Crisis. http://news.bbc.co.uk/2/hi/7851853.stm.

BBC. 2010. Japan Passes New $61bn Stimulus Package. http://www.bbc.co.uk/news/business-11844483.

BBC. 2012a. Timeline: The Unfolding Eurozone Crisis. February 13. http://www.bbc.co.uk/news/business-13856580.

BBC. 2012b. Eurozone Crisis Explained. *BBC News*, July 23.

Beaudreau, Bernard C. 2005. *How the Republicans Caused the Stock Market Crash of 1929*. Bloomington, IN: iUniverse Publishing.

Beck, Thortsen and Asli Demirgüç-Kunt. 2009. Financial Institutions and Markets Across Countries and Over Time: Data and Analysis. World Bank Policy Research Working Paper No. 4943.

Beirne, John and Marcel Fratzscher. 2013. The Pricing of Sovereign Risk and Contagion during the European Sovereign Debt Crisis. ECB Working Paper No. 1625.

Belaisch, Agnes, Charles Collyns, Paula De Masi, Guy Meredith, Anoop Singh, Reva Krieger, and Robert Rennhack. 2005. Stabilization and Reforms in Latin America: A Macroeconomic Perspective of the Experience Since the 1990s. IMF Occasional Paper. Washington, DC: IMF.

Benedictus, Luca de. 2011. Africa and the World Trade Network: Persistence, Change and the Aftermath of the Global Financial Crisis. Paper prepared for the European Report on Development.

Benigno, Gianluca, Huigang Chen, Christopher Otrok, Alessandro Rebucci, and Eric R. Young. 2013. Financial Crises and Macro-Prudential Policies. *Journal of International Economics* 89: 453–470.

Berg, Andrew. 1999. The Asia Crisis: Causes, Policy Responses, and Outcomes. IMF Working Paper 99/138.

Bergmann, Carl. 1930. Germany and the Young Plan. *Foreign Affairs* 8(4): 583–597.

Bernanke, Ben. 1983. Non-Monetary Effects of the Financial Crisis in the Propagation of the Great Depression. NBER Working Paper 1054.

Bernanke, Ben S. 1995. The Macroeconomics of the Great Depression: A Comparative Approach. *Journal of Money, Credit and Banking* 27(1): 1–28.

Bernanke, Ben S. 2000. Japanese Monetary Policy: A Case of Self-Induced Paralysis? Presentation at the ASSA meetings, Boston, MA, January 9.

Bernanke, Ben S. 2002. Remarks by Governor Ben S. Bernanke At the Conference to Honor Milton Friedman, University of Chicago, Chicago, IL. On Milton Friedman's Ninetieth Birthday. November 8.

Bernanke, Ben S. 2005. The Global Saving Glut and the US Current Account Deficit. The Sandridge Lecture, Virginia Association of Economics, Richmond, VA. March 10.

Bernanke, Ben S. and Kevin Carey. 1996. Nominal Wage Stickiness and Aggregate Supply in the Great Depression. *Quarterly Journal of Economics* 111(3): 853–883.

Bertola, Luis and Jose Antonio Ocampo. 2012. *The Economic Development of Latin America since Independence*. New York: Oxford University Press.

Best, Jacqueline. 2004. Hollowing out Keynesian Norms: How the Search for a Technical Fix Undermined the Bretton Woods Regime. *Review of International Studies* 30(3): 383–404.

Bhagat, Sanjai, Brian Bolton, and Jun Lu. 2015. Size, Leverage, and Risk-Taking of Financial Institutions. *Journal of Banking and Finance* 59: 520–537.

Bhagwati, Jagdish. 1998. The Capital Myth – The Difference between Trade in Widgets and Dollars. *Foreign Affairs* 77(3): 7–12.

Bicaba, Zorobabel, Daniel Kapp, and Francesco Molteni. 2015. Stability Periods between Financial Crises: The Role of Macroeconomic Fundamentals and Crises Management Policies. *Economic Modelling* 43: 346–360.

Bird, Graham. 2007. The IMF: A Bird's Eye View of Its Role and Operations. *Journal of Economic Surveys* 21(4): 683–745.

Bank for International Settlements (BIS). 2009. Bank for International Settlement Statistics. http://www.bis.org/statistics/index.htm.

Bank for International Settlements (BIS). 2010. Basel III: A Global Regulatory Framework for More Resilient Banks and Banking Systems. BIS Publication.

Bank for International Settlements (BIS). 2011. Capital Treatment for Bilateral Counterparty Credit Risk Finalized by the Basel Committee. June 1. http://www.bis.org/press/p110601.htm.

Bank for International Settlements (BIS). 2012. Basel Committee on Banking Supervision reforms – Basel III. http://www.bis.org/bcbs/basel3/b3summarytable.pdf.

Blanchard, Olivier, Giovanni Dell'Ariccia, and Paolo Mauro. 2010. Rethinking Macroeconomic Policy. *Journal of Money, Credit and Banking* 42(s1): 199–215.

Blanton, Robert, Shannon Blanton, and Dursun Peksin. 2015. Financial Crises and Labor: Does Tight Money Loosen Labor Rights? *World Development* 76: 1–12.

Blecker, Robert. 1999. *Taming Global Finance*. Washington, DC: Economic Policy Institute.

Bogdanowicz-Bindert, Christine A. 1986. The Debt Crisis: The Baker Plan Revisited. *Journal of Interamerican Studies and World Affairs* 28(3): 33–45.

Bongini, Paola, Stijn Claessens, and Giovanni Fern. 2001. The Political

Economy of Distress in East Asian Financial Institutions. *Journal of Financial Services Research* 19(1): 5–25.

Bordo, Michael D. 1992. The Gold Standard and Other Monetary Regimes. *NBER Reporter* Spring: 7–10.

Bordo, Michael D. 2008. Gold Standard. In *Concise Encyclopedia of Economics*, ed. David R. Henderson. Indianapolis, IN: Liberty Fund.

Bordo, Michael D. and Barry Eichengreen. 1993. *A Retrospective on the Bretton Woods System: Lessons for International Monetary Reform.* Chicago, IL: University of Chicago Press.

Bordo, Michael D., Christopher J. Erceg and Charles L. Evans. 2000. Money, Sticky Wages, and the Great Depression. *American Economic Review* 90(5): 1447–1463.

Bordo, Michael D., Claudia Dale Goldin, and Eugene Nelson White. 1998. *The Defining Moment: The Great Depression and the American Economy in the Twentieth Century.* Chicago, IL: University of Chicago Press.

Bordo, Michael and Harold James. 2001. The Adam Klug Memorial Lecture: Haberler versus Nurske: The Case for Floating Exchange Rates as an Alternative to Bretton Woods? NBER Working Paper 8545.

Bordo, Michael and Harold James. 2010. The Past and Future of IMF Reform. http://sciie.ucsc.edu/JIMF/bordojamesimfmarch09V3.pdf.

Bordo, Michael and Harold James. 2014. The European Crisis in the Context of the History of Previous Financial Crises. *Journal of Macroeconomics* 39(B): 275–284.

Bordo, Michael D. and John S. Landon-Lane. 2010. The Global Financial Crisis of 2007–08: Is It Unprecedented? NBER Working Paper 16589.

Bordo, Michael D. and C.M. Meissner. 2012. Does Inequality Lead to a Financial Crisis? *Journal of International Money and Finance* 31: 2147–2161.

Bordo, Michael D. and David C. Wheelock. 1998. Price Stability and Financial Stability: The Historical Record. *Federal Reserve Bank of St Louis Review*. September–October: 41–62.

Borio, Claudio and Piti Disyatat. 2011. Global Imbalances and the Financial Crisis: Link or No Link? BIS Working Paper 346.

Boschi, Melisso and Aditya Goenka. 2012. Relative Risk Aversion and the Transmission of Financial Crises. *Journal of Economic Dynamics and Control* 36: 85–99.

Boughton, James M. 2009. A New Bretton Woods? IMF. http://www.imf.org/external/pubs/ft/fandd/2009/03/boughton.htm.

Boughton, James M. 2012. *Tearing Down Walls: The International Monetary Fund 1990–1999.* Washington, DC: IMF.

Bouzas, Roberto. 1996. The Mexican Peso Crisis and Argentina's Convertibility Plan: Monetary Virtue or Monetary Impotence? In

The Mexican Peso Crisis, ed. Riordan Roett. London: Lynne Rienner Publishers.

Brenner, Michael J. 1976. *The Politics of International Monetary Reform: The Exchange Crisis.* Cambridge, MA: Ballinger Publishing Company.

Brenner, Robert. 2006. *The Economics of Global Turbulence.* New York: Verso.

Bretschger, Lucase, Vivien Kappel, and Therese Werner. 2012. Market Concentration and the Likelihood of Financial Crises. *Journal of Banking and Finance* 36: 3336–3345.

Brumbaugh, Jr, R. Dan and Andrew S. Carron. 1987. Thrift Industry Crisis: Causes and Solutions. *Brookings Papers on Economic Activity* 2: 349–388.

Bruner, Fernando A. and Jaume Ventura. 2010. Rethinking the Effects of Financial Liberalization. http://www.econ.upf.edu/docs/papers/down loads/1128.pdf.

Bruner, Robert F. and Sean D. Carr. 2007. *The Panic of 1907: Lessons Learned from the Market's Perfect Storm.* Hoboken, NJ: John Wiley & Sons.

Brunila, Anne and Kari Takala. 1993. Private Indebtedness and the Banking Crisis in Finland. Bank of Finland Discussion Papers 9/93.

Brunnermeier, Markus, Andrew Crockett, Charles Goodhart, Avinash D. Persaud, and Hyun Shin. 2009. The Fundamental Principles of Financial Regulation. Geneva Reports on the World Economy – Preliminary Conference Draft.

Buchs, Thierry D. 1999. Financial Crisis in the Russian Federation: Are the Russians Learning to Tango? *Economics of Transition* 7(3): 687–715.

Buiter, Willem H. 2007. The Central Bank as Market Maker of Last Resort. *Maverecon.com.* August 12.

Buiter, Willem H. 2009. Too Big to Fail is Too Big. *Financial Times* blog. June 24.

Buiter, Willem H., Giancarlo Corsetti, and Paolo A. Pesenti. 1998. *Financial Markets and European Monetary Cooperation.* New York: Cambridge University Press.

Bulmer-Thomas, Victor. 1999. The Brazilian Devaluation: National Responses and International Consequences. *International Affairs* 75(4): 729–741.

Bussiere, Matthieu, Gong Cheng, Menzie Chinn, and Noemie Lisack. 2015. For a Few Dollars More: Reserves and Growth in Times of Crises. *Journal of International Money and Finance* 52: 127–145.

Caballero, Julian. 2015. Banking Crises and Financial Integration: Insights from Networks Science. *International Financial Markets, Institutions, and Money* 34: 127–146.

Caballero, Ricardo J. 2010. The "Other" Imbalance and the Financial Crisis. NBER Working Paper 15636.

Caballero, Ricardo J., Takeo Hoshi, and Anil K Kashyap. 2008. Zombie Lending and Depressed Restructuring in Japan. *American Economic Review* 98(5): 1943–1977.

Caballero, Ricardo J. and Pablo Kurlat. 2009. The "Surprising" Origin and Nature of Financial Crises: A Macroeconomic Policy Proposal. MIT Department of Economics Working Paper No. 09–24.

Calavita, Kitty, Henry N. Pontell, and Robert H. Tillman. 1997. *Big Money Crime*. Berkeley, CA: University of California Press.

Calice, Giovanni, Jing Chen, and Julian Williams. 2013. Liquidity Spillovers in Sovereign Bond and CDS Markets: An Analysis of the Eurozone Sovereign Debt Crisis. *Journal of Economic Behavior and Organization* 85: 122–143.

Calomiris, Charles W. and Gary Gorton. 1991. The Origins of Banking Panics: Models, Facts, and Bank Regulation. In *Financial Markets and Financial Crises*, ed. R. Glenn Hubbard. Chicago, IL: University of Chicago Press.

Calomiris, Charles, Daniela Klingebiel, and Luc Laeven. 2004. A Taxonomy of Financial Crisis Resolution Mechanisms: Cross-Country Experience. World Bank Working Paper 3379.

Calomiris, Charles and Joseph R. Mason. 2003. Fundamentals, Panics, and Bank Distress During the Depression. *American Economic Review* 93: 1615–1647.

Calvo, Guillermo A. and Carmen Reinhart. 2000. When Capital Inflows Come to a Sudden Stop: Consequences and Policy Options. In *Reforming the International Monetary and Financial System*, ed. P. Kenen and A. Swoboda. Washington, DC: International Monetary Fund.

Cantero-Saiz, Maria, Sergio Sanfilippo-Azofra, Begoña Torre-Olmo, and Carlos López-Gutiérrez. 2014. Sovereign Risk and the Bank Lending Channel in Europe. *Journal of International Money and Finance* 47: 1–20.

Carron, Andrew S. and Benjamin M. Friedman. 1982. Financial Crises: Recent Experience in US and International Markets. *Brookings Papers on Economic Activity* 1982(2): 395–422.

Carstens, Agustín G. and Alejandro M. Werner. 1999. Mexico's Monetary Policy Framework under a Floating Exchange Rate Regime. Banco de Mexico Documento de Investigación No. 9905.

Case–Shiller Home Price Index, S&P Case–Shiller Home Price Indices. http://us.spindices.com/index-family/real-estate/sp-corelogic-case-shiller.

Cavallo, Domingo. 2002. The Fight to Avoid Default and Devaluation. April 25. http://www.cavallo.com.ar/wp-content/uploads/the_fight.pdf.

Cesarano, Filippo. 2006. *Monetary Theory and Bretton Woods*. New York: Cambridge University Press.

Chang, Ha-Joon. 2000. The Hazard of Moral Hazard: Untangling the Asian Crisis. *World Development* 28(4): 775–788.

Chang, Roberto. 2007. Financial Crises and Political Crises. *Journal of Monetary Economics* 54: 2409–2420.

Chang, Roberto and Andres Velasco. 1998. Financial Crises in Emerging Markets. NBER Working Paper No. 6606.

Chen, Qianying, Andrew Filardo, Dong He, and Feng Zhu. 2015. Financial Crisis, US Unconventional Monetary Policy and International Spillovers. IMF Working Paper 15/85.

Chinn, Menzie and Jeffrey Frankel. 2008. The Euro May over the Next 15 Years Surpass the Dollar as Leading International Currency. Harvard University JFK School of Government Working Paper RWP08–016.

Chinn, Menzie and Hiro Ito. 2005. *What Matters for Financial Development? Capital Controls, Institutions, and Interactions*. UC Santa Cruz: Santa Cruz Center for International Economics.

Chiodo, Abbigail J. and Michael T. Owyang. 2002. A Case Study of a Currency Crisis: The Russian Default of 1998. *Federal Reserve Bank of St Louis Review* November–December: 7–17.

Chor, Davin and Kalina Manova. 2010. Off the Cliff and Back? Credit Conditions and International Trade during the Global Financial Crisis. NBER Working Paper 16174.

Christofides, Charis, Theo S. Eicher, and Chris Papageorgiou. 2015. Did Established Early Warning Signals Predict the 2008 Crises? *European Economic Review* 81: 1–202.

Chudik, Alexander and Marcel Fratzscher. 2012. Liquidity, Risk and the Global Transmission of the 2007–2008 Financial Crisis and the 2010–11 Sovereign Debt Crisis. European Central Bank Working Paper 1416.

Chudnovsky, Daniel and Andres Lopez. 2007. *The Elusive Quest for Growth in Argentina*. New York: Palgrave Macmillan.

Claessens, Stijn, Giovanni Dell'Ariccia, Deniz Igan, and Luc Laeven. 2010. Lessons and Policy Implications from the Global Financial Crisis. IMF Working Paper WP/10/44.

Claessens, Stijn, Simeon Djankov, and Lixin Colin Xu. 2000. Corporate Performance in the East Asian Financial Crisis. *World Bank Research Observer* 15(1): 23–46.

Cline, William R. 2015. From Populist Destabilization to Reform and Possible Debt Relief in Greece. Peterson Institute for International Economics Policy Brief PB15–12.

CNN. 2010. Greece's Financial Crisis Explained. *CNN.com*, March 26.

Cogley, Timothy. 1999. FRBSF Economic Letter 99–10. Federal Reserve Bank of San Francisco online. March 26.

Cohen, Adam. 2009. Franklin D. Roosevelt: The First 100 Days. *Time*. June 24.

Cohen, Benjamin J. 2002. Bretton Woods System. *Routledge Encyclopedia of International Political Economy*. New York: Routledge

Cohen, Daniel. 1992. The Debt Crisis: A Postmortem. *NBER Macroeconomics Annual* 7: 65–105.

Cohen, Daniel and Sebastien Villemot. 2015. Endogenous Debt Crises. *Journal of International Money and Finance* 51: 337–369.

Colander, David, Hans Föllmer, Armin Haas, Michael Goldberg, Katarina Juselius, Alan Kirman, Thomas Lux, and Brigitte Sloth. 2009. The Financial Crisis and the Systemic Failure of Academic Economics. Kiel Institute Working Paper No. 1489.

Cole, H. and L. Ohanian. 2000. New Deal Policies and the Persistence of the Great Depression: A General Equilibrium Analysis. Federal Reserve Bank of Minneapolis, Discussion Paper.

Collás-Monsod, Solita. 1989. Management of the Debt Crisis: A Debtor's Viewpoint. In *Solving the Global Debt Crisis*, ed. C.A. Bogdanowicz-Bindert. New York: Harper & Row.

Collyns, Charles and Abdelhak Senhadji. 2002. Lending Booms, Real Estate Bubbles, and The Asian Crisis. IMF Working Paper No. 02/20.

Columbia Electronic Encyclopedia. 2001. Dawes Plan. http://www. infoplease.com/ce6/history/A0814823.html.

Committee for the Study of Economic and Monetary Union. 1989. Report on Economic and Monetary Union in the European Community. European Community.

Conway, Edmund. 2008. Dollar's Golden Era is Ending, Warns Soros. *Telegraph*. January 23.

Coolidge, Calvin. 1924. Speech on Taxes, Liberty, and the Philosophy of Government, delivered August 11 1924, White House Grounds, Washington, DC.

Corsetti, Giancarlo, Keith Kuester, Andre Meier, and Gernot J. Mueller. 2012. Sovereign Risk, Fiscal Policy, and Macroeconomic Stability. IMF Working Paper WP/12/33.

Corsetti, Giancarlo, Paolo Pesenti, and Nouriel Roubini. 1998. Paper Tigers? A Model of the Asian Crisis. NBER Working Paper No. 6783.

Coudert, Virginie, Cecile Couharde, and Valerie Mignon. 2011. Exchange Rate Volatility Across Financial Crises. *Journal of Banking and Finance* 35: 3010–3018.

Crotty, James. 2009. Structural Causes of the Global Financial Crisis:

A Critical Assessment of the "New Financial Architecture." *Cambridge Journal of Economics* 33(4): 563–580.

Curry, Timothy and Lynn Shibut. 2000. The Cost of the Savings and Loan Crisis: Truth and Consequences. *FDIC Banking Review* 13(2): 26–35.

Cypher, James M. 1996. Mexico: Financial Fragility or Structural Crisis? *Journal of Economic Issues* 30(2): 451–461.

D'Arista, Jane. 2002. Financial Regulation in a Liberalized Global Environment. In *International Capital Markets*, ed. J. Eatwell and L. Taylor. New York: Oxford University Press.

D'Arista, Jane. 2006. The Implications of Aging for the Structure and Stability of Financial Markets. Background paper prepared for the World Economic and Social Survey 2007 on Ageing and Financial Markets. December 7.

D'Arista, Jane and Stephany Griffith-Jones. 2009. G-24 Agenda and Criteria for Financial Regulatory Reform. G-24 paper.

Da Costa, G.C. 1991. External Debt of Developing Countries: Crisis of Growth. *Economic and Political Weekly* 26(8): 433–438.

Da Rocha, Bruno T. and Solomos Solomou. 2015. The Effects of Systemic Banking Crises in the Inter-War Period. *Journal of International Money and Finance* 54: 35–49.

Dabla-Norris, Era and Yasemin Bal Gunduz. 2014. Exogenous Shocks and Growth Crises in Low Income Countries: A Vulnerability Index. *World Development* 59: 360–378.

Davar, Ezra. 2015. General Equilibrium Theory – Walras versus Post-Walras Economists: "Finding Equilibrium" – Losing Economics. Institute of Economic Research Working Papers 46.

Davidson, Paul. 2009. *The Keynes Solution: The Path to Global Economic Prosperity*. New York: Palgrave Macmillan.

Davison, Lee. 2005. Politics and Policy: The Creation of the Resolution Trust Corporation. *FDIC Banking Review* 17(2): 17–44.

De Bruyckere, Valerie, Maria Gerhardt, Glenn Schepens, and Rudi Vander Vennet. 2013. Bank/Sovereign Risk Spillovers in the European Debt Crisis. *Journal of Banking and Finance* 37: 4793–4809.

De Krivoy, Ruth. 2003. Banking Crises in Latin America: Regulatory and Supervisory Issues. In *Financial Crises in Latin America*, ed. Edgardo Demaestri and Pietro Maschi. Washington, DC: IADB.

De Paiva Abreu, Marcelo and Rogerio L.F. Werneck. 2005. The Brazilian Economy from Cardoso to Lula: An Interim View. Catholic University of Rio de Janiero Discussion Paper 504.

De Santis, Roberto A. 2015. A Measure of Redenomination Risk. European Central Bank Working Paper 1785.

Deaton, Angus. 2011. The Financial Crisis and the Well-Being of Americans. The Hicks Lecture, Oxford, May 16.

DeLong, J. Bradford and Barry Eichengreen. 1991. The Marshall Plan: History's Most Successful Structural Adjustment Program. NBER Working Papers 3899.

Demirgüç-Kunt, Asli and Luis Servén. 2009. Are All the Sacred Cows Dead? Implications of the Financial Crisis for Macro and Financial Policies. World Bank Policy Research Paper 4807.

Desai, Padma. 2003. *Financial Crisis, Contagion, and Containment: From Asia to Argentina*. Princeton, NJ: Princeton University Press.

Despres, Emile, Charles P. Kindleberger, and Walter S. Salant. 1966. The Dollar and World Liquidity. A Minority View. *The Economist*, February 5.

Devlin, Robert. 1989. *Debt and Crisis in Latin America*. Princeton, NJ: Princeton University Press.

Dewatripont, Mathias, Jean-Charles Rochet, and Jean Tirole. 2010. *Balancing the Banks: Global Lessons from the Financial Crisis*. Princeton, NJ: Princeton University Press.

Diaz Sanchez, Jose Luis, and Aristomene Varoudakis. 2013. Growth and Competitiveness as Factors of Eurozone External Imbalances. World Bank Policy Research Working Paper 6732.

Djiwandono, J. Soedradjad. 2007. Ten Years After the Asian Crisis: An Indonesian Insider's View. In *Ten Years Later: Revisiting the Asian Financial Crisis*, ed. Bhumika Muchhala. Washington, DC: Woodrow Wilson International Center for Scholars.

Dobbin, Frank R. 1993. The Social Construction of the Great Depression: Industrial Policy during the 1930s in the United States, Britain and France. *Theory and Society* 22(1): 1–56.

Dodd, Randall. 2007. Subprime: Tentacles of a Crisis. *IMF Finance and Development* 44(4): 15–19.

Dodd, Randall. 2008. Over-the-Counter Markets: What are They? *IMF Finance and Development* 45(2). http://www.imf.org/external/pubs/ft/fandd/2008/06/basics.htm.

Domac, I. and M.S. Martinez Peria. 2003. Banking Crises and Exchange Rate Regimes: Is there a Link? *Journal of International Economics* 61: 41–72.

Dominguez, Jorge I. 2008. Explaining Latin America's Lagging Development in the Second Half of the Twentieth Century. In *Falling Behind: Explaining the Development Gap between Latin America and the United States*, ed. Francis Fukuyama. New York: Oxford University Press.

Dooley, Michael P. 2000. A Model of Crises in Emerging Markets. *Econometric Journal* 110: 256–272.

Dooley, Michael P. and Michael M. Hutchison. 2009. Transmission of the US Subprime Crisis to Emerging Markets: Evidence on the Decoupling–Recoupling Hypothesis. *Journal of International Money and Finance* 28(8): 1331–1349.

Drees, Burkhard and Ceyla Pazarbaşıoğlu. 1998. The Nordic Banking Crises: Pitfalls in Financial Liberalization? IMF Occasional Paper 161.

Dungey, Mardi, Jan P.A.M. Jacobs, and L. Lestano. 2015. The Internationalization of Financial Crises: Banking and Currency Crises 1883–2008. *North American Journal of Economic and Finance* 32: 29–47.

Easterly, William. 1989. Fiscal Adjustment and Deficit Financing during the Debt Crisis. In *Dealing with the Debt Crisis*, ed. I. Husain and I. Diwan. Washington, DC: World Bank.

Eatwell, John and Lance Taylor. 2000. *Global Finance at Risk: The Case for International Regulation*. New York: New Press.

The Economist. 2008. China Seeks Stimulation. November 10.

Edlin, Aaron S. and Dwight M. Jaffee. 2009. Show Me The Money. *Economists' Voice*. March.

Edwards, Sebastian. 1989. Structural Adjustment Policies in Highly Indebted Countries. In *Developing Country Debt and Economic Performance, Volume One*, ed. Jeffrey D. Sachs. Chicago, IL: University of Chicago Press.

Edwards, Sebastian. 2005. Capital Controls, Sudden Stops and Current Account Reversals. NBER Working Paper No. 11170.

Eggertsson, Gauti B. 2006. Fiscal Multipliers and Policy Coordination. Federal Reserve Bank of New York Staff Reports 241.

Eichengreen, Barry. 1992. *Golden Fetters: The Gold Standard and the Great Depression, 1919–1939*. New York: Oxford University Press.

Eichengreen, Barry. 1999. *Toward a New International Financial Architecture: A Practical Post-Asia Agenda*. Washington, DC: Institute for International Economics.

Eichengreen, Barry. 2000. The EMS Crisis in Retrospect. NBER Working Paper 8035.

Eichengreen, Barry. 2007. *Global Imbalances and the Lessons of Bretton Woods*. Cambridge, MA: MIT Press.

Eichengreen, Barry. 2012. European Monetary Integration with Benefit of Hindsight. *JCMS: Journal of Common Market Studies* 50: 123–136.

Eichengreen, Barry. 2014. *Hall of Mirrors: The Great Depression, the Great Recession, and the Uses – and Misuses – of History*. New York: Oxford University Press.

Eichengreen, Barry, Ricardo Hausmann, and Ugo Panizza. 2004. The Pain of Original Sin. In *Other People's Money*, ed. B. Eichengreen and R. Hausmann. Chicago, IL: University of Chicago Press.

Eichengreen, Barry and Peter B. Kenen. 1994. Managing the World

Economy Under the Bretton Woods System: An Overview. In *Managing the World Economy: Fifty Years After Bretton Woods*, ed. Peter Kenen. Washington, DC: Institute for International Economics.

Eichengreen, Barry and Kevin H. O'Rourke. 2009. A Tale of Two Depressions. *www.voxeu.org*. September 1.

Eichengreen, Barry and Andrew Rose. 1998. Staying Afloat When the Wind Shifts: External Factors and Emerging-Market Banking Crises. NBER Working Paper No. 6370.

Eichengreen, Barry, Andrew K. Rose, and Charles Wyplosz. 1996. Contagious Currency Crises. NBER Working Paper 5681.

Eichengreen, Barry and Jeffrey Sachs. 1985. Exchange Rates and Economic Recovery in the 1930s. *Journal of Economic History* 45: 925–946.

Eichengreen, Barry and Peter Temin. 1997. The Gold Standard and the Great Depression. NBER Working Paper No. W 6060.

Elizalde, Abel. 2007. From Basel I to Basel II: An Analysis of the Three Pillars. CEMFI Working Paper No. 0704.

Englund, Peter. 1999. The Swedish Banking Crisis: Roots and Consequences. *Oxford Review of Economic Policy* 15(3): 80–97.

Enrich, David, Liz Rappoport, and Jenny Strasburg. 2009. Banks Aiming to Play Both Sides of Coin. *Wall Street Journal*, March 27.

Ergungor, O. Emre. 2007. On the Resolution of Financial Crises: The Swedish Experience. Federal Reserve Bank of Cleveland, Policy Discussion Paper 21.

Esaka, Taro. 2014. Are Consistent Pegs Really More Prone to Currency Crises? *Journal of International Money and Finance* 44: 136–163.

European Commission. 2009. Commission Adopts European Economic Recovery Plan. http://ec.europa.eu/economy_finance/articles/eu_econ-omic_situation/article13502_en.htm.

European Commission. 2010. http://ec.europa.eu/internal_market/finances/committees/index_en.htm.

European Council and European Commission. 1992. *Treaty on European Union*. Luxembourg: Office for Official Publications of the European Communities.

European Systemic Risk Board. 2015. ESRB Report on the Regulatory Treatment of Sovereign Exposures. March. http://www.esrb.europa.eu/pub/pdf/other/esrbreportregulatorytreatmentsovereignexposures032015.en.pdf?c0cad80cf39a74e20d9d5947c7390df1.

Euzéby, Alain. 2010. Economic Crisis and Social Protection in the European Union: Moving Beyond Immediate Responses. *International Social Security Review* 63(2): 71–86.

Evans-Pritchard, Ambrose. 2012. Portugal Props Up Banks with €6.6bn. *Telegraph*, June 4.

FDIC. 1997. *History of the Eighties*. Washington, DC: FDIC.

Feldstein, Martin. 2002. Argentina's Fall: Lessons from the Latest Financial Crisis. *Foreign Affairs* 81(2): 7–14.

Felices, Guillermo and Tomasz Wieladek. 2012. Are Emerging Market Indicators of Vulnerability to Financial Crises Decoupling from Global Factors? *Journal of Banking and Finance* 36: 321–331.

Fender, I. and J. Gyntelberg. 2008. Overview: Global Financial Crisis Spurs Unprecedented Policy Actions. *BIS Quarterly Review* December: 1–24.

Ferguson, Thomas and Robert Johnson. 2009. Too Big to Bail: The "Paulson Put," Presidential Politics, and the Global Financial Meltdown. *International Journal of Political Economy* 38(1): 3–34.

Fernandez, Ana I., Francisco Gonzalez, and Nuria Suarez. 2013. How Do Bank Competition, Regulation, and Institutions Shape the Real Effect of Banking Crises? International Evidence. *Journal of International Money and Finance* 33: 19–40.

Ferraro, Vincent and Melissa Rosser. 1994. Global Debt and Third World Development. In *World Security: Challenges for a New Century*, ed. M. Klare and D. Thomas. New York: St Martin's Press.

Ferri, Giovanni, L.G. Liu, and Joseph E. Stiglitz. 1999. The Procyclical Role of Rating Agencies: Evidence from the East Asian Crisis. *Economic Notes by Banca Monte dei Paschi di Siena SpA* 28(3): 335–355.

Ffrench-Davis, Ricardo. 1987. Latin American Debt: Debtor–Creditor Relations. *Third World Quarterly* 9(4): 1167–1183.

Financial Stability Forum. 2009. Report of the Financial Stability Forum on Addressing Procyclicality in the Financial System. FSF Report April 2.

Fisher, Irving. 1929 [1931]. *New York Herald Tribune*. October 24. Reprinted (1931) in Edward Angly, *Oh Yeah?* New York: Viking Press.

Fisher, Irving. 1933. The Debt–Deflation Theory of Great Depressions. *Econometrica* 1: 337–357.

Fisher, Irving. 1934. *Are Booms and Depressions Transmitted Internationally Through Monetary Standards?* 2nd rev. edn. New Haven, CT: Irving Fisher.

Flatters, Frank. 2000. Thailand and the Asian Crisis. In *The Asian Financial Crisis*, ed. W.T. Woo, J.D. Sachs, and K. Schwab. Cambridge, MA: MIT Press.

Floros, Christos, Renatas Kizys, and Christian Pierdzioch. 2013. Financial Crises, the Decoupling–Recoupling Hypothesis, and the Risk Premium on the Greek Stock Index Futures Market. *International Review of Financial Analysis* 28: 166–173.

Flynn, Peter. 1999. Brazil: The Politics of Crisis. *Third World Quarterly* 20(2): 287–317.

Ford, Gerald. 1979. *A Time to Heal: The Autobiography of Gerald R. Ford.* New York: Harper & Row.

Fouad, Mahmoud H. 1978. Petrodollars and Economic Development in the Middle East. *Middle East Journal* 32(3): 307–321.

Fraga, Arminio. 2000. Monetary Policy During the Transition to a Floating Exchange Rate: Brazil's Recent Experience. *Finance and Development* March: 16–18.

Frankel, Jeffrey. 2009. What's "In" and What's "Out" in Global Money. Adapted from keynote speech for workshop on Exchange Rates: The Global Perspective, sponsored by the Bank of Canada and the European Central Bank, Frankfurt, June 19.

Fratzscher, Marcel. 2011. Capital Flows, Push versus Pull Factors and the Global Financial Crisis. 2011 Bretton Woods Conference.

Frenkel, Roberto and Martin Rapetti. 2009. A Developing Country View of the Current Global Crisis: What Should Not Be Forgotten and What Should Be Done. *Cambridge Journal of Economics* 33: 685–702.

Fried, Edward R. and Charles L. Schultze. 1975. Overview. In *Higher Oil Prices and the World Economy*, ed. E.R. Fried and C.L. Schultze. Washington, DC: Brookings Institution.

Friedman, Milton. 1992[1976]. Prize Lecture: Inflation and Unemployment, Lecture to the Memory of Alfred Nobel, December 13, 1976. In *Nobel Lectures, Economics 1969–1980*, ed. Assar Lindbeck. Singapore: World Scientific Publishing.

Friedman, Milton and Anna J. Schwartz 1963. *A Monetary History of the United States, 1867–1960*. Princeton, NJ: Princeton University Press.

Friedman, Milton and Anna J. Schwartz 2008. *The Great Recession, 1929–1933*. Princeton, NJ: Princeton University Press.

Fukao, Mitsuhiro. 2003. Japanese Financial Deregulation and Market Discipline. In *Financial Crises in Japan and Latin America*, ed. E. Demaestri and P. Masci. Washington, DC: Inter-American Development Bank.

Furceri, Davide and Annabelle Mourougane. 2012. The Effect of Financial Crises on Potential Output: New Empirical Evidence from OECD Countries. *Journal of Macroeconomics* 34(3): 822–832.

G-20. 2009. Declaration on Strengthening the Financial System. G20 Document. April 2.

Gaddy, Clifford G. and Barry W. Ickes. 2010. Russia after the Global Financial Crisis. *Eurasian Geography and Economics* 51(3): 281–311.

Galbraith, James K. 2008. *The Predator State: How Conservatives Abandoned the Free Market and Why Liberals Should Too*. New York: Simon & Schuster.

Galbraith, James. 2014. *The End of Normal: The Great Crisis and the Future of Growth*. New York: Simon & Schuster.

Galbraith, John Kenneth. 1955. *The Great Crash of 1929*. New York: Mariner Books.

Galbraith, John Kenneth. 1994. *A Journey through Economic Time*. New York: Houghton Mifflin.

Gallagher, Kevin. 2007. Toward a Theory of Innovation and Industrial Pollution: Evidence from Mexican Manufacturing. In *Industrial Innovation and Environmental Regulation: Developing Workable Solutions*, ed. S. Parto and B. Herbert-Copley. Tokyo: UNU Press.

Gao, Bai. 2001. *Japan's Economic Dilemma*. Cambridge: Cambridge University Press.

Garcia-Palacios, Jaime H., Augusto Hasman, and Margarita Samartin. 2014. Banking Crises and Government Intervention. *Journal of Financial Stability* 15: 32–42.

Gardó, Sándor and Reiner Martin. 2010. The Impact of the Global Economic and Financial Crisis on Central, Eastern, and South-Eastern Europe: A Stock-Taking Exercise. European Central Bank Occasional Paper 114.

Gätjen, Rebekka and Melanie Schienle. 2015. Measuring Connectedness of Euro Area Sovereign Risk. SFB 649 Discussion Paper 2015-019.

Gauthier-Villars, David. 2012. Europe Hit by Downgrades. *Wall Street Journal*, January 14.

Gavin, Michael and Roberto Perotti. 1997. Fiscal Policy in Latin America. In *NBER Macroeconomics Annual 1997, Volume 12*, ed. Ben Bernanke and Julio Rotemberg. Cambridge, MA: MIT Press.

Gay, Edwin F. 1932. The Great Depression. *Foreign Affairs* 10(4): 529–540.

Gialis, Stelios and Maria Tsampra. 2015. The Diverse Regional Patterns of Atypical Employment in Greece: Employment Restructuring, Re/Deregulation and Flexicurity Under Crisis. *Geoforum* 62: 175–187.

Giambiagi, Fabio and Marcio Ronci. 2004. Fiscal Policy and Debt Sustainability: Cardoso's Brazil, 1995–2002. IMF Working Paper 156.

Gibson, Heather D., Stephen G. Hall, and George S. Tavlas. 2014. Fundamentally Wrong: Market Pricing of Sovereigns and the Greek Financial Crisis. *Journal of Macroeconomics* 39: 405–419.

Giddy, Ian H. 1994. *Global Financial Markets*. Lexington, MA: D.C. Heath & Company.

Gilman, Martin. 2010. *No Precedent, No Plan*. Cambridge, MA: MIT Press.

Gilpin, Robert. 1987. *The Political Economy of International Relations*. Princeton, NJ: Princeton University Press.

Glencross, Andrew. 2014. The Eurozone Crisis as a Challenge to Democracy and Integration in Europe. *Orbis* 58(1): 55–68.

Goddard, John, Phil Molyneux, and John O.S. Wilson. 2009. The Financial

Crisis in Europe: Evolution, Policy Responses and Lessons for the Future. *Journal of Financial Regulation and Compliance* 17(4): 362–380.

Goldstein, Morris. 1998. The Asian Financial Crisis: Causes, Cures, and Systemic Implications. Institute for International Economics Policy Analyses in International Economics.

Gomez-Puig, Marta, Simon Sosvilla-Rivero, and Maria del Carmen Ramos-Herrera. 2014. An Update on EMU Sovereign Yield Spread Drivers in Times of Crisis: A Panel Data Analysis. *North American Journal of Economic and Finance* 30: 133–153.

Goodfriend, Marvin. 2005. The Monetary Policy Debate Since October 1979: Lessons for Theory and Practice. *Federal Reserve Bank of St Louis Review* 87(2): 243–262.

Gorton, Gary B., Stefan Lewellen, and Andrew Metrick. 2012. The Safe-Asset Share. NBER Working Paper 17777.

Grammatikos, Theoharry and Robert Vermeulen. 2012. Transmission of the Financial and Sovereign Debt Crises to the EMU: Stock Prices, CDS Spreads, and Exchange Rates. *Journal of International Money and Finance* 31: 517–533.

Greenspan, Alan. 2008. Testimony before the House Committee on Oversight and Government Reform.

Griffith-Jones, Stephany and Osvaldo Sunkel. 1986. *Debt and Development Crises in Latin America*. New York: Oxford University Press.

Gruben, William C. and John H. Welch. 2001. Banking and Currency Crisis Recovery: Brazil's Turnaround of 1999. Federal Reserve Bank of Dallas Economic and Financial Review, Fourth Quarter.

Guillén, Mauro F. 2009. The Global Economic and Financial Crisis: A Timeline. http://lauder.wharton.upenn.edu/pdf/Chronology%20Economic%20%20 Financial%20Crisis.pdf.

Gündüz, Yalin and Orcun Kaya. 2014. Impacts of the Financial Crisis on Eurozone Sovereign CDS Spreads. *Journal of International Money and Finance* 49: 425–442.

Haggard, Stephen. 2000. *The Political Economy of the Asian Financial Crisis*. Washington, DC: Institute for International Economics.

Hahn, J., H.S. Shin, and K. Shin. 2011. Non-core Bank Liabilities and Financial Vulnerability. Paper presented at the Fed and JMCB Conference in September.

Hanna, Don. 2000. Restructuring Asia's Financial System. In *The Asian Financial Crisis*, ed. W.T. Woo, J. Sachs, and K. Schwab. Cambridge, MA: MIT Press.

Hannsgen, Greg and Dimitri B. Papadimitriou. 2009. Lessons from the New Deal: Did the New Deal Prolong or Worsen the Great Depression? Levy Institute Working Paper No. 481.

Harrison, Mark. 1998. The Economics of World War II: An Overview. In *The Economics of World War II: Six Great Powers in International Comparison*, ed. Mark Harrison. Cambridge: Cambridge University Press.

Hartland-Thunberg, Penelope. 1977. Oil, Petrodollars and the LDC's. *Financial Analysts Journal* 33(4): 55–58.

Hausmann, Ricardo and Andrés Velasco. 2002. Hard Money's Soft Underbelly: Understanding the Argentine Crisis. *Brookings Trade Forum* 2002: 59–104.

Healy, Jack. 2009. Dow, First Time in a Year, Breaks Through 10 000. *New York Times*. October 14.

Helleiner, Eric. 1994. *States and the Reemergence of Global Finance: From Bretton Woods to the 1990s*. Ithaca, NY: Cornell University Press.

Helleiner, Eric. 2005. The Strange Story of Bush and the Argentine Debt Crisis. *Third World Quarterly* 26(6): 951–969.

Hénin, Pierre-Yves and Marie Podevin. 2002. Assessing the Effects of Policy Changes: Lessons from the European 1992 Experience. *Econometrics of Policy Evaluation* July–December: 435–461.

Hernández-Murillo, Rubén. 2007. Experiments in Financial Liberalization: The Mexican Banking Sector. *Federal Reserve Bank of St Louis Review* 89(5): 415–432.

Higgins, Bryon. 1993. Was the ERM Crisis Inevitable? *Federal Reserve Bank of Kansas City Economic Review* 4: 27–40.

Hirsch, Fred. 1967. *Money International*. Harmondsworth: Penguin Press.

Hockett, Robert. 2002. From Macro to Micro to Mission-Creep: Defending the IMF's Emerging Concern with the Infrastructural Prerequisites to Global Financial Stability. *Columbia Journal of Transnational Law* 41: 153–193.

Holinski, Nils, Clemens Kool, and Joan Muysken. 2012. Persistent Macroeconomic Imbalances in the Euro Area: Causes and Consequences. *Federal Reserve Bank of St Louis Review* 94(1): 1–20.

Hong, Kiseok and Johng-Wha Lee. 2000. Korea: Returning to Sustainable Growth? In *The Asian Financial Crisis*, ed. W.T. Woo, J. Sachs, and K. Schwab. Cambridge, MA: MIT Press.

Honkapohja, Seppo. 2014. Financial Crises: Lessons from the Nordic Experience. *Journal of Financial Stability* 13: 193–201.

Honkapohja, Seppo, Erkki Koskela, Stefan Gerlach, and Lucrezia Reichlin. 1999. The Economic Crisis of the 1990s in Finland. *Economic Policy* 14(29): 399–436.

Hoover, Herbert. 1952. *The Memoirs of Herbert Hoover*. New York: Macmillan Company.

Hornbeck, Jeffrey. 2004. Argentina's Sovereign Debt Restructuring. Congressional Research Service Report for Congress 32637.

Hoshi, Takeo and Anil K. Kashyap. 2004. Japan's Financial Crisis and Economic Stagnation. *Journal of Economic Perspectives* 18(1): 3–26.

Humphreys, Charles and John Underwood. 1989. The External Debt Difficulties of Low-Income Africa. In *Dealing with the Debt Crisis*, ed. I. Husain and I. Diwan. Washington, DC: World Bank.

Husain, Ishrat and Ishac Diwan. 1989. Introduction. In *Dealing with the Debt Crisis*, ed. I. Husain and I. Diwan. Washington, DC: World Bank.

Hussain, Mumtaz and Steven Radelet. 2000. Export Competitiveness in Asia. In *The Asian Financial Crisis*, ed. W.T. Woo, J. Sachs, and K. Schwab. Cambridge, MA: MIT Press.

Illing, Gerhard and Philipp König. 2014. The European Central Bank as Lender of Last Resort. DIW Economic Bulletin 9.

IMF. 1995. IMF Praises Argentine Measures, Sees US$2b Loan Increase. News Brief No. 95/9, March 13.

IMF. 1998. Brazil and IMF Announce Successful Conclusion to Negotiations on Economic, Financial Program. *IMF Survey* 27(21), November 16.

IMF. 2002. IMF Executive Board Approves New Conditionality Guidelines. Press Release No. 02/43. September 26.

IMF. 2003. Lessons from the Crisis in Argentina. Policy Development Paper. October 8.

IMF. 2010a. Special Drawing Rights. Factsheet. January 31.

IMF. 2010b. IMF Board Approves Far-Reaching Governance Reforms. http://www.imf.org/external/pubs/ft/survey/so/2010/NEW110510B.htm.

IMF. 2011. About the IMF. http://www.imf.org/external/about.htm.

Ingves, Stefan. 2002. The Nordic Banking Crisis from an International Perspective. Speech for Seminar on Financial Crises, Kredittilsynet, The Banking, Insurance and Securities Commission of Norway, September 11.

Irwin, Gregor and David Vines. 1999. A Krugman–Dooley–Sachs Third Generation Model of the Asian Financial Crisis. CEPR Discussion Papers 2149.

Ivanova, Anna, Wolfgang Mayer, Alex Mourmouras, and George Anayiotas. 2003. What Determines the Implementation of IMF-Supported Programs? IMF Working Paper 03/8.

Jackson, James K. 2008. The US Financial Crisis: Lessons from Sweden. CRS Report for Congress. September 29.

Jaffee, Dwight M. 1994. The Swedish Real Estate Crisis. Report prepared for the Studieförbundet Näringsliv och Samhälle, Center for Business and Policy Studies, Stockholm, Sweden, October.

Jeanne, Olivier and Jeromin Zettelmeyer. 2004. In *Other People's Money*, ed. B. Eichengreen and R. Hausmann. Chicago, IL: University of Chicago Press.

Jing, Zhongbo, Jakob de Haan, Jan Jacobs, and Haizhen Yang. 2014. Identifying Banking Crises Using Money Market Pressure: New Evidence for a Large Set of Countries. *Journal of Macroeconomics* 43: 1–20.

Johanssen, Anders C. 2010. Financial Markets in East Asia and Europe During the Global Financial Crisis. Stockholm School of Economics CERC Working Paper 13.

Johnson, Simon. 2009a. Too Big to Fail, Politically. *Baseline Scenario* blog. https://baselinescenario.com/2009/06/18/too-big-to-fail-politically/.

Johnson, Simon. 2009b. "Large Integrated Financial Groups": Can't Live Without 'Em? Simon Johnson's blog on *The New Republic*. December 8.

Johnson, Simon. 2009c. What Did TARP Accomplish? *New York Times Economix Blog*, November 19. http://economix.blogs.nytimes.com/2009/11/19/what-did-tarp-accomplish/?_r=0.

Johnson, Simon and Todd Mitton. 2001. Cronyism and Capital Controls: Evidence from Malaysia. NBER Working Paper 8521.

Jones, Erik. 2009. The Euro and the Financial Crisis. *Survival* 51(2): 41–54.

Jonung, Lars. 2009. Financial Crisis and Crisis Management in Sweden: Lessons for Today. ADBI Working Paper 165.

Joyce, J.P. 2011. Financial Globalization and Banking Crises in Emerging Markets. *Open Economic Review* 22: 875–895.

Kahler, Miles. 1985. Politics and International Debt. *International Organization* 39(3): 357–382.

Kamin, Steven B. and Laurie Pounder DeMarco. 2010. How Did a Domestic Housing Slump Turn into a Global Financial Crisis? Board of Governors of the Federal Reserve System, International Finance Discussion Papers 994.

Kaminsky, Graciela L. and Carmen M. Reinhart. 1999. The Twin Crises: The Causes of Banking and Balance-of-Payments Problems. *American Economic Review* 89(3): 473–500.

Kaminsky, Graciela L. and Sergio L. Schmukler. 1999. What Triggers Market Jitters? A Chronicle of the Asian Crisis. *Journal of International Money and Finance* 18: 537–560.

Kanaya, Akihiro and David Woo. 2000. The Japanese Banking Crisis of the 1990s: Sources and Lessons. IMF Working Paper No. 7.

Kapstein, Ethan. 1994. *Governing the Global Economy*. Cambridge, MA: Harvard University Press.

Kato, Takao. 2001. The End of Lifetime Employment in Japan?: Evidence from National Surveys and Field Research. *Journal of the Japanese and International Economies* 15: 489–514.

Katz, Ellen Florian. 2007. The Risk in Subprime. *Fortune Magazine*. March 1.

Kaufman, Robert R. and Barbara Stallings. 1991. The Political Economy of Latin American Populism. In *The Macroeconomics of Populism in Latin America*, ed. Rudiger Dornbusch and Sebastian Edwards. Chicago, IL: University of Chicago Press.

Kauko, Karlo. 2014. How to Foresee Banking Crises? A Survey of the Empirical Literature. *Economic Systems* 38: 289–308.

Kazanas, Thanassis and Elias Tzavalis. 2014. Comment on "Fundamentally Wrong: Market Pricing of Sovereigns and the Greek Financial Crisis." *Journal of Macroeconomics* 39: 420–423.

Keynes, John Maynard. 1920. *The Economic Consequences of the Peace*. New York: Harcourt Brace.

Keynes, John Maynard. 1924. Alfred Marshall, 1842–1924. *Economic Journal* 34(135): 311–372.

Keynes, John Maynard. 1936. *The General Theory of Employment, Interest and Money*. London: Palgrave Macmillan.

Kindleberger, Charles P. 1937. *International Short-Term Capital Movements*. New York: Columbia University Press.

Kindleberger, Charles P. 1951. Bretton Woods Reappraised. *International Organization* 5(1): 32–47.

Kindleberger. Charles P. 1978. *Manias, Panics and Crashes: A History of Financial Crises*. New York: John Wiley.

Kindleberger, Charles P. 1986. *The World in Depression, 1929–1939*. Berkeley, CA: University of California Press.

Kindleberger, Charles P. and Robert Aliber. 2005. *Manias, Panics and Crashes: A History of Financial Crises*. New York: John Wiley.

Kissinger, Henry. 1998. How US Can End Up as the Good Guy. *Los Angeles Times*. February 8.

Kleimeier, Stefanie, Harald Sander, and Sylvia Heuchemer. 2013. Financial Crises and Cross-Border Banking: New Evidence. *Journal of International Money and Finance* 32: 884–915.

Klein, Michael W. 1998. European Monetary Union. *New England Economic Review* March–April: 3–12. Federal Reserve Bank of Boston.

Knot, Klaas, Jan-Egbert Sturm, and Jakob de Haan. 1998. The Credibility of the European Exchange Rate Mechanism. *Oxford Economic Papers* 50: 186–200.

Kohonen, Anssi. 2014. Transmission of Government Default Risk in the Eurozone. *Journal of International Money and Finance* 47: 71–85.

Korte, Josef, and Sascha Steffen. 2014. Zero Risk Contagion – Banks' Sovereign Exposure and Sovereign Risk Spillovers. Working Paper.

Koskeynkylä, Heikki and Jukka Vesala. 1994. Finnish Deposit Banks 1980–1993: Years of Rapid Growth and Crisis. Bank of Finland Discussion Papers 16/94.

Kouretas, Georgios. 2010. The Greek Crisis: Causes and Implications. *Panoeconomicus* 57(4): 391–404.

Kowalik, Michal. 2011. Countercyclical Capital Regulation: Should Bank Regulators Use Rules or Discretion? *Federal Reserve Bank of Kansas City* Second Quarter: 63–84.

Krueger, Anne. 2002. Crisis Prevention and Resolution: Lessons from Argentina. IMF Conference on "The Argentina Crisis," Cambridge, July 17.

Krugman, Paul. 1979. A Model of Balance-of-Payments Crises. *Journal of Money, Credit and Banking* 11: 311–325.

Krugman, Paul. 1994. The Myth of Asia's Miracle. *Foreign Affairs* 73: 62–78.

Krugman, Paul. 1996. Are Currency Crises Self-Fulfilling? In *NBER Macroeconomics Annual*, ed. B.S. Bernanke and J.J. Rotemberg. Cambridge, MA: NBER.

Krugman, Paul. 1999. Balance Sheets, the Transfer Problem, and Financial Crises. *International Tax and Public Finance* 6(4): 459–472.

Krugman, Paul. 2007. Is This the Wile E. Coyote Moment? *New York Times* blog. http://krugman.blogs.nytimes.com/2007/09/20/is-this-the-wile-e-coyote-moment/.

Kunz, Diane. 1997. The Marshall Plan Reconsidered. *Foreign Affairs* 76(3): 162–170.

Kushida, Kenji E. and Kay Shimizu. 2014. Introduction: Syncretism in Japan's Political Economy Since the 1990s. In *Syncretism*, ed. Kenji E. Kusida and Kay Shimizu. Stanford, CA: Walter H. Shorenstein Asia-Pacific Research Center.

Lainà, Patrizio, Juhi Nyholm, and Peter Sarlin. 2015. Leading Indicators of Systemic Banking Crises: Finland in a Panel of EU Countries. *Review of Financial Economics* 24: 18–35.

Lamdany, Ruben. 1989. The Market-Based Menu Approach in Action: The 1988 Brazilian Financing Package. In *Dealing with the Debt Crisis*, ed. I. Husain and I. Diwan. Washington, DC: World Bank.

Landler, Mark. 2008. Credit Crisis Triggers Downturn in Iceland. *New York Times Online*, April 17.

Larrain, Felipe and Andres Velasco. 1990. Can Swaps Solve the Debt Crisis? Lessons from the Chilean Experience. Princeton Studies in International Finance 69.

Latin American Shadow Financial Regulatory Committee. 2002. Resolution of Argentina's Financial Crisis. Latin American Shadow Financial Regulatory Committee Meeting, May 5, Statement No. 5.

Laubsch, Alan. 2009. Navigating the Global Crisis. Presentation at Riskmetrics Conference, Hong Kong, June 4.

Levy, Walter J. 1980. Oil and the Decline of the West. *Foreign Affairs* 58(5): 999–1015.

Lewis, Michael. 2011. When Irish Eyes Are Crying. *Vanity Fair*, March.

Lischinsky, Bernardo. 2003. The Puzzle of Argentina's Debt Problem: Virtual Dollar Creation? In *The Crisis That Was Not Prevented: Argentina, the IMF, and Globalisation*, ed. J.J. Teunissen and A. Akkerman. Amsterdam: FONDAD.

Lokshin, Michael and Martin Ravallion. 2000. Welfare Impacts of Russia's 1998 Financial Crisis and the Response of the Public Safety Net. *Economics of Transition* 8(2): 269–295.

Lowrey, Annie. 2012. Regulators Move Closer to Oversight of Nonbanks. *New York Times*, April 3.

Ludwig, Alexander. 2014. A Unified Approach to Investigate Pure and Wake-Up Call Contagion: Evidence from the Eurozone's First Financial Crisis. *Journal of International Money and Finance* 48: 125–146.

MacDonald, Ronald, Vasilos Sogiakas, and Andreas Tsopanakis. 2015. An Investigation of Systemic Stress and Interdependence within the Eurozone and Euro Area Countries. *Economic Modelling* 48: 52–69.

Maddison, Angus. 1995. *Monitoring the World Economy, 1820–1992*. Paris: OECD Development Centre Studies.

Mai, Nicola. 2008. Lessons from the 1990s Scandinavian Banking Crises. JP Morgan Chase Research Note. May 9.

Mainwaring, Scott, Daniel Brinks, and Aníbal Pérez-Liñán. 2001. Classifying Political Regimes in Latin. *Studies in Comparative International Development* 36(1): 37–65.

Mamudi, Sam. 2008. Lehman Folds with Record $613 billion debt. *Market Watch*. September 15.

Mankoff, Jeffrey. 2010. The Russian Economic Crisis. Council on Foreign Relations Special Report 53.

Marshall, Alfred. 1890. *Principles of Economics*. London: Macmillan & Co.

Massa, Isabella, Jodie Keane, and Jane Kennan. 2012. The Eurozone Crisis and Developing Countries. Overseas Development Institute Working Paper 345.

Matousek, Roman, Aarti Rughoo, Nicholas Sarantis, and A. George Assaff. 2015. Bank Performance and Convergence during the Financial Crisis: Evidence from the "Old" European Union and Eurozone. *Journal of Banking and Finance* 52: 208–216.

McCracken, Paul W. 1996. Economic Policy in the Nixon Years. *Presidential Studies Quarterly* 26(1): The Nixon Presidency: 165–177.

McDonald, Donogh C. 1982. Debt Capacity and Developing Country Borrowing: A Survey of the Literature. *Staff Papers – International Monetary Fund* 29(4): 603–646.

McKinnon, Ronald. 1988. Monetary and Exchange Rate Policies for International Financial Stability: A Proposal. *Journal of Economic Perspectives* 2: 83–103.

McKinnon, Ronald I. 1993. Rules of the Game: International Money in Historical Perspective. *Journal of Economic Literature* 31(1): 1–44.

McKinnon, Ronald. 2005. Trapped by the Dollar Standard. *Journal of Policy Modeling* 27: 477–485.

Meissner, Charles F. 1984. Debt: Reform Without Governments. *Foreign Policy* 56: 81–93.

Meltzer, Allan H. 1991. US Policy in the Bretton Woods Era. *Federal Reserve Bank of St Louis Review* May–June: 54–83.

Meyer, Laurence H., Brian M. Doyle, Joseph E. Gagnon, and Dale W. Henderson. 2002. International Coordination of Macroeconomic Policies: Still Alive in the New Millennium? International Finance Discussion Papers 723.

Miao, Jianjun and Pengfei Wang. 2015. Banking Bubbles and Financial Crises. *Journal of Economic Theory* 157: 763–792.

Mihaljek, Dubravko. 2009. The Spread of the Financial Crisis to Central and Eastern Europe: Evidence from BIS Data. BIS Working Paper, October 15.

Mikdashi, Zuhayr. 1981. Oil Price and OPEC Surpluses: Some Reflections. *International Affairs* 57(3): 407–427.

Minsky, Hyman. 1977. A Theory of Systemic Fragility. In *Financial Crises: Institutions and Markets in a Fragile Environment*, ed. Edward I. Altman and Arthur W. Sametz. Hoboken, NJ: Wiley.

Minsky, Hyman. 1980 [1982]. Finance and Profits, the Changing Nature of Business Cycles, The Business Cycle and Public Policy. 1929–1980, Joint Economic Committee, Congress of the United States, United States Government Printing Office, Washington, DC. Reprinted 1982 in Hyman P. Minsky, *Can It Happen Again?* Armonk, NY: M.E. Sharpe & Co.

Minsky, Hyman. 1991. Financial Crises: Systemic or Idiosyncratic. Levy Institute Working Paper No. 51.

Mishkin, Frederic S. 1999. Lessons from the Asian Crisis. *Journal of International Money and Finance* 18: 709–723.

Mishkin, Frederic S. 2011. Over the Cliff: From the Subprime to the Global Financial Crisis. *Journal of Economic Perspectives* 25(1): 49–70.

Mizen, Paul and Serafeim Tsoukas. 2012. The Response of the External Finance Premium in Asian Corporate Bond Markets to Financial Characteristics, Financial Constraints, and Two Financial Crises. *Journal of Banking and Finance* 36: 3048–3059.

Mohanty, Mritiunjoy. 1992. Strategies for Solution of Debt Crisis: An Overview. *Economic and Political Weekly* 27(9): 465–476.

Montoro, Carlos and Ramon Moreno. 2011. The Use of Reserve Requirements as a Policy Instrument in Latin America. *BIS Quarterly Review* March: 53–65.

Morales, Isidro. 1997. The Mexican Crisis and the Weakness of the NAFTA Consensus. *Annals of the American Academy of Political and Social Science* 550: 130–152.

Morales, Jeremy, Yves Gendron, and Henri Guenin-Paracini. 2014. State Privatization and the Unrelenting Expansion of Neoliberalism: The Case of the Greek Financial Crisis. *Critical Perspectives on Accounting* 25: 423–445.

Moravcsik, Andrew. 2012. Europe After the Crisis: How to Sustain a Common Currency. *Foreign Affairs* 91(3): 54–68.

Mundell, Robert A. 1973a. Uncommon Arguments for Common Currencies. In *The Economics of Common Currencies*, ed. H.G. Johnson and A.K. Swoboda. Crows Nest, Australia: Allen & Unwin.

Mundell, Robert A. 1973b. A Plan for a European Currency. In *The Economics of Common Currencies*, ed. H.G. Johnson and A.K. Swoboda. Crows Nest, Australia: Allen & Unwin.

Musacchio, Aldo. 2012. Mexico's Financial Crisis of 1994–1995. Harvard Business School Working Paper, No. 12–101, May.

Nabli, Mustapha K. 2010. Growth after the Global Recession in Developing Countries. In *The Great Recession and Developing Countries*, ed. Mustapha K. Nabli. Washington, DC: World Bank.

Nakaso, Hiroshi. 2001. The Financial Crisis in Japan during the 1990s: How the Bank of Japan Responded and the Lessons Learnt. BIS Papers No. 6.

NBER Macrohistory Database. 2010. Cambridge, MA: NBER.

Neely, Christopher J. 1999. An Introduction to Capital Controls. *Federal Reserve Bank of St Louis Review* November–December: 13–30.

Neftci, Salih N. 2002. FX Short Positions, Balance Sheets, and Financial Turbulence. In *International Capital Markets*, ed. J. Eatwell and L. Taylor. New York: Oxford University Press.

Nelson, Rebecca M., Paul Belkin, and James K. Jackson. 2015. The Greek Debt Crisis: Overview and Implications for the United States. Congressional Research Service Report 7–5700.

Newman, Jay H. 1989. Developing Country Debt and Market Reality. In *Solving the Global Debt Crisis*, ed. C.A. Bogdanowicz-Bindert. New York: Harper & Row.

Nixon, Richard. 1971. Address to the Nation Outlining a New Economic Policy: "The Challenge of Peace." August 15. Television address.

Nyberg, Peter and Vesa Vihriälä. 1993. The Finnish Banking Crisis and Its Handling. Bank of Finland Discussion Paper 8.

Obstfeld, Maurice. 1994. The Logic of Currency Crises. *Cahiers Economique et Monetaires* 43: 189–212.

Obstfeld, Maurice. 2012. Financial Flows, Financial Crises, and Global Imbalances. *Journal of International Money and Finance* 31(3): 469–480.

Obstfeld, Maurice and Kenneth Rogoff. 2009. Global Imbalances and the Financial Crisis: Products of Common Causes. CEPR Discussion Paper No. DP7606.

OECD. 1995. *OECD Economic Surveys 1995: Mexico*. Paris: OECD.

Okubo, Yoshio. 2003. Financial Sector Reform in Japan: Progress and Challenges. In *Financial Crises in Japan and Latin America*, ed. E. Demaestri and P. Masci. Washington, DC: Inter-American Development Bank.

Ongena, Steven, David C. Smith, and Dag Michalsen. 2000. Firms and their Distressed Banks: Lessons from the Norwegian Banking Crisis. Board of Governors of the Federal Reserve System, International Finance Discussion Papers No. 686.

Oudiz, Gilles and Jeffery Sachs. 1984. Macroeconomic Policy Coordination Among the Industrial Economies. *Brookings Papers on Economic Activity* 1: 1–64.

Palley, Thomas I. 2015. Milton Friedman's Economics and Political Economy: An Old Keynesian Critique. In *Milton Friedman: Contributions to Economics and Public Policy*, ed. Robert Cord. New York: Oxford University Press.

Palma, Gabriel. 2000. The Magical Realism of Brazilian Economics: How to Create a Financial Crisis by Trying to Avoid One. CEPA Working Paper No. 17.

Papanikos, Gregory T. 2015. The Real Exchange Rate of Euro and Greek Economic Growth. *Journal of Economic Asymmetries* 12: 100–109.

Paulson, Henry. 2010. *On the Brink*. New York: Business Plus.

Pehle, John W. 1946. The Bretton Woods Institutions. *Yale Law Journal* 55(5): 1127–1139.

Pempel, T.J. 1999. *The Politics of the Asian Economic Crisis*. Ithaca, NY: Cornell University Press.

Penrose, Edith. 1976. The Development of Crisis. In *The Oil Crisis*, ed. Raymond Vernon. New York: W.W. Norton & Company.

Perkins, Dwight Heald and Wing Thye Woo. 2000. Malaysia: Adjusting to Deep Integration. In *The Asian Financial Crisis*, ed. W.T. Woo, J. Sachs, and K. Schwab. Cambridge, MA: MIT Press.

Perotti, Enrico C. 2002. Lessons from the Russian Meltdown: The Economics of Soft Legal Constraints. CEPR Policy Paper No. 9.

Perry, Guillermo and Luis Servén. 2004. The Anatomy of a Multiple

Crisis: Why was Argentina Special and What Can We Learn from It? *Monetary Unions and Hard Pegs* 57: 231–287.

Pinto, Brian and Sergei Ulatov. 2010. Financial Globalization and the Russian Crisis of 1998. World Bank Policy Research Working Paper 5312.

Poledna, Sebastian, José Luis Molina-Borboa, Serafín Martínez-Jaramillo, Marco van der Leij, and Stefan Thurner. 2015. The Multi-Layer Network Nature of Systemic Risk and its Implications for the Costs of Financial Crises. *Journal of Financial Stability* 20: 70–81.

Pop-Eliches, Grigore. 2008. *From Economic Crisis to Reform: IMF Programs in Latin America and Eastern Europe.* Princeton, NJ: Princeton University Press.

Powell, Andrew. 2002. Argentina's Avoidable Crisis: Bad Luck, Bad Economics, Bad Politics, Bad Advice. *Brookings Trade Forum* 2002: 1–58.

Powell, Jim. 2003. *FDR's Folly.* New York: Three Rivers Press.

Pozsar, Zoltan. 2011. Institutional Cash Pools and the Triffin Dilemma of the US Banking System. IMF Working Paper 11/190.

Prakash, Aseem. 2001. The East Asian Crisis and the Globalization Discourse. *Review of International Political Economy* 8(1): 119–146.

Pratap, Sangeeta and Carlos Urrutia. 2012. Financial Frictions and Total Factor Productivity: Accounting for the Real Effects of Financial Crises. *Review of Economic Dynamics* 15: 336–358.

Prodi, Romano and Alberto Clo. 1976. Europe. In *The Oil Crisis*, ed. Raymond Vernon. New York: W.W. Norton & Company.

Pronobis, Michal. 2014. Is Monetary Policy of ECB the Right Response to the Eurozone Crisis? 19th International Scientific Conference; Economics and Management 2014, ICEM 2014, April 23–25, Riga, Latvia.

Qin, Xiao and Chengying Luo. 2014. Capital Account Openness and Early Warning System for Banking Crises in G20 Countries. *Economic Modelling* 39: 190–194.

Quigley, John M. 2001. Real Estate and the Asian Crisis. *Journal of Housing Economics* 10(2): 129–161.

Radelet, Steven and Jeffrey Sachs. 1998. The Onset of the East Asian Financial Crisis. NBER Working Paper 6680.

Radelet, Steven and Wing Thye Woo. 2000. Indonesia: A Trouble Beginning. In *The Asian Financial Crisis*, ed. W.T. Woo, J. Sachs, and K. Schwab. Cambridge, MA: MIT Press.

Rajan, R. 2010. *Fault Lines.* Princeton, NJ: Princeton University Press.

Ramirez de la O, Rogelio. 1996. The Mexican Peso Crisis and Recession of 1994–1995: Preventable Then, Avoidable in the Future? In *The Mexican Peso Crisis*, ed. Riordan Roett. London: Lynne Rienner Publishers.

Rappoport, Peter and Eugene N. White. 1994. Was the Crash of 1929 Expected? *American Economic Review* 84(1): 271–281.

Reinhart, Carmen, Morris Goldstein, and Graciela Kaminsky. 2000. Assessing Financial Vulnerability: An Early Warning System for Emerging Markets: Introduction. MPRA Paper No. 13629.

Reinhart, Carmen and Ken Rogoff. 2009. *This Time is Different: A Panoramic View of Eight Centuries of Financial Crises.* Princeton, NJ: Princeton University Press.

Reinhart, Carmen M. and Kenneth S. Rogoff. 2014. Recovery from Financial Crises: Evidence from 100 Episodes. *American Economic Review Papers and Proceedings* 104 (5): 50e55.

Rhodes, William R. 1989. A Negotiator's View. In *Solving the Global Debt Crisis*, ed. C.A. Bogdanowicz-Bindert. New York: Harper & Row.

Riding, Alan. 1987. Brazil to Suspend Interest Payment to Foreign Banks. *New York Times*, February 21.

Riedel, James. 1988. Industrialization and Growth: Alternative Views of East Asia. In *Achieving Industrialization in East Asia*, ed. Helen Hughes. Cambridge: Cambridge University Press.

Ries, Philippe. 2000. *The Asian Storm.* Boston, MA: Tuttle Publishing.

Righi, Marcelo Brutti and Paulo Sergio Ceretta. 2013. Risk Prediction Management and Weak Form Market Efficiency in Eurozone Financial Crisis. *International Review of Financial Analysis* 30: 384–393.

Robinson, Bruce. 2009. World War Two: Summary Outline of Key Events. *BBC Online.* November 5. http://www.bbc.co.uk/history/worldwars/wwtwo/ww2_summary_01.shtml.

Robinson, Neil. 2007. So What Changed? The 1998 Financial Crisis and Russia's Economic and Political Development. *Demokratizatsiya* 15(2): 245–259.

Rodrik, Dani. 2004. Getting Institutions Right. Institute for Advanced Study Working Paper. https://www.sss.ias.edu/files/pdfs/Rodrik/Research/getting-institutions-right.pdf.

Rodrik, Dani. 2006. Goodbye Washington Consensus, Hello Washington Confusion? A Review of the World Bank's "Economic Growth in the 1990s: Learning from a Decade of Reform." *Journal of Economic Literature* 44: 973–987.

Rodrik, Dani. 2009. A Plan B for Global Finance. *The Economist.* March 12.

Roett, Riordan. 1996. The Mexican Devaluation and the US Response: Potomac Politics, 1995-Style. In *The Mexican Peso Crisis*, ed. Riordan Roett. London: Lynne Rienner Publishers.

Rogoff, Kenneth. 2003. The IMF Strikes Back. *Foreign Policy* 134: 38–47.

Romer, Christina. 2004. The Great Depression. *Britannica Encyclopedia.* https://www.britannica.com/event/Great-Depression.

Rotberg, Eugene. 1989. The Politics of the Debt Crisis. In *Solving the Global Debt Crisis*, ed. C.A. Bogdanowicz-Bindert. New York: Harper & Row.

Rothermund, Dietmar. 1996. *The Global Impact of the Great Depression, 1929–1939*. New York: Routledge.

Rural Migration News. 1995. Devaluation and Emigration From Mexico. *Rural Migration News* 1(1). http://migration.ucdavis.edu/rmn/more.php?id=31_0_4_0.

Saccomanni, Fabrizio. 2010. The Global Crisis and the Future of the International Monetary System. Speech by Mr Fabrizio Saccomanni, Director General of the Bank of Italy, at the Chinese Academy of Social Sciences, Beijing, April 15.

Sachs, Jeffrey. 1989a. Making the Brady Plan Work. *Foreign Affairs* 68(3): 87–104.

Sachs, Jeffrey. 1989b. Introduction. In *Developing Country Debt and Economic Performance, Volume One*, ed. Jeffrey D. Sachs. Chicago, IL: University of Chicago Press.

Sachs, Jeffrey D. and Wing Thye Woo. 2000. Understanding the Asian Financial Crisis. In *The Asian Financial Crisis*, ed. W.T. Woo, J. Sachs, and K. Schwab. Cambridge, MA: MIT Press.

Sachs, Jeffrey. 1996. Alternative Approaches to Financial Crises in Emerging Markets. *Revista de Economic Politica* 16(2): 40–52.

Sachs, Jeffrey, Aaron Tornell, and Andres Velasco. 1996. The Mexican Peso Crisis: Sudden Death or Death Foretold? NYU Starr Center Research Report 96–20.

Salmon, Felix. 2009. Recipe for Disaster: The Formula That Killed Wall Street. *Wired Magazine*, January 23.

Sandal, Knut. 2004. The Nordic Banking Crises in the Early 1990s: Resolution Methods and Fiscal Costs. In *The Norwegian Banking Crisis*, ed. T.G. Moe, J.A. Solheim, and B. Vale. Norges Bank Occasional Paper No. 33.

Sarafrazi, Soodabeh, Shawkat Hammoudeh, and Paulo AraújoSantos. 2014. Downside Risk, Portfolio Diversification, and the Financial Crisis in the Eurozone. *Journal of International Financial Markets, Institutions, and Money* 32: 368–396.

Sato, Takafumi. 2003. Changes in the Japanese Financial Failure Resolution System. In *Financial Crises in Japan and Latin America*, ed. E. Demaestri and P. Masci. Washington, DC: Inter-American Development Bank.

Schlesinger, Jr, Arthur Meier. 2003. *The Coming of the New Deal, 1933–1935*. New York: Mariner Books.

Schubert, Aurel. 1991. *The Credit-Anstalt Crisis of 1931*. Cambridge: Cambridge University Press.

Serven, Luis and Andres Solimano. 1993. Debt Crisis, Adjustment Policies, and Capital Formation in Developing Countries: Where Do We Stand? *World Development* 21(1): 127–140.

Sevilla, Christina R. 1995. Explaining the September 1992 ERM Crisis: The Maastricht Bargain and Domestic Politics in Germany, France, and Britain. Presented at the European Community Studies Association, Fourth Biennial International Conference, May 11–14, Charleston, SC.

Shambaugh, Jay C. 2012. The Euro's Three Crises. *Brookings Papers on Economic Activity* Spring: 157–207.

Shirakawa, Masaaki. 2009. International Policy Response to Financial Crises. Remarks at the Federal Reserve Bank of Kansas City, Jackson Hole, Wyoming, Symposium.

Shwadran, Benjamin. 1986. *Middle East Oil Crises Since 1973*. London: Westview Press.

Singh, Ajit. 2002. "Asian Capitalism" and the Financial Crisis. In *International Capital Markets*, ed. J. Eatwell and L. Taylor. New York: Oxford University Press.

Smimou, K. and W. Khallouli. 2015. On the Intensity of Liquidity Spillovers in the Eurozone. *International Review of Financial Analysis* 25C: 125–153.

Smith, Clint E. 1996. International Perspectives on the Mexican Peso Crisis: An Introduction. In *The Mexican Peso Crisis*, ed. Riordan Roett. London: Lynne Rienner Publishers.

Sobel, Mark and Louellen Stedman. 2006. The Evolution of the G-7 and Economic Policy Coordination. Department of the Treasury Office of International Affairs, Occasional Paper No. 3.

Sobel, Robert. 1968. *Panic on Wall Street: A History of America's Financial Disasters*. Washington, DC: Beard Books.

Sooklal, Jai. 2012. Funding and Liquidity Risk Considerations. Speech at the Federal Reserve in the 21st Century Conference. March 20.

Soros, George. 2012. *Financial Turmoil in Europe and the United States*. New York: PublicAffairs.

Spero, Joan E. 1999. *The Failure of the Franklin National Bank: Challenge to the International Banking System*. Washington, DC: Beard Books.

Springer, Gary L. and Jorge L. Molina. 1995. The Mexican Financial Crisis: Genesis, Impact, and Implications. *Journal of Interamerican Studies and World Affairs* 37(2): 57–81.

Sprinkel, Beryl Wayne. 1952. Economic Consequences of the Operations of the Reconstruction Finance Corporation. *Journal of Business of the University of Chicago* 25(4): 211–224.

Steigum, Erling. 2004. Financial Deregulation with a Fixed Exchange

Rate: Lessons from Norway's Boom–Bust Cycle and Banking Crisis. In *The Norwegian Banking Crisis*, ed. T.G. Moe, J.A. Solheim, and B. Value. Norges Bank Occasional Paper No. 33.

Steigum, Erling. 2011. The Norwegian Banking Crisis in the 1990s: Effects and Lessons. Centre for Monetary Economics, BI Norwegian School of Management, Working Paper 5/11.

Steinbeck, John. 1939. *The Grapes of Wrath*. New York: Viking Books.

Steiner, Andreas. 2014. Reserve Accumulation and Financial Crises: From Individual Protection to Systemic Risk. *European Economic Review* 70: 126–144.

Stiglitz, Joseph E. 2004. The Post Washington Consensus Consensus. Paper presented at a conference sponsored by Foundation CIDOB and the Initiative for Policy Dialogue, Barcelona, September, "From the Washington Consensus towards a New Global Governance."

Stiglitz, Joseph E. 2009. A Bank Bailout that Works. *Nation*. March 4.

Stockhammer, Engelbert. 2015. Rising Inequality as a Cause of the Present Crisis. *Cambridge Journal of Economics* 39(3): 935–958.

Storm, Servaas and C.W.M. Naastepad. 2015. Crisis and Recovery in the German Economy: The Real Lessons. *Structural Change and Economic Dynamics* 32: 11–24.

Strange, Susan. 1972. The Dollar Crisis 1971. *International Affairs (Royal Institute of International Affairs 1944–)* 48(2): 191–216.

Straetmans, Stefan and Sajid M. Chaudhry. 2015. Tail Risk and Systemic Risk of US and Eurozone Financial Institutions in the Wake of the Global Financial Crisis. *Journal of International Money and Finance* 58: 191–223.

Sundaram, Jomo Kwame. 2007. What Did We Really Learn from the 1997–98 Asian Debacle? In *Ten Years Later: Revisiting the Asian Financial Crisis*, ed. Bhumika Muchhala. Washington, DC: Woodrow Wilson International Center for Scholars.

Süppel, Ralph. 2003. *Russia's Financial Markets Boom, Crisis and Recovery, 1995–2001: Lessons for Emerging Markets Investors*. Vienna: SUERF.

Sutela, Pekka. 1999. The Financial Crisis in Russia. Bank of Finland Online Publication 11. http://www.suomenpankki.fi/pdf/92222.pdf.

Takagi, Shinji. 2007. The Legacy of the East Asian Crisis: An Academic Perspective on Four Great Lessons. Paper presented at the International Symposium "Ten Years after the East Asian Crisis: Lessons and Future Economic Prospects," Waseda University, Tokyo, October 6.

Takagi, Shinji. 2009. The Global Financial Crisis and Macroeconomic Policy Issues in Asia. Asian Development Bank Research Policy Brief 32.

Takahashi, Wataru. 2013. Japanese Monetary Policy: Experience from the Lost Decades. *International Journal of Business* 18(4): 277–306.

Taylor, Jason E. 2002. The Output Effects of Government Sponsored Cartels During the New Deal. *Journal of Industrial Economics* 50(1): 1–10.

Tel Aviv Stock Exchange. 2011. Tel Aviv Stock Exchange. http://www.tase.co.il/TASEEng/.

Temin, Peter. 1976. *Did Monetary Forces Cause the Great Depression?* New York: W.W. Norton.

Temin, Peter. 1989. *Lessons from the Great Depression.* Cambridge, MA: MIT Press.

Ter-Minassian, Teresa and Gerd Schwartz. 1997. The Role of Fiscal Policy in Sustainable Stabilization: Evidence from Latin America. IMF Working Paper WP/97/94.

Teslik,LeeHudson.2009.TheUSEconomicStimulusPlan.CouncilonForeign Relations. http://www.cfr.org/united-states/us-economic-stimulus-plan/p18348.

Thornton, Mark. 2008. The Great Depression: Mises vs. Fisher. *Quarterly Journal of Austrian Economics* 11: 230–241.

Tobin, James. 1998. Asian Financial Crisis. *Japan and the World Economy* 10: 351–353.

Trevino, José Angel Curria. 1989. The LDC Debt Crisis: A Debtor's View. In *Solving the Global Debt Crisis,* ed. C.A. Bogdanowicz-Bindert. New York: Harper & Row.

Triantis, Stephen G. 1967. *Cyclical Changes in Trade Balances of Countries Exporting Primary Products, 1927–1933.* Toronto: University of Toronto Press.

Triffin, Robert. 1960. *Gold and the Dollar Crisis.* New Haven, CT: Yale University Press.

Tsafos, Nikos. 2013. *Beyond Debt: The Greek Crisis in Context.* North Charleston, SC: CreateSpace Independent Publishing Platform.

UN. 2009a. World Financial and Economic Crisis and its Impact on Development. Conference Draft Outcome Document. May 8.

UN. 2009b. The Commission of Experts of the President of the UN General Assembly on Reforms of the International Monetary and Financial System. http://www.un-ngls.org/docs/ga/cfr/key_perspectives.pdf.

UnitedSteelworkersUnion.2008.SteelworkersLettertoPaulson.October28. http://blog.usw.org/2008/10/29/paulson-deal-cheats-american-taxpayers/.

US Senate Banking Committee. 2010. Brief Summary of the Dodd–Frank Wall Street Reform and Consumer Protection Act. http://banking.senate.gov/public/_files/070110_Dodd_Frank_Wall_Street_Reform_comprehensive_summary_Final.pdf.

US Treasury Department. 2009. Financial Regulatory Reform: A New Foundation. White Paper Report on Financial Regulatory Reform.

Vale, Bent. 2004. The Norwegian Banking Crisis. In *The Norwegian Banking Crisis*, ed. T.G. Moe, J.A. Solheim, and B. Value. Norges Bank Occasional Paper No. 33.

Van Wijnbergen, Sweder, Mervyn King, and Richard Portes. 1991. Mexico and the Brady Plan. *Economic Policy* 6(12): 14–56.

Varoufakis, Yanis. 2013. *The Global Minotaur: America, the True Origins of the Financial Crisis and the Future of the World Economy*. London: Zed Books.

Vasquez, Ian. 1996. The Brady Plan and Market-Based Solutions to Debt Crises. *Cato Journal* 16(2): 233–243.

Vasquez, Ian. 2002. A Retrospective on the Mexican Bailout. *Cato Journal* 21(3): 545–551.

Vavilov, Andrey. 2010. *The Russian Public Debt and Financial Meltdowns*. New York: Palgrave Macmillan.

Volcker, Paul and Toyoo Gyohten. 1992. *Changing Fortunes*. New York: Times Books.

Wachtel, Howard M. 1980. A Decade of International Debt. *Theory and Society* 9(3): 504–518.

Wade, Robert. 2001. Explaining the Great Asian Slump. In *Financial Liberalization and the Asian Crisis*, ed. Ha-Joon Chang, Gabriel Palma, and D. Hugh Whittaker. New York: Palgrave.

Wade, Robert. 2007. The Aftermath of the Asian Financial Crisis. In *Ten Years Later: Revisiting the Asian Financial Crisis*, ed. Bhumika Muchhala. Washington, DC: Woodrow Wilson International Center for Scholars.

Wade, Robert and Frank Veneroso. 1998. The Asian Crisis: The High-Debt Model vs. The Wall Street–Treasury–IMF Complex. *New Left Review* March–April: 3–23.

Walton, John and Charles Ragin. 1990. Global and National Sources of Political Protest: Third World Responses to the Debt Crisis. *American Sociological Review* 55(6): 876–890.

Warren, Robert B. 1937. The International Movement of Capital. *Proceedings of the Academy of Political Science* 17(3): 65–72.

Weiner, Joann M. 2009. Biggest Mistake of the Financial Crisis: Lehman Bros. Bankruptcy. *Politics Daily*, September 15.

Weisbrot, Mark. 2007. Ten Years After: The Lasting Impact of the Asian Financial Crisis. CEPR Policy Paper, August.

Whitt, Joseph A. 1996. The Mexican Peso Crisis. *Federal Reserve Bank of Atlanta Economic Review* January/February: 1–20.

Wicker, Elmus. 1980. A Reconsideration of the Causes of the Banking Panic of 1930. *Journal of Economic History* 40(3), 571–583.

Wicker, E. 1996. *The Banking Panics of the Great Depression*. Cambridge: Cambridge University Press.

Williamson, John. 2004. A Short History of the Washington Consensus. Paper commissioned by Fundación CIDOB for the conference "From the Washington Consensus Towards a New Global Governance," Barcelona, September 24–25.

Williamson, John and Molly Mahar. 1998. A Survey of Financial Liberalization. Princeton Essay in International Finance 211.

Woodruff, David M. 2014. Governing by Panic: The Politics of the Eurozone Crisis. LSE "Europe in Question" Discussion Paper 81/2014.

Woods, Ngaire. 2010. Global Governance after the Financial Crisis: A New Multilateralism or the Last Gasp of the Great Powers? *Global Policy* 1(1): 51–63.

World Bank. 1993. *The East Asian Miracle: Economic Growth and Public Policy*. World Bank Policy Research Reports. New York: Oxford University Press.

World Bank. 2011. Developing Countries Are Driving Global Growth, but Risks Remain. January 12. http://econ.worldbank.org/WBSITE/EXTERNAL/EXTDEC/0,,contentMDK:22806935~pagePK:64165401~piPK:64165026~theSitePK:469372,00.html.

World Bank. 2012. World Development Indicators Database. www.databank.worldbank.org.

Yeyati, Eduardo and Tomas Williams. 2012. Emerging Economies in the 2000s: Real Decoupling and Financial Recoupling. *Journal of International Money and Finance* 31(8): 2102–2126.

Yuan, Chunming and Tanu J. Pongsiri. 2015. Fiscal Austerity, Growth Prospects, and Sovereign CDS Spreads: The Eurozone and Beyond. *International Economics* 141: 50–79.

Yurdakul, Funda. 2014. Factors that Trigger Financial Crises: The Case of Turkey. *Procedia – Social and Behavioral Sciences* 109: 896–901.

Zacharias, Ajit, Thomas Masterson, and Kijong Kim. 2009. Who Gains From President Obama's Stimulus Package . . . And How Much? Levy Institute of Bard College Special Report, June 12.

Index

Note: Personalities are indexed under their last name but appear as First Name Last Name to distinguish them from cited authors who are also indexed by last name but appear in the conventional form Last Name, First Name.